Shadow of
the New Deal

THE HISTORY OF
COMMUNICATION

Robert W. McChesney and
John C. Nerone, editors

*A list of books in the series
appears at the end of this book.*

Shadow of the New Deal

The Victory of Public Broadcasting

JOSH SHEPPERD

UNIVERSITY OF ILLINOIS PRESS
Urbana, Chicago, and Springfield

Library of Congress Cataloging-in-Publication Data
Names: Shepperd, Josh, 1977– author.
Title: Shadow of the New Deal : the victory of public broadcasting
    / Josh Shepperd.
Description: Urbana : University of Illinois Press, [2023] |
    Series: The history of communication | Includes bibliographical
    references and index.
Identifiers: LCCN 2022049985 (print) | LCCN 2022049986
    (ebook) | ISBN 9780252045110 (hardback) | ISBN
    9780252087257 (paperback) | ISBN 9780252054488 (ebook)
Subjects: LCSH: Public broadcasting—United States—History. |
    Television broadcasting—United States—History. | Radio
    broadcasting—United States—History. | National Association
    of Educational Broadcasters.
Classification: LCC HE8689.7.P82 S56 2023 (print) | LCC
    HE8689.7.P82 (ebook) | DDC 384.540973—dc23/eng/20230106
LC record available at https://lccn.loc.gov/2022049985
LC ebook record available at https://lccn.loc.gov/2022049986

*This book is dedicated to my grandmother, Helene Gordon.
Her formidable intellect and natural curiosity inspired me
to become a researcher.*

Contents

Acknowledgments

The framing of this book reflects years of study, conversations with friends, public talks, and apprenticeships that I picked up across degrees in Philosophy, Educational Policy, and Media and Cultural Studies.

This book owes a huge debt to Michele Hilmes, Dean of Radio Studies and mentor extraordinaire. It can be reasonably stated that I work in the "Hilmesian" Media History Research Tradition. The book's faults are mine, and its successes are due to her training. Deep thanks for helping me conceptualize this research project also goes to Alexander Russo, Jack Mitchell, Allison Perlman, Victor Pickard, Colin Burnett, Rich Halverson, Ken Saltman, Quentin Wheeler-Bell, Douglas Gomery, Christopher Sterling, Julie D'Acci, David Park, Shawn Vancour, Brent Malin, Paddy Scannell, Sonja Williams, Bill Siemering, Bob Avery, Kevan Harris, Katherine Jewell and Christopher Ali (both who generously reviewed chapters), Sam Rocha, Dan Marcus, Jason Loviglio, Laura Garbes, Mike Janssen, Eric Hayot, Susan Douglas, Rosa Eberly, Robert McChesney, John Nerone, Brian Kane for his invitation to present a chapter at the Yale Franke Lectures in the Humanities series, David Craig, David Park, Jay Needham, Neil Verma, Eric Hoyt, Dan Streible, Mark Williams, Danny Nasset, Mariah Schaefer, and Michael Apple, who put aside numerous hours to engage in long, detailed conversations about social theory and educational historiography. Special thanks to Jonathan Gray for helping me to position my archival work among contemporary media studies discourses.

I highly valued my undergraduate and M.A. studies at DePaul University with Bill Martin, William McNeill, Graham Harman, Stephen Haymes, and Gayle Mindes, as well as my time with Timothy Stock, Hillary Johnson, Ben Bigler, Diane Nititham, Aga Michalak, Nicole Jurek, and Miles Levy.

My first academic position brought me to Washington, DC, where I was fortunate to land in a terrific collegial network based at Catholic University. Thanks to Niki Akhavan, Stephen McKenna, Martin Johnson, Abby Moser, Chelsea Stieber, Lev Weitz, Michele Averchi, Anton Barba-Kay, Jonathan Monaghan, Julia Young, Patricio Simari, Lisa Lynch, Jennifer Fleeger, Larry Poos, Jennifer Horne, Kate Jansen, Maura Ugarte, and Lisa Gitelman.

A big emphasis of my time in DC included intensive training in public history and policy work with the world class staff at the Library of Congress, particularly Steve Leggett, Cary O'Dell, Matt Barton, Gregory Lukow, David Pierce, Patrick Mityling, Sam Brylawski, Karen Fishman, Guha Shankar, and Julie Drizen.

Seven years of my life were spent in Madison, Wisconsin, where I was fortunate to learn from strong and dedicated scholars and an active alumni network: Phil Sewell, Mary Beltran, Dave Black, Jim Baughman, Jeremy Morris, Brian Fauteaux, Kyle Conway, Bill and Wanda Kirkpatrick, Scot Barnett, Gregory Katz, Sreya Mitra, Andrew Bottomley, Chris Cwynar, Kit Hughes, Jennifer Wang, Bill Whitney, Nora Patterson, Joe Abisaid, John Powers, Jake Smith, Aswin Punathambekar, Michael Curtin, Mary Beth Haralovich, Kyra Hunting, Derek Kompare, James Dietrich, and John Fiske.

Much of this research is indebted to the relationships with archivists that I've built along the way. A historian's work is always already partly completed thanks to archivist help in locating materials and understanding finding aids at the Rockefeller Archive, Ohio State University, Wisconsin Center for Film and Theater Research, University of Maryland Hornbake Library, Library of Congress, and National Archives. Thanks also to Mike Henry, Laura Schnitker, Jim Baxter, Chuck Howell, Sarah Cunningham, Rodney Ross, William Davis, Dara Baker, Richard McCulley, Eric Schwartz, and David Weinstein.

One of my favorite parts of conducting research is meeting with friends and colleagues to talk about history and ideas. Thanks to everyone who's been there, helped, and listened along the way: Bill Blattner, Craig Kridel, Hugh Slotten, Michael Socolow, Noah Arceneaux, Margaret Schwartz, Amanda Keeler, Sreya Mitra, Brian Gregory, Catherine Martin, Helen Forgasz, Ethan Plaut, Todd Hyman, Susan Persky, Jason Hoffman, Kieran Kelley, Dave Kozin, Emily Goodmann, Ingrid Ockert, Rick Popp, Maristella Feustle, Patrick Feaster, Brandon Burke, Yuri Shimoda, John Vallier, Lauren Bratslavsky, Stephanie Sapienza, Allison Schein Holmes, Jim Buhler, Rebecca Wanzo, Bala Baptiste, Alejandra Bronfmann, Meghan Sitar, Jennifer Waits, Tanya Zuk, Kathleen Battles, Ines Casillas, Sonia Robles, Gregory Jones-Katz, David Seubert, William Vanden Dries, Christine Ehrick, Derek Vaillant, Ian Whittington, Ruta Abolins, Frank Absher, Ernesto Aguilar, Tim Anderson, Joshua Glick, Patricia Aufderheide, Michael Austin, Glenda Balas, Kyle Barnett, A.J. Bauer,

Aniko Bodrokhosy, Jack Brighton, Lauren Bratskavsky, Tim Brooks, Claudia Calhoun, Debra Rae Cohen, Mike Conway, Paul Conway, Amalia Cordova, Jane Curry, Vinzenz Hediger, Josh Davis, Brecht Declercq, Brian DeShazor, Thomas Doherty, Ralph Engelman, Jim Farrington, Dylan Flesch, Will Floyd, Kevin Erickson, Karma Foley, Ken Freedman, Bob Friedman, Anna Friz, Kathy Fully-Seely, Josh Garret-Davis, Matthew Kirshenbaum, Brian Real, Jose Luis Ortiz Garza, Kenneth Goldsmith, Katie Day Good, David Goodman, David Goren, Jonathan Auerbach, Mary Beth Haralovich, Joy Hayes, Nicole Hemmer, Heather Hendershot, Bob Horton, Debora Jaramillo, David Jenemann, Phylis Johnson, Sally Kane, Anna Kornbluh, Christine Acham, Michael Keith, Mary Ann Watson, Janet Wasko, Carol Stabile, Laura Wagner, David Walker, Monica de la Torre, Chris Terry, Jennifer Stoever, Kyle Stine, Carlene Stephens, Al Stavitsky, Michael Stamm, Marissa Moorman, Steve Fabian, Lynn Spigel, Susan Smulyan, Suzy Smith, Wendy Shay, Tim Shaffer, Toby Seay, Peter Schaefer, Eric Rothenbuhler, Jocelyn Robinson, Elena Razlogova, Jeff Pooley, Michael Pahn, Marcus Breen, David Plotkin, Jeff Place, Brenda Nelson-Strauss, Shirley Goldyn, Julie Beth Napolin, Cynthia Meyers, Ross Melnick, Charlie McGovern, Anne MacLennan, Sam Litzinger, Larry Lichty, Elana Levine, Andy Lanset, Alex Kupfer, Michael Kramer, Lina Ortega, Alex Sayf Cummings, Swagato Chakrovorty, Mary Myers, Pamela Vanhaitsma, Asheesh Siddique, Grant Wythoff, Jeffrey Binder, Chris Willoughby, Jen Shook, Georgia Ennis, Jocelyn Rodel, Dyfrig Jones, Phil Skepanski, Mark Poepsel, Ella Klik, Michael Peters, Will Mari, Scott Ferguson, John Shane, Dan Olson, Naomi Olson, Kerry Kelly, Wendy Guyer, Argie Berou, Charlie Schmidt, John Dorsey, Daniel Murphy, Michael Ahs, Manu Chandar, David Ben-Marre, Lisa Rabin, Jason Alston, Ran Zwigenberg, Tom Muhlren, Chris and Jennifer Millard, Chris Loomis, Oliver Gaycken, Michael Huntsberger, Sherman Dorn, Stephen Nelson, and Bill Reese.

Thank you to my new colleagues at the University of Colorado Boulder for their support as I completed this book (alphabetically): Lori Bergen, August Black, Andrew Calabrese, Shu-Ling Chen Berggreen, Nabil Echchaibi, Lori Emerson, Patrick Ferrucci, Steven Frost, Helen Gurnee, Cheryl Higashida, Stewart Hoover, Jeanne Liotta, Polly Bugros McLean, Elika Ortega, Janice Peck, Colette Perold, Samira Rajabi, Bill Riordan, Sandra Ristovska, Wick Rowland, Nathan Schneider, Hanna Rose Shell, Pete Simonson, Rick Stevens, and Ted Striphas, Emilie Upczak, Jamie Wagner. RA Matthew Pickard conducted some bibliographic research for the final draft.

Finally, my family has always supported my interest in scholarship. My partner Betsy Mulet is a brilliant researcher and has been there every step of the way. Betsy, I love you. Thanks also to Helene, Bill, Sid, Rae, Charlotte, Ileane, Joel, Mike, Sydney, Gail, Lou, and Dana.

Shadow of
the New Deal

Introduction

Public Media's
Economy of Promise

In 1936 a young Edward R. Murrow was sent by the Rockefeller Foundation to study standardized enunciation practices at the BBC.[1] When Murrow returned, he brought word of a skilled young Director of Regional Talks named Charles Siepmann. Siepmann joined the BBC in 1927 and was known for voicing opinion about radio's social responsibilities. His politics had run afoul with BBC Director-General John Reith, who was irritated by Siepmann's "liberal positions on controversial issues." Reith placed Siepmann on a Rockefeller exchange fellowship to evaluate the state of the BBC's closest US counterpart—university broadcasting. As soon as he arrived, Siepmann embarked on a national tour of university stations.

By 1936 the BBC was already developing its first television service.[2] The US educational broadcasting was a comparatively incipient endeavor. When Siepmann reached Iowa State University in Ames, he found a station lacking in vision beyond provincial public service such as farm reports. Expecting to find a parallel to the BBC, an annoyed Siepmann noted a "pathetically limited staff" of "rough cut, pitiable, poor, down at the heel people," led by a "rather heavy uncongenial type, with a rather subnormal culture."[3] Visiting the University of Illinois station he was equally disappointed in their receiving representative, who he described as an "insensitive and not very intelligent man, who had produced odd programs."[4] In the 1930s, US educational media was received less a parallel to the BBC than a ramshackle assemblage of Midwestern state university employees filling the airwaves with monotone lectures, poorly staged drama, and disorganized instruction.

At the end of his tour Siepmann surmised that educational broadcasters were comparatively lacking in "execution," not only to the BBC, but the networks CBS and NBC,[5] who as Kathy Fuller-Seeley has written, had recruited vaudevillian and tin pan alley performers to develop program aesthetics.[6] But one broadcaster's plight impressed upon Siepmann. The University of Iowa station in Iowa City was uniquely neglected, to the point that it had almost become a one-man operation. To meet criteria for a full broadcast day, engineer, announcer, and station manager Carl Menzer had taken to playing solo violin on air for hours, to an unknown audience.[7] Siepmann reported Menzer as having the demeanor of a man who had been "crushed," carrying on without institutional support. Siepmann returned to New York pessimistic about university broadcasting's prospects, and he advised the Rockefeller Foundation to cut funding for several university experiments,[8] leaving nonprofit broadcasters without a patron until the Ford Foundation's educational television program began in 1952.[9]

Yet, despite Siepmann's condescending remarks, educators had been inspired by his expertise. His cutting report aside, in person he was a generous consultant, providing despondent university broadcasters with some hope and direction for the country's first educational technology project. He would ultimately stay in America, work with the Office of War Information (OWI) and Federal Communications Commission (FCC) and help to found NYU's communication department. Siepmann inspired Menzer in particular. Evidence of BBC best practices[10] encouraged Menzer that noncommercial media was not only possible but could thrive in an American setting. Just not in Iowa, yet.

One night after a particularly lonely interlude on his violin, Menzer was resolute that he had come to a solution. For several years, he and University of Oklahoma colleague T. M. Beaird had considered what would happen if university stations were to form a decentralized network, one that could, as he would write a few years later, "tie up" stations from Wisconsin to South Dakota?[11] Such an educational chain might extend over the entire United States and exchange the best programs produced at each university. Menzer and Beaird's concept resonated with similarly struggling colleagues at state universities, from Iowa State, to Illinois, to Ohio State, which they discussed under a new and loosely united clearing house called the Association of University and College Broadcasting Stations (ACUBS), later renamed the National Association of Educational Broadcasters (NAEB) in 1934.[12] Carl Menzer happened to be a core member and rotating president of its board. It would take fifteen more years, but the NAEB eventually built something very close to Menzer's vision, which they called the "bicycle network," setting the stage for future NAEB members to populate NPR and PBS in the late 1960s.[13] Iowa State and Illinois joined Menzer at the University of Iowa as core administrators on the project, forging the scaffolding for what would become the protoversion of US public media by the early 1950s.

Between the 1930s and 1960s, the NAEB grew to represent and chronicle the multi-tiered work of largest media reform movement of the New Deal, one that covered hundreds of institutions and employed thousands of practitioners, policymakers, and advocates. University broadcasters began as disorganized, underfunded, and under-supported, but evolved beyond the ivory console to become a sustained media advocacy campaign, one that would transform an aspiration—in this case the belief that media could improve equal access to education through technology—into a sustainable media industry. Over the next fifteen years, advocates strategically absorbed, analyzed, and observed best practices, advice, and criticisms, calling upon transnational advisors such as Siepmann,[14] while synthesizing methodologies from philanthropic, federal, public educational, and even commercial sectors, into a bottom-up, decentralized network that became the largest public system in the world. The US public media emerged from an infrastructure built between the 1930s and 1960s that thrived without advertising income and called upon a different understanding of the purpose of mass media than commercial industries.[15]

Among strategies pursued by proto public broadcasting advocates after 1936, universities built the first educational program networks, with experiments in Chicago and in the Rocky Mountains, in the process coining the term "public broadcasting service" thirty years before the Public Broadcasting Act of 1967. School systems sought alternative funding beyond advertising income to signal fidelity to communications technology as a democratic tool.[16] And a strategic alliance between federal agencies and activist groups emerged to mitigate the influence of free markets upon civic imagination. Perhaps the most influential strategy was the development of academic research to understand educational technology's effects upon politics and culture of the national psyche.

This book looks at the strategic influences of players, institutions, and policies that inspired how the NAEB eventually overcame its early disarray to ultimately build NPR and PBS. Nothing about the process was inevitable. Through a series of setbacks, small victories, and trial-and-error experiments, public media in the United States emerged as a unique noncommercial media industry, one that began as an inefficient experiment but grew during the New Deal to innovate media production, genre, and approaches to media advocacy, fashioning an alternative infrastructure with an alternative vision to commercial broadcasting. Noncommercial media advocates conceptualized a system dedicated democratic, educational, and civic principles, in the process developing a different economy of scale predicated on the *promise* that technology could reconcile social inequalities by increasing informational access. Over the first fifteen years of development, this "economy of promise" synthesized the work of separate sectors into one institutional voice that engendered new cultural and analytical programs.

Public Media and Public Interest

To this point no literature has accounted for the transitional period between 1934 and 1952, when noncommercial media advocates and practitioners received protected frequencies for educational television. It was a remarkable turnaround, eighteen years before educators had been almost completely shut out of frequency allocations by a newly constituted FCC. The events leading up to the Communications Act of 1934 have been widely discussed and debated. As Robert McChesney has argued in his foundational book *Telecommunications, Mass Media, and Democracy,*[17] the Act consolidated privatization-friendly policies put in motion during the Hoover administration into a privatized US media landscape.[18] "Public interest" nomenclature that first appeared in the 1920s became a shorthand term stipulated in the Act by which regulators would determine if broadcasters were deserving of points on a dial. Instead of focusing on the importance of civic content or public service, the language of public interest came to equate with technocratic criteria such as maintenance of facilities or producing a full day of broadcasts, two operations that university broadcasters had not yet streamlined in the early 1930s.[19] But the tenor of FCC investment in educational broadcasting changed after the Act due to a series of regulatory events.

In 1935 Congressman Anning Prall was appointed Chair of the FCC, tasked with allocating frequencies for radio stations in line with the public interest mandate.[20] When it came time for Prall's office to review over 1,500 applications in consultation with twenty-one departments of government, the FCC stripped licenses from over 70 percent of all educational stations for not meeting criteria in the Act for public interest.[21] Businesses were able to manage facilities and support continuous broadcasts through the accumulation of revenue, which required little government investment. Universities intended for radio to be a classroom extension service. By the time educators were ready to logistically organize in line with public interest it was too late, communication regulators settled on the convenience of a privatized system that began with a head start. Despite a robust activist trade group presence, and some light negotiation with regulators between 1931 and 1934, when the

Communications Act of 1934 was passed Congress resolutely settled on the technically reliable commercial framework.

Congress assumed that there would be several benefits to a private system arrangement—free market media hypothetically allowed more voices through the door,[22] which commercial media lobbyists contended would diversify airwaves and provide better content localism.[23] As Alexander Russo notes, regional commercial broadcasting made significant strides in technical, distribution, and content development areas between the 1920s and 1950s, while breaking new ground in researching audiences.[24] In contrast, primary documents between 1921 and 1934 point to early educational radio as a classroom extension service in which lecturers were by and large unable to even understand the equipment, with few notable exceptions. Educational broadcasting was strong in concept and weak in practice, while commercial broadcasting carried the facilities, money, and talent to continuously streamline content and operations. But the networks were not invested in low-listenership programming.[25]

Typically painted as the victory of privatization, of a paradise lost that precluded the United States from developing its own BBC, reception to the public interest mandate of the Communications Act took several unexpected turns. Unfriendly to educational broadcasters in 1934, I argue both parallel and in contrast to Robert McChesney, and in line with recent scholarship by Allison Perlman[26] and Victor Pickard,[27] that while the Communications Act effectively ended early distance-learning experiments at dozens of universities, it also articulated the first institutional conditions for broadcasting practice, which set in motion a series of strategic decisions about how tenacious media reformers would organize during the New Deal.[28] As a modest revisionist history, this book argues that the Communications Act signaled the end of the first wave of educational radio, but it also signified the commencement of a massive coalition that anticipated public media.

As Prall and the FCC deliberated about the fate of educational licenses in early 1935, several path dependencies became clear to the Commission. Although most educational stations were not prepared to run a full broadcast day or fund facilities maintenance, the regulation did not forbid educational stations from receiving frequencies.[29] While inconsistencies in best practices and lack of funding had hampered educational applications, the FCC believed that the Act had set clear parameters for licensure that could be met by educational institutions by clarifying management rules for cultural, technological, and labor sectors through its articulation of a logistical framework for media production and distribution.

Indeed, in 1935 educators still needed more time to hone their craft, and they soon realized that they too could implement professional station practices in the public interest, without losing their ambition to produce democratic programming. After the Act educational radio practice evolved into a multi-sector reform movement. Noncommercial broadcasters were galvanized to transform early experiments in radio instruction into educational content produced with the aesthetics and technical conventions of commercial stations.[30]

It would take another thirty years, and support across five unique sectors, but the vision for public media eventually became a national agency, as Robert Avery[31] has written about in foundational analysis of the Public Broadcasting Act of 1967. This book focuses on the crucial exploratory period of 1935 to 1952, when many of the characteristics that we associate with the US public system emerged due to federal pressures, shifts in activist strategy, and academic research into how to understand educational listeners.

Why Public Media Matters for Media Studies: Evidentiary Challenges to Dominant Narratives of Media Research

As Sonja Williams has argued in her groundbreaking research, examining the organizational genealogy of noncommercial media challenges several working assumptions about media and communication history.[32] Reports like Siepmann's can serve to bookend and confirm disciplinary assumptions about the fate of democratic media. If one examines the plight of university stations based upon documents immediately preceding and proceeding the Communications Act, the educational broadcasting landscape might be interpreted as an inverted reprisal of Professor Pangloss in Candide articulated the eyes of Siepmann. One can imagine Siepmann wandering agrarian America, witnessing the struggles of a few stations, declaring the *worst* of all possible worlds for the likes of poor Carl Menzer. But just a few years later, the genres, practices, and policies that we associate with public media began to formularize.[33] Much has been written about the fragmentation of the US media system due to commodification of the conditions of distribution and engagement.[34] More must be written about how historical media reformers, for better and worse, attempted to and sometimes *succeeded* at evoking a functional public sphere, as David Goodman and Joy Hayes have recently chronicled regarding the US Office of Education's New Deal Educational Radio Project.[35]

As David Goodman[36] has further argued, it can fairly be argued that early commercial media had its own civic impulse, and even put resources and labor into improving educational programming. And further, for many commercial media actually served as the default public sphere for the United States,[37] one that occasionally provided some degree of diversity in representation and ownership, but has, as Jennifer Stoever has written, largely reproduced dominant contradictions regarding racial and gender biases.[38] The US commercial industry was shaped to avoid the trappings of state-based media through its capacity to dynamically adjust to the demands of audience response.[39] At the same time, commercial media was fundamentally and philosophically different from noncommercial media, in that for-profit industries were organized around questions of scale, profit, and audience data derived from content, circulated and measured to sustain continuance of its productive and distributive divisions. As Michele Hilmes has written,[40] the public interest mandate set a precedent for privatization of American media by fastening the FCC with a set of contradictions, which made it difficult for FCC Commissioners to reconcile civic goals with the bill's requirements. At the same time, as Hilmes has discovered in her foundational research, the Act built momentum for the US commercial media sector to define its strength in dialectical contrast to the BBC.

Calling upon Susan Douglas's work,[41] this book looks at how noncommercial media history provides a different kind of media industry case study, however contradictory, that details the limits and capacities of how advocates explored strategies to achieve parity in depiction, access, and labor.[42] Public media hasn't always been successful at meeting its mission statement.[43] The content of early broadcasts tended toward paternalism, very few minority experiences were invited into public media's production culture,[44] and it can be fairly observed that many audiences were poorly represented and not invited to participate in content production by educational media's self-appointed stewards.[45] One of the hypothetical strengths of a nonprofit system is that it can equally target small and large audiences without worrying about advertiser pressures, and public media has regularly failed to realize its discursive goals in this way. Recent scholarship by Laura Garbes[46] and Christopher Chavez[47] have considered how some of the foundational decisions of the service influenced these administrative and representational exclusions. In terms of gender equality, university broadcasting featured a more diverse distribution of female voices than network radio.[48] But as Laurie Ouellette[49] has observed about the early period of public media, representational distribution almost universally skewed white, middle class, and carrying nationalistic and sometimes neoliberal beliefs.

Public media's origin story is not the same type of reform movement that one finds in crucial civil rights, gender,[50] orientation equity, or antiwar activist movements. At the same time, broadcasts were produced with the intent to encourage social equilibrium by offering extension systems for educational institutions. One discovers few egregiously racist texts such as *Amos 'n' Andy* in the educational radio archive, for example, and to its credit the belief in the primacy of equal access to education held by media technologists[51] preceded national educational policy by decades. Educational media was earnest in its dedication to improving social relations, yet rife with paternalistic assumptions inherent to its moment,[52] especially in its conspicuous lack of diversity in administration, leadership, and willingness to provide a forum for diverse talent in its early development.[53] Diversity remains a major omission in the administrative public media archive. It's nearly impossible to locate a document in which advocates between the 1920s and 1950s discussed how their agenda would have been strengthened by expanding partnerships with rights activists or groups. Reform media advocacy worked from a paradoxical impulse. Its proponents endeavored to build a better society using technology, yet the reform agenda was guided exclusively by a white positionality.[54]

From the perspective of gender representation public media has always been the American pioneer in putting women at the front of anchor, reporting, and program development positions. This has not been true in terms of race, and largely not for orientation. Public media was advocated, lobbied for, and constructed with an imagined expectation of public participation that its content would be available to everyone. But implementation of this aspiration was rarely even discussed until the late 1950s, with some genuinely diverse and experimental content produced in the 1960s and 1970s.

The contradictions of public media history in mind,[55] noncommercial media history reveals that alternative production cultures have not only been envisioned but have been implemented and continue to exist.[56] Analyzing media history through a "public service" lens reveals to what extent American media studies discourses have closely orbited the gravity of the dominant system.[57] As Ralph Engelman pointed out in his important book on the relationship between public and community media,[58] there's comparably little scholarship that approaches media industries through non-corporate eyes.

Because advocates tended to be based at university, government, and grantwriting agencies, they left hundreds of thousands of pages of correspondence, ledgers, memos, and reports detailing every step of institutional organization, every policy that they interpreted and contested, and key players who participated in the movement.[59] The public media archive provides critical media studies with an opportunity to study not just contradictions in regulation, but when, how, and which reform strategies *succeeded*. Stories of critical media intervention abound at state archives, scattered at regional historical societies, and in the hundreds of books of reform scholarship between the 1920s and 1960s that populate our library shelves.[60] As Katherine Rye Jewell has written, in this way noncommercial media represents an exciting path for new media industry research.[61]

Approaching Public Media as a Noncommercial Media Industry

This book explores the emergence of an alternative broadcasting infrastructure in the United States. The logic for this system finds its roots in public education. Famous examples such as the Wisconsin Idea, discussed by Jack Mitchell[62] in his exemplary history, posited the maxim that a public university's reach should only be the limited by the borders of the state.[63] Public media's regulatory roots are additionally traceable to educational policy.[64] University broadcasters understood themselves as professors and university administrators utilizing technology to interpret compulsory education recommendations from the federal government and distance-learning programs.

After 1934 much of public media's proto history consisted of investigating and meeting requirements for media practice set by regulators in conversation with government agencies. Federal agencies tended to encourage clearinghouse and research work, which in turn opened a unique space in between public and private sectors for activists and practitioners to influence how the government deliberated upon media regulation. Philanthropic groups by and large underwrote these educational projects during the 1930s, if a project fit a regulatory mandate and served in a complementary role to the goals of a national agency. Grass roots practitioners and activists focused on reaching regional audiences and improving the quality of their broadcasts, and over time the activist spirit of the work carved out a stable space for the genres now associated with public media. Institutional voices worked in parallel toward civic goals allowed by each sector. At times federal, philanthropic, and practitioner spheres worked in direct contact, at other times they worked separately, but always to actualize the common endeavor of building a "fourth network" dedicated to education. By the time educational broadcasting was institutionalized as public broadcasting in 1967, university broadcasters and federal advocates had influenced three national educational policies and nurtured a national network.[65]

Much of the methodological approach of media industry studies[66] can be applied to the study of public media. By media industry studies I refer to sociological and historical scholarship that looks at economic, structural, creative cultural, and receptive contours surrounding a content-producing studio. This book focuses on how university broadcasters became a stable institutional voice with a unique economy of scale, with self-sustaining divisions organized to contribute to the production, distribution, activism, management, facilities, and content development. Noncommercial media industries rejected logics of accumulation early in their development, and this orientation became a rallying cry during the New Deal that culminated as an institutional identity.

At the same time public media industries emulated innovations of the commercial networks and regional broadcasting units.[67] They remained different from commercial industries because their mission statement called upon discourses in progressive social organization.[68] Noncommercial media industries exhibited a different cultural gatekeeping logic, had fewer funds to utilize, and worked more from principles than an audience metric model. Broadcasts were developed to contribute to a national infrastructure in which every student could take coursework no matter their location, and activists genuinely believed that radio lessons would unify disparate parts of the country while addressing inequalities in classroom access. The fledgling noncommercial media industry of the 1930s and 1940s sought to spread academic disciplines such as economics and political science to the masses through genres of public affairs, interviews, drama, music appreciation, and policy analysis.

While there were palpable differences between commercial and noncommercial media industries, and conflicts between its stakeholders, by the early 1950s best practices in production and content delivery were standardized due to interplay between both models.[69] Since educational media lacked a stable funding source until the late 1940s, its early history was replete with collaborative projects across universities, cities, regions, and sectors. Documents show that while educators and commercial broadcasters often skirmished over frequency licenses, commercial broadcasters were not ideologically opposed to educational broadcasts.[70] After the Communications Act commercial broadcasters invited educators to learn production practices, hired the best talent from early educational stations, and convened projects in which audience studies were developed by a mix of academic and private researchers. In fact, as Amanda Keeler has written, commercial media produced many of the strongest educational programs of the 1930s.[71] The networks later invested in the stability of university broadcasting after the FCC issued them sustaining broadcasting responsibilities. Though sustaining programs did not have to be explicitly educational, such broadcasts still had to meet criteria for non-advertising content and were considered unprofitable. By the 1960s both sectors were in favor of a carved-out role for educational media.

Public/private collaboration also influenced the trajectory of media reform strategy. Between 1935 and 1950 reform strategy had moved beyond mission statements alone to strategically interrogate how their programs were produced and how content spoke to target age groups. Due to public/private collaboration, university broadcasts accumulated the characteristics of aesthetic, production value, and audience engagement of commercial broadcasters. American public media learned from the innovations in aesthetics,[72] broadcast flow, and technical practices of the networks. Over the 1950s educational broadcasts became something more like educational entertainment, and content was produced to materialize socio-cultural goals associated with cultural uplift and skill acquisition. Public media retained its founding principles and dedicated itself to inform and encourage "understanding" and "appreciation" of "events, ideas, and culture, even if some of the instructional dimensions of educational broadcasting dissipated in the 1970s."[73]

Public Media as a Case Example of a Successful Media Advocacy Project

Robert McChesney discusses two activist case examples that that competed to define the meaning of noncommercial media in the 1920s and 1930s. The first was an activist lobby to secure set-aside experimental frequencies, pursued by the National Committee on Education by Radio (NCER). The second was a cross-sector technocratic model embodied by Levering Tyson of the National Advisory Council on Education by Radio (NACRE), which worked in a space between commercial and educational approaches. The Communications Act of 1934 changed both media reform groups.

With a year of the Act, these lobby groups continued, adjusted, and synthesized their work with dozens of additional institutions, while new institutions joined the movement. Among allies that began to advocate for noncommercial media, a newly constituted FCC began to work with the Office of Education, whose new Commissioner took an interest in radio to promote national curricular standards. And an emergent NAEB explored logistical and practice-based work as core strategies of media reform. These agencies and associations laid the groundwork for educators to organize as a decentralized network through the NAEB in the late 1940s.

One central takeaway from this history is that reform strategy typically failed until abstract ideals were translated into logistical practices.[74] This book interprets reform activity (pre and post 1934) by looking at which strategies were implemented before and after the Communications Act, and how reform strategies changed with the introduction of new political and economic pressures. Before 1934 most activism took a rhetorical approach, with distributed memos, ledgers, and correspondence that delineated the difference between commercial and educational media, including a letter-writing campaign to the Federal Radio Commission (FRC). Literature produced by pre-New Deal practitioners, and in this case activists, remains some of the most vivid, clearly stated, and persuasive modeling of the role of media in American democracy. After 1934, reformers transitioned to system-building advocates who focused on bureaucratic, research, and collaborative frameworks. More institutions participated with reform work after 1934, and the eventual centralization of communication at the NAEB provided a continuity line for the movement to keep tabs on different initiatives, opened a robust discussion regarding which steps to take, and provided regulators and a broader public with a coherent apparatus to associate with noncommercial media. This book argues that it's crucial to look at reform history as a series of institutional, regulatory, and cultural experiments. Advocates and practitioners slowly developed a material infrastructure that included production standards, methods of analysis, and inter-institutional connectivity.

Public Media as an Intellectual History of the US Public Sphere

This book examines the figures, agencies, players, and grassroots activists who transformed university broadcasting into a viable alternative system, one able to meet pedagogical goals, retain listeners, and sustain a full broadcast day.[75] Three events stood out in defining early public media. First, the Sixth Report and Order of 1952, in which a portion of future television frequencies were allocated to educational broadcasters after years of lobby, signaled an important regulatory victory for reform work. Second was the constitution of the bicycle network, the distribution mechanism of educational broadcasting that got its start in 1949 but had been conceived as early as 1931 and was worked on by NAEB members starting in 1939.[76] The bicycle network synthesized the production, research, and talent of dozens of institutions into one production culture. By creating a mechanism to share content produced at multiple universities, educators resembled an independent network with multiple development sites. Finally, the three Titles of the Public Broadcasting Act reflect an idiosyncratic pastiche of the different policies, innovations, and concessions that it took to build a federally funded system.[77]

The American public media experiment predates Habermas's work on the public sphere[78] by some years, and is better understood as practitioners attempting to realize a Deweyan vision of a society built around science, rationality, and experiential learning.[79] Advocates believed in modeling behavior and awareness about one's community through inculcation, guided by the assumption that unfettered informational exchange (instead of unfettered financial exchange) would constitute a marketplace of ideas to increase democratic awareness.[80] This distinction is important because it's not clear that media reformers ever envisioned themselves as a critical social movement. At the same time, advocates believed that educational media would provide a corrective to social and economic inequities that limited public access, and consequent equity.[81] Less concerned with broad structural realignment than a firm belief in the transformative power of skill acquisition and cultural uplift, US public media is better thought about as a "small p" public sphere, a reform movement that followed the modest goal of expanding public *services*.[82]

Put in conceptual terms, the early history of public media should be understood as fidelity to an aspiration, which engendered the creation of a media industry. This is a crucial distinction from a case study of a media industry that produced aspirational content. Public media history provides a case example for how grass roots organization and program design culminated in a self-sustaining institution. While educational broadcasting after 1934 might be characterized as a public project without a dominant leader or institution, there is no question that educational broadcasting proponents were unified in their aspiration to increase equal access to public education. Different than arguing that media reform worked as a united political bloc dedicated to achieving broad structural realignment, this book contends that advocates worked in concert to streamline best practices within the limits and pressures of public educational and communication regulatory bodies.

If one accepts that the *idea* of public media is a core protagonist of this history, it's not a big leap to envision how a fomenting post-Act reform landscape helped to inspire the intellectual pillars of an academic discipline (communication studies),[83] a concept-inflected media industry, and as David Park and Jefferson Pooley[84] have discussed, participated in intellectual debates, explorations of methodology, and experimentation with research techniques. In the fifteen years after the Act reformers coordinated with movements in folklore, critical theory, public policy, propaganda, and advertising research.

The surprise appearance and rejection of Theodor Adorno by the Princeton Radio Research Project (PRRP) concluded the early stages of educational audience research, leading the nascent discipline communication studies to choose political economy as its qualitative policy method instead of critical theory. The resolutely empirical direction that reformers took after the Act proved to be successful at convincing regulators that educational broadcasting deserved special frequency assignments. The marriage of three major empirical approaches to media: mass communication, political economy, and broadcast production, ultimately shaped the influential early communication program at the University of Illinois. Illinois' basic departmental structure—research, political advocacy, and media practice—became the model not only for the communication discipline, but the support system for public broadcasting itself. The complexity of this historical case begs a reader to contemplate about how grass roots organization can be both decentralized and unified around a concept, and how consequent coalitional fidelity might inform media advocacy historiography.

Chapter 1. Advocacy: Media Reform, from Activism to Advocacy: Before and After the Communications Act of 1934

Chapter 1 looks at how public education influenced early educational broadcasters to become invested in a noncommercial service. Universities believed that technology could be of service in providing equal access to education for all residents of a state. The first articulated difference between commercial and nonprofit models appeared in the 1920s, when practitioners decided that they would not accept advertising dollars. But early advocacy was not without its contradictions. Pre-Act practitioners were strong in concept but weak in techniques of broadcasting practice.

Most educational broadcasting exchanges between 1925 and 1933 revolved around the difficulty of producing quality content and reaching listeners. While educators explored best practices, two advocacy models materialized to articulate a philosophy of educational radio. The NCER was a Payne-Funded activist lobby inspired by the US Office of Education to secure set-aside frequencies. Levering Tyson of the National Advisory Council on Education by Radio (NACRE), worked for the Carnegie Fund in a technocratic space between commercial and educational approaches, tasked with eliminating misunderstanding between sectors. The Communications Act of 1934 cut both early reform models short. Yet within a year of the Act, these lobby groups adjusted to respond to new institutional interest in radio from federal institutions. A newly constituted FCC began to work with the Office of Education, whose new Commissioner took an interest in radio to teach as many students as possible. In the post Communications Act Landscape, the three primary practitioner and reform organizations—the Association for College and University Broadcasting Stations (ACUBS), NCER, and NACRE—set the groundwork for regulatory victories when they realized that they would have to reorganize to address rules of the Communications Act.

Chapter 2. Funding without Advertising: The Philanthropic Mandate for Collaboration between Educational and Commercial Broadcasters

Chapter 2 looks at how the uniquely American model of public broadcasting developed as a collaboration between public and private sectors, due to the foundational support of the Rockefeller Foundation. It discusses how the Rockefeller Foundation functioned as what Michele Hilmes has called a "shadow government" for media production during the New Deal. Projects funded by the Rockefeller Foundation ultimately anticipated the contours of public media's infrastructure.

In the late 1920s the Payne Fund embraced educational radio as a strategy to promote nation building and to combat what they viewed as film and radio's roles in public deliberation. The Rockefeller Foundation was recruited to work with a fomenting post-Act media reform movement when FCC Commissioner E.O. Sykes wrote a 1935 Pursuant mandating that the future of educational broadcasters should endeavor to meet the new public interest mandate, which meant production of more "entertaining" educational programs and locating strategies to better understand how students learned through radio. The FCC partnered with the Office of Education and founded the Federal Radio Education Committee (FREC). In 1935 and 1936 FREC organized two conferences that brought together the commercial, educational, research, philanthropic, and manufacturing sectors. These conferences inspired the Rockefeller Foundation to assign John Marshall to fund educational broadcasting experimentation. The Rockefeller Foundation had recently worked with educators on an Eight Year Study to improve assessment and pedagogy for compulsory education, and saw an opportunity to influence standardized practices in educational radio in a similar manner. Over the next five years, Marshall funded and meticulously detailed multiple experiments, infrastructure projects, internships with commercial broadcasters, and exchanges with the BBC.[85] Marshall underwrote almost every single experiment in educational broadcasting during this time, and the early infrastructure for public media emerged in three areas: technical best practices, audience research, and philanthropic support.

Chapter 3. Infrastructure and Facilities: America's Public Media Industry: From the Rocky Mountain Radio Council to the National Bicycle Network

Chapter 3 examines how media reformers built a sustainable production and distribution model for public media industries, from the bottom up and without advertising income. As illustrated by Hugh Slotten and Jack Mitchell, early experiments in educational broadcasting were primarily composed of classroom extension services for local schools, immigrants, or farmers. For this reason, most early programs were instructional. Educational stations were understaffed and often did not have the resources to fill a broadcast day. NAEB stations explored strategies for how to standardize quality content and fill airtime. Their first breakthrough came from the University of Iowa. Broadcaster Carl Menzer posited that NAEB members might utilize new technologies to relay educational content.

Over the next seven years, the NAEB pursued several stages of trial-and-error experiments modeled upon Menzer's concept that the NAEB should network content. At the same time John Studebaker at the Office of Education provided valuable federal support by organizing the first clearinghouse for scripts and program transcriptions, while he consulted with educational stations. Meanwhile, three experiments in public media production got off the ground thanks to newly available Rockefeller Foundation Funds. The University Broadcasting Council of Chicago networked citywide broadcasts. The Payne Fund-connected Rocky Mountain Radio Council designed the first regional educational network, in the process coining the term "public broadcasting." And John Marshall invited BBC Director of Talks Charles Siepmann to the United States. In 1936 Siepmann visited and consulted with dozens of university stations, ultimately influencing the course of NAEB station practice.

The final steps in the development of a public media industry were consolidated in 1949 and 1950. The NAEB held a major conference in conjunction with Wilbur Schramm's newly founded University of Illinois Institute of Communications Research, which came to be known as the Allerton House Seminars. The seminars concluded with an agreement across dozens of stations that universities would pool their talent and resources to build a decentralized alternative to commercial broadcasting, which they nicknamed the "bicycle network." The bicycle network was facilitated by the University of Illinois and WYNC and made educational content available to every interested station.

Chapter 4. Research and Development: Communications Research, the Most Persuasive Strategy of the Media Reform Movement

Chapter 4 looks at how media reformers sought to persuade policymakers that educational content was deserving of special treatment and reserved frequencies. Their most persuasive lobby strategy turned out to be early communications research, which was developed to explore educational broadcasting reception. FREC assigned a small group of researchers called the Princeton Radio Research Project (PRRP) to explore how to gauge when educational broadcasting was effective. The findings of the PRRP, coupled with simultaneous projects at Ohio State University and the University of Wisconsin Madison were so successful that they became core techniques of research and development practices, engendered the academic study of communication, and persuaded policymakers that a noncommercial media outlet could work in service of public interest.

Originally titled "Project 15," the PRRP began as an ad hoc committee comprised of volunteers and nominees from the FREC conferences: Ivy League professors, the Rockefeller Foundation, and the Columbia Broadcasting System (CBS). Headed by Hadley Cantril, a young Princeton professor, the PRRP was mandated to develop an empirical "technique" to assess audience reception to programming. Paul Lazarsfeld, Herta Herzog, and a young CBS-appointed representative named Frank Stanton joined Cantril.[86] The PRRP made their first major breakthrough by synthesizing social psychology methods with advertising demographic research. The new method was unexpectedly effective at encapsulating and then predicating reception among targeted listeners, and was able to produce similar survey responses across geographic spaces based upon demographic affiliation. The PRRP's first national test became a national sensation when they assessed response to the *War of the Worlds* "panic."[87] The WOTW analysis became so influential that public media advocacy henceforth included audience response as a tool for regulatory lobby.[88]

To compose policy language that described project findings for the FCC, PRRP researcher Paul Lazarsfeld persuaded the Rockefeller Foundation's John Marshall to underwrite political theorist Theodor Adorno to join the project. Adorno's brief engagement with the PRRP has been well chronicled by multiple works. However, Adorno's critical theory approach was rejected by the project's empirical researchers. The BBC's Charles Siepmann equally articulated a critical vision for reform research, but also understood production and development practices. Siepmann replaced Adorno as FREC's advocacy model, which carried far-reaching ramifications for both public media, and the emerging field of Communication.

When founding Chair of the Illinois Institute of Communication Research Wilbur Schramm wrote the first text assessing the pre-history of communication studies, he looked to the PRRP as the foundational research consortium and went about hiring multiple Rockefeller Foundation-connected researchers to populate the Institute of Communications Research. Dallas Smythe, who would go on to become one of the founders of political economy of media research, was recommended to Schramm by Paul Lazarsfeld for his work on Siepmann's "Blue Book";[89] Schramm specialized in mass communications research; and Robert Hudson of the Rocky Mountain Radio Council was hired to conduct research into broadcast and development. The first communication program was in part predicated on Rockefeller Foundation-funded educational broadcasting research.

Chapter 5. Policy: Public Media Policy, 1934–1967—Lessons from Reform History

Chapter 5 looks at the broad policy arc of noncommerical media from the Communications Act to the Public Broadcasting Act of 1967, focusing on how media reformers responded to changes in communications policy. Archives reveal that public media's most effective lobby concentrated on reporting its technical needs and contributions as an educational extension service. In every case that media reformers successfully influenced noncommercial policy and practice between 1934 and 1967, their winning argument revolved around strategically combining advocacy around Communications Act's "public interest" mandate and arguments for expanded educational access through technology. After 1934, media reformers learned to successfully manage the logistics of a radio station. In 1945 the FCC awarded universities new FM frequencies. During the FCC "TV Freeze" advocates framed their work as a logistical implementation of compulsory education policies.

The Communications Act of 1934 imagined radio as both an ethereal extension of interstate commerce, and framed language in the bill as meeting these goals through maintenance of facilities and uninterrupted access to content. Since the Communications Act broadly defined frequency allocation criteria as requiring continuous institutional maintenance—such as funding, facilities, and standardized content—educational broadcasters were at first unable to meet requirements of this mandate, leading to station closure. However, the public interest mandate later became the precedent by which reformers were able to position themselves as meeting the same technical standards as commercial industries, while providing an additional public service that complemented educational reform discourses.

A series of educational policies—from the Lanham Act of 1941 to the National Defense of Education Act of 1958—became tools of the media reform movement to change broadcasting policy. By the 1960s, broadcasting policy was more inclusive of educational policy. The Educational Television Facilities Act of 1962 and the Public Broadcasting Act of 1967 were framed with the same language of educational bills, that the system was not meeting its mandate unless it reached every listener. Until 1967, public media was tied to the educational sector. The Public Broadcasting Act of 1967 was even drafted out of the Department of Health, Education, and Welfare.

Conclusion

The book ends with the argument that to understand public media's history, it must be understood as a long advocacy that ultimately changed communications policy by synthesizing successful reform strategies across multiple sectors. Attention to public media's educational policy work can still be of service to public media's broader project. A US public media infrastructure with increased focus on educational outreach programs—such as podcasting, multi-medial interfaces, inter-sector collaboration, and public forums—would buttress established support, expand funding opportunities, and reconnect public media with a gigantic and already-diverse constituency of target listeners: students.

CHAPTER 1

Advocacy

Media Reform, from Activism to Advocacy: Before and After the Communications Act of 1934

This book argues that public media in the United States began with strategic reform work conducted after the Communications Act of 1934.
Defined in the context of this history, media reform is the transmission
of a social vision into sustainable institutional and technological practices
that circulate a group, discourse, or agency's perspective to the broadest
possible receptive sphere.[1] Reform work attempts to reconcile a regulatory
or cultural contradiction in line with a perceived public good, and includes
evaluation, organization, and implementation of a social vision among productive, regulatory, and distributive machinations. Media reform strategy
sometimes takes a rhetorical form, such as awareness raising, challenging
of dominance, and "spreading the word." Strategy can also take the form of
organizing, system building, technical experimentation, and research into
policy and media phenomena. Associated media reform scholarship tends
to center on how political and industrial groups set precedents that influence
subsequent regulatory decision-making.[2]

Media reform is not the same thing as a rights movement, though reform
often overlaps and intersects with rights movements, and rights movements
regularly develop their own media reform strategies. Reform might first and
foremost be thought about as an organized form of mobilization to shape
policy and culture to reflect a specific vision of public participation. It's important to not associate reform work solely with rights work, because it's
possible that a regressive political operation might envision and successfully
implement an anti-rights vision of reform. Reform work is a mechanism that
increases or decreases access to information and opportunities for ownership
and participation. In this way media reform should not be received as an

inherent social good but as the strategic push and pull between competing, organized institutional interests, that aspire to standardize a set of beliefs and practices to promote a desired structure of relations.

This book examines one of the earliest and largest media reform movements of US history: the advocacy by educators, activists, philanthropic groups, and federal agencies to accumulate frequencies for educational, nonprofit media. Much of the energy of this reform movement was built on a vision of technology as an extension of civic, educational, and participatory initiatives already in progress across public, governmental, and local institutions.[3] The type of reform taken up by the advocates covered in this book, which eventually numbered hundreds of institutions and thousands of participants, was not fully activated until the first major media regulation indirectly restricted nonprofit media. As described across multiple foundational texts, the Communications Act of 1934 effectively ended the first American experiment in noncommercial radio. But, this book argues, the Act also engendered the unintended consequence of galvanizing multiple sectors to create a secure, ethereal public infrastructure to increase access to information. By examining archival materials across five sectors, it's possible to chronicle the slow, ad hoc, trial-and-error implementation of educational reform strategy, to carve out a special cultural role for education among commercial media industries.

Commercial broadcasters played a major role in the development of noncommercial media practice in the United States. At the same time, they exerted dominance over access points and the aesthetic predilections of listeners. The ideology of early commercial media industries should be qualified as a balancing act of increasing revenue while observing federal policy, broadcasting in the national interest, entertaining audiences, maintaining advertising income, and building infrastructure.[4] Whereas the ideology of early noncommercial media industries might be thought about as an attempt to materialize principles about public participation into media practice.[5] The history of media reform breaks commonly held assumptions about the distinction between public and private in US media history. Educational media in the United States was irrefutably a central concern of New Deal media reformers, yet at the same time the shape of what became public media emanated from simultaneous influences, within the constraints of how those sites interpreted their institutional goals.

The dialectical interplay between different reform interests, the government, commercial agencies, and researchers developed into something like a coalition to carve out a special space for noncommercial media. Each sector repeatedly adjusted their procedures, strategies, and perspectives about the purpose of noncommercial media until a national system was in place.[6] With reference to Victor Pickard, Allison Perlman, and Christopher Ali's scholarship, it's crucial to point out that media reform is a story of grassroots organizing. Yet it was not always grassroots groups that implemented or inspired reform, as Mary Beltran[7] and Aniko Bodroghkozy[8] have expertly detailed their research.

It is further important to note that individual reform agents belong to the arc of this history in shorter participatory periods than the duration of the movement itself; it was the shared vision of social parity that survived into posterity more than the work of a single actant.[9] For this reason this book is interested in exploring the conditions in which a reform vision became sustainable beyond a specific activist, agency, or group.[10] The history of media reform after the Communications Act is one in which nearly every stakeholder of US broadcasting laid the groundwork for the possibility of a noncommercial infrastructure, albeit for contrasting reasons. By the end of the first major period of post-regulatory foment, between 1935 and 1952, grassroots practitioners were prepared to synthesize the contributions of different sectors into the auspice of a single institutional voice by retroactively calling upon the previous decade's points of progress.[11]

This book provides an unusual case study in that the protagonists of public media in the United States, the National Association of Educational Broadcasters (NAEB) play a secondary role in rise of New Deal media research. The aspiration to extend education into a media practice slowly coalesced as a patchwork through continuous remediation of the work of different sectors, until the NAEB eventually synthesized the approaches of previous institutions to construct a recognizable "network" within the US context. Pre-1930 educational reform work took an *activist* bent and attempted to influence regulatory and institutional decisions made by other institutions. After 1934 the same institutions changed their approach into something more like a system-building *advocacy* that balanced theory, production, and audience research into a single voice. The shift from activism to advocacy[12] aided the innovation of noncommercial content, connectivity between stations, and helped to meet criteria of "public interest" broadcasting.[13]

The distinction between pre-and post-act organizational strategies is observable across four major institutions. The first is the NAEB, which began as the Association of College and University Broadcasting Stations (ACUBS), a loosely organized clearinghouse for educational broadcasters to report on program content.[14] After the Act their constellation of members experimented with the craft of broadcasting, eventually combining the work of hundreds of institutions into a single voice. The National Committee on Education by

Radio (NCER) and National Advisory Council on Radio in Education (NA-CRE), famously chronicled in Robert McChesney's book, were both launched from the same source—Commissioner William John Cooper of the Office of Education—while Cooper worked with the Carnegie and Payne groups to fund educational radio advocacy.[15] They diverged on strategy based upon their different institutional mandates. The NCER began as a foundational voice of political economic analysis before the Act, just to become one of the great educational media producers after the Act. The NACRE took a middle-of-the-road approach, and encouraged cross-sector collaboration among stakeholding groups, accidentally becoming a crucial cog in the development of early communications research. Neither NCER nor NACRE approaches were successful in procuring protected frequencies for educators, and both fizzled out by WWII. But between these groups, the philosophy and practices of public media emerged, with the NACRE closely advising the fourth major group of this period: the Office of Education and Federal Communication Commission's Federal Radio Education Committee (FREC).

Public Media as a System Building Strategy to Advocate for Principles of Educational Access and Practice

The original principles for public media came from Progressive-Era philosophies such as John Dewey, who argued that democracy benefited from convening institutional practices that would raise awareness about one's community. Dewey promoted understanding of democracy through training, and believed that specific institutions could be tasked with the promotion of equity, which he called "intentional agencies."[16] Roughly the same time as Dewey's educational concepts, states began to look to universities as bureaucratic sites for economic, public, and cultural extension work.[17] Dewey's concepts, when combined with bureaucratic mandates to expand the reach of public education to every resident of a state, gave public education the veneer that access was not only a service but a right, and that it was the responsibility of educational institutions to locate strategies to reach every student. Educators received radio as one possible strategy to expand access to public education.

It is the argument of this book that public media can be traced from Progressive-Era concepts about equal access to education, through reform advocacy, to the Public Broadcasting Act, which was instituted through three Titles. First, construction grants for educational broadcasting; second, maintenance of facilities; third, study of educational and instructional broadcasting.[18] Each title was written to address different institutional pressures that had been initiated before to the Act itself. For example, the history of construction grants (Title I) can be traced back to state requirements to provide facilities for compulsory education. Maintenance of facilities (Title II) was necessary so that a school, and later educational broadcasting, continued to meet regulatory approval for license renewal. And research into public and instructional broadcasting (Title III) was implemented to make sure that best practices in educational facilities met regulatory mandates. Funding for the Public Broadcasting Act hedged upon the fundamental concept that noncommercial media served an educational purpose similar to compulsory education. The Act itself contained dozens of traces of past events to realize this goal going back to the 1930s.

Compulsory Educational Policies and Practices and the first Distance-Learning Mandates

Early public media emerged in a symbiotic relationship with the growth of compulsory state education. To understand the mindset of those who built the educational radio system, and the strategic decisions that reformers made in the 1930s, it's crucial to frame radio work within the logic of 1920s distance-learning and classroom extension services. As early as the 1910s educational advocates searched for strategies to streamline reception for agrarian and immigrant access: distance-learning initiatives appear in roughly the early 1910s, audio visual organizations and the first multiple choice tests were implemented at roughly the same time.[19] Once educational radio appeared in the early 1920s, it was situated against a robust discussion regarding how to increase training in speech and trade.[20] The first compulsory education regulation was passed in Massachusetts in 1852, and mandatory schooling became associated with modernization theses through the Progressive Era.[21] It took until 1918 that every state had compulsory education laws.[22] Education was typically concerned with skill acquisition in a fixed occupational landscape.[23] By the late Progressive Era, schools were designed to increase attendance, inclusion of immigrant families, and to provide a constructive environment after Child Labor laws were passed, the last in place by 1914.[24] By the 1920s it had become a tacit assumption that every child should be in school, and if services were not available, that strategies to reach distance learners should be explored.

In the years preceding radio, school districts had focused on what William Reese has aptly called "technologies of progressivism"—which included handwriting, mass production of working pencils, playgrounds as public meeting places, and by the 1910s Audio-Visual (AVI) materials.[25] Both in and outside of the classroom, information required access to equipment.[26] It's under these discourses, as an extension not only of distance learning but the assumption that everyone must be "educated" that educational radio materialized in the late 1910s. And like public schools, radio required a lot more than curriculum to succeed—namely buildings, training, and consistency of content delivery.

The Earliest Aspirations of Educational Broadcasting: The Association of College and University Broadcasting Stations and the Educational Principles of Noncommercial Media

The earliest Schools of the Air were distance-learning extension services. The first distance-learning program was founded at Pennsylvania State University in 1892 to serve rural and adult learners.[27] It wasn't until the 1910s that most universities were offering correspondence services. Educators began to congregate over the question of how radio might be put in service of compulsory educational strategies in the late 1910s. The Association of Colleges and University Broadcasting Stations (ACUBS) was founded in November of 1925 as a distance-learning trade ledger[28] after the Fourth National Radio Conference in Washington, DC. Stations were widely geographically separated, and most early discussions revolved how to best reach rural populations.[29] ACUBS' mission statement captured most of the early activities of the organization.

> "Believing that radio is in its very nature one of the most important factors in our national and international welfare, we, the representatives of institutions of higher learning, engaged in educational broadcasting, do associate ourselves together to promote, by mutual cooperation and united effort, the dissemination of knowledge to the end that both the technical and educational features of broadcasting may be extended to all."[30]

Although there was a shared mission—expanding access to education—there was no unified sense of how educational radio should be practiced in the 1920s. The group struggled greatly in these earliest years; by 1927 membership had dropped and the group only had an end of the year balance of $15. As Harold Hill (1954) states in his brief history, ACUBS members were primarily occupied with the basic problem of keeping stations on the air and trying to "arouse the interest" of listeners.[31] The Association looked doomed to failure by 1929 for lack of interest, but their luck temporarily shifted after the first annual convention held in Columbus, Ohio, on July 1, 1930, attracted representatives from many of the country's top land grant universities.

Taking their cue from the precedent of the "modern school"[32] early practitioners believed that the creation of an ethereal "social center" would encourage a civic-based democratic sphere that would promote social equity through continuous participation.[33] In determining how technology might be used for educational purposes, practitioners emphasized basic tenets of equal access to education across three areas: 1) educational radio should be a nonprofit institution, 2) its purpose was to serve underrepresented populations and educational efforts, and 3) a national Association's mission was to describe the state of the union of what amounted to a university service.

Early officeholders of the Association were especially invested in the notion that educational radio had a different mission than commercial broadcasters. Board member B.B. Brackett of the University of South Dakota was an especially outspoken voice. "What is the fundamental purpose of any school owned broadcast organization? To educate as many personas as possible and to disseminate as much accurate and reliable information as it can."[34] The founding of NCER in 1929 further incited ACUBS members to articulate a clear vision of nonprofit radio with an active nonprofit media lobby.[35] Tracy Tyler of the NCER encouraged the organization that their work was "one of the most powerful and effective existent tools for popular education" and adult education. "[D]evelopment of programs of adult education will help offset the present tendency toward centralization and network monopoly."[36]

Problems with Educational Broadcasting Practice and Early Distance-Learning Experiments with Broadcast Aesthetics

As the ACUBS grew, it sought to aggregate information about work of educational stations. Of the roughly 70–80 stations accounted for by an ACUBS internal survey, at the peak moment of early educational broadcasting only 8–10 stations were actively on the air more than a few hours per day if at all.[37] Universities obtained licenses before 1925 on behalf of engineering and physics departments' experimentation with radio waves[38]—before the rise of commercial network broadcasting—but universities had generally taken their frequencies for granted. Stations aired without university support and were often staffed by local amateur broadcasters.[39]

Educational radio stations further lacked coherent pedagogical standards. Records are replete with anecdotal reports of failure, such as professors with "high nasal voices" speaking indistinctly into a microphone at unannounced times during the week, or the development of unpopular programs on the West Coast dedicated to teaching state residents "how to use modern plumbing."[40] The discrepancy between institutional quality and broadcasting was noted almost immediately by Ohio State University (OSU), the first university to take radio serious as an object of cultural research.[41] Ohio State developed the first effective correspondence classes by radio. As Al Stavitsky has written, Ohio State pioneered broadcasting into Cleveland classrooms.[42] WOSU's adult education series, *Emergency Radio Junior College* ran on a budget of $2000 a month and enrolled around 400 students. Students were issued a book with enrollment.[43] And the program ran five to eight courses per quarter, with proficiency examinations and mimeographed texts distributed free of charge. Between 1932 and 1933, enrollment mounted from 624 to 1538 total, with 1200 in a single class. Approximately eighty Ohio counties were represented in the registered listening audience. One internal report noted that at least fifteen to twenty radio supervisors were needed to maintain OSU's successful output.[44]

Ohio State attempted several interventions to improve educational radio, including holding yearly radio education conferences, and in 1931 they announced the formation of an institute for education by radio that would be devoted to examining technical aspects, program management, and broadcast administration. To encourage other stations to devote time to best broadcast practices they held drama contests that demanded significant work in preparation on subjects like memorization, voice intonation, aural spatialization, etc. Ohio State was also the first university to realize the importance of radio aesthetics, with internal documents that issued recommendations, for example, that "cues must be quickly picked up and tempo is faster in radio drama, and that diction, pronunciation and breathing are to be noted."[45]

Despite the early technical scaffolding set by Ohio State, it became clear to ACUBS members that classroom practices at almost every other university had not translated into successful curriculum. Between 1931 and 1933 ACUBS bulletins spoke to the pervasive problem of developing educational content on a shoestring budget, with a lack of trained practitioners, and little understanding of radio as a medium. Shows were poorly promoted, would air once or twice and then never again.[46] In one letter B.B. Brackett wrote that the "larger perception is that universities don't broadcast well and are hard to hear."[47] Canadian radio pioneer Merrill Denison devised a document for the ACUBS regarding "five conditions" that he felt "handicapped the development of the educational medium."[48] Among problems were lack of publicity for educational programs, "appropriateness of presentation," and "adequate remuneration for talent." Ben Darrow, early pioneer of educational broadcasting at Ohio State, had similarly attempted to address problems of "best practices" by circulating a 10-point Special Bulletin to the ACUBS in 1931 with boilerplate recommendations such as "stations need to provide satisfactory equipment," and "treat radio received information the same as other information and include it in exams so students dutifully listen."[49]

As Robert McChesney has shown, the NCER realized just how close educators were to losing their frequencies due to inefficiency and emergent commercial-friendly policies under Herbert Hoover. Armstrong Perry of the NCER wrote to ACUBS officials that the "average listener" was in a state of "hopeless confusion as far as knowledge or programs."[50] Besides being scheduled unpredictably, educational programs were rarely longer than fifteen minutes. Full length programs featuring dialogue, drama, and music were necessary to persuade the Federal Radio Commission (FRC) that quality programming was being produced at universities.[51]

Indeed by 1933 educational radio practice had become cause for alarm. Morse Salisbury of the US Department of Agriculture distributed a departmental report titled "Educational Broadcasting in 1928–1933" that painted a grim picture of the performance of educational radio. "Previous hopes surged high and public prints teemed with glowing predictions," but by 1933 the poor quality of educational broadcasts had "exploded" his belief that radio had "magical powers of education."[52] The Department of Agriculture ceased its support of educational broadcasters in 1933, and distributed announcements through commercial networks. Radio education simply could not compare in effective instruction value with courses given in residence to a few people.

"You can't expect the radio organization of a university or a college to do a good job unless you give it authority. Further, stations need the editorial workers and production men and women and clerical help necessary to ask the good radio talent of the faculty and assist that talent in preparing and producing and following up really educational programs. And you can't expect the good radio talent of the faculty to continue indefinitely piling more and more radio work on top of a full-time teaching or research program."[53]

The Office of Education noticed that the predominantly state and region-based experiments of universities little resembled the progress made by public education's curricular standards. In a 1931 letter the Office of Education implored universities to prepare speakers through broadcast instruction, and to train listener groups in how to understand live lectures, especially adult listeners.[54] The letter noted that broadcasting was evolving to become a "highly specialized art," and that microphone technique related to diction, pronunciation, articulation, tone quality, accent, and general cultural effect needed to be addressed for pedagogy to be effective.[55]

Core ACUBS members took note of these warnings but could offer little in the way of solutions to the problem of curricular standards.[56] ACUBS president and University of Illinois Director of Broadcasting Josef Wright wondered if educational stations should look to the "radio-formatting success of NBC?" to streamline content. He distributed recommendations for radio practices, with bullet points such as: "program contributors should be at station at least ten minutes before advertised hour for broadcasting. Observance will save announcer many anxious moments."[57] But stations simply could not afford experienced staff or remuneration of talent. In 1932, a report noted that one-third of educational stations were forced to sell time to advertisers to subsidize the station's activities and fees just to pay for transmitter or line rental costs.[58] These same stations put little if any of those funds into development. It became clear that a concerted effort would be necessary to influence upcoming regulation about the fate of educational broadcasts.[59]

Two Early Activist Models: The National Committee on Education by Radio and the National Advisory Council on Radio in Education

While educators attempted to address deficiencies of university radio, federal regulation was shaping how stations would obtain licenses. Institutional leaders had sounded the alarm about problems with providing compulsory educational as early as the Radio Act of 1927.[60] The origins of media reform began somewhat from the top-down. In the late 1920s Fredrick Paul Keppel of the Carnegie Corporation and American Association for Adult Education (AAAE) met with General Charles McKinley Salzman of the FRC to inquire about how radio might serve national interest through education, but without interfering with developing industry, government, or general public.[61] They determined to organize a group to maintain communication between each sector. Keppel persuaded John Rockefeller Jr. to finance preliminary steps into opening a discussion about collaboration.

In 1928 Herbert Hoover appointed Ray Wilbur as the Secretary of the Interior. At a White House dinner Keppel persuaded Wilbur that his AAAE should collaborate with the FRC to address broadcasting access under conditions of frequency scarcity, a term that described how demand exceeded available licensure for radio channels.[62] Wilbur compelled Commissioner of Education William John Cooper to initiate Keppel's concept by organizing a conference for the industry and educators. In 1930 Levering Tyson was hired by Keppel to form the National Advisory Council on Radio in Education (NACRE), tasked with putting different sectors into conversation regarding identification of a common social goal for radio.[63]

Commissioner Cooper's meeting also inspired the foundation of the NCER, which grew out of early reform work conducted by Ben Darrow at Ohio State University. Darrow wrote a persuasive survey in 1928 that identified overwhelming public interest in radio as a classroom extension tool, which caught the attention of the Payne Fund philanthropy group.[64] Prompted by Darrow's work, John Clifton, Director of Education of Ohio, green lit a state-wide trial, paid for by a Payne Fund grant.[65] The project's advisory committee contacted Payne to cover survey and research expenses, leading to the NCER's first major lobbyist hire, Armstrong Perry, educational radio specialist at the Office of Education.[66] The NCER was organized to "receive and collect" documents for resources, "organize some materials into bulletins," and "outline techniques for research and carry on investigations into best methods of broadcasting and compare results of lessons sent to schools by radio," to raise awareness about the importance of "this new instrument as an educational tool."[67] The NCER was tasked with preventing conflicts and duplication of effort between various broadcasting efforts, to "furnish advice on educational soundness of programs suggested and to supply typical programs upon the request of any station." NCER appointed Joy Elmer Morgan of the National Education Association (NEA) as chair. Clifton was then appointed to support Morgan, along with President of the University of Wyoming A.G. Crane. The NCER was instructed by Cooper to "bring about legislation to permanently and exclusively assign 15%" of radio frequencies, and support research into radio education.[68] They were further mandated to "safeguard and serve the interests" of broadcasting stations associated with educational institutions, to encourage development, and promote coordination of existing facilities. The Payne Fund gave the NCER a 5-year grant, and its first office was in the NEA building in Washington, DC, in 1930.

The NCER's 15 percent mandate picked up immediate support from Senator Simeon D. Fess of Ohio, who introduced an early bill on the matter. Fess believed that it was possible to set aside special frequencies due to a regulatory tradition in which westward land was granted for the public education. As Hugh Slotten has shown in his remarkably researched work on early communication regulation, the Fess bill failed.[69] But in the process, the NCER's activism set an important early distinction between public and privately run media.

NACRE and NCER were founded as two different strategic groups stemming from the same recommendations made by the AAAP and Office of

Education: 1) to organize a committee for the purpose of formulating definite plans and recommendations for protecting and promoting broadcasting originating in educational institutions, with the Office of Education be taking responsibility of notification. And 2) to lobby for future radio allocations to be set aside for educational use.[70] Appropriately identified as the two pillars of early educational lobby, Robert McChesney paints one group as strong (NCER) versus another group of complacent (NACRE) activists. Yet both the NCER and NACRE shared the same origin in philanthropically funded mandates to address insufficiencies of the Radio Act of 1927, and the work of each group was to some extent predetermined by their respective funding bodies. Tyson, in particular, was quite limited in his technocratic role, in accordance with his assignment and the influence of his philanthropic underwriters. But Tyson would go on to play a crucial role in the development of public media.

A New Deal Project: Commissioner John Studebaker and the US Office of Education's Investment in Educational Radio

While educators and lobbyists searched for methods to secure frequencies for educational experimentation, the idea that technology might serve a public good gained traction in the federal sector.[71] Upon Franklin Roosevelt's election, educational radio was seen as a tool to combat fascism, communicate with the public during the Great Depression, and increase the pace of work training.[72] As discussed in David Goodman's work on civic broadcast history, New Deal Commissioner of Education John Studebaker played a central role in the early stages of the development of public media. Studebaker was a serendipitous appointment in many ways.[73] A Midwest progressive with strong institutional supervisory experience as Des Moines School Superintendent, in 1931 Studebaker applied for and received $125,000 in grants from the Carnegie Corporation to begin a five-year experiment in the Des Moines Public School system in the institution of "public forums."[74] As Kunzman and Tyack have illustrated, there were practical reasons to begin this experiment, especially regional expansion of public engagement.[75] Studebaker was also informed by progressive educational thought.[76] Over past decades educators had envisioned the space of public schools as a necessary extension of progressive public service ideals.[77] Studebaker posited that besides training education should increase democratic participation through community access.[78]

Studebaker developed public forums in Des Moines to promote public discourse through a weekly assembly hour comprised of panels, visual aids, and prepared speeches. To prepare individuals for continuous growth as civic actors, he contended that education should influence the future decisions of individual citizens, and therefore concern itself with questions that challenged the notion that any idea or person is infallible. "First we teach young children to read and write, second we teach or should teach the young child how to observe the kind of world he lives in, and help him by the use of his tools of learning to discover for himself what is in that world."[79] Education, according to Studebaker, should urge the complete and impartial survey of all theories and ideas, as well as critical testing of these ideas through analysis and experimentation. If democratic participation were modeled around public participatory dissent, it would be less likely that an unchallenged fascist impulse would appear as an affiliation in the face of widespread economic or social unrest.[80]

Forum leaders were trained to facilitate the exchange of information and points of view among citizens to cultivate tolerance and develop "critical intelligence,"[81] no specific program for social indoctrination was planned for participation in a public space.[82] For his concept of educational initiatives to be accessible to large audiences, which he called "assemblages,"[83] additional resources would have to be funneled into extension services. Studebaker buttressed his experiment with an expansion of the forum idea into a *Radio School of the Air* in 1934[84] to supplement extant initiatives for students unable to attend school or workers unable to attend forums, which gained the attention of officials at the United States Office of Education. Originally hired as a one-year appointment, Studebaker at first found a national institution having "little to do with settling educational policies," directing most of its attention to statistical measurements and minimal bureaucratic oversight.[85] His one-year appointment turned into a three, and he eventually became the country's longest-serving Commissioner, ending his tenure in 1948 before going into the private sector.[86] A crucial component of his time included translating his concept of democratic education from an Iowan experiment into radio practice.[87]

"Public Interest" and Public Infrastructure: The Communications Act of 1934 and the Convening of a Media Reform Coalition

While educational broadcasters and the Office of Education identified radio as a tool for classroom extension services, regulators were persuaded that radio should serve a different purpose.[88] Previous to 1927, radio regulation was overseen by the Commerce Department.[89] To balance the responsibility over frequency allocations, Senators Clarence Dill and Wallace H. White passed a bill that authorized the Federal Radio Commission, which was ratified as the Radio Act of 1927. The bill separated the United States into five regional zones, and the FRC was granted authority to determine conditions for frequency licenses. But there was no mechanism for how to deliberate about the strength of individual applications. As McChesney and Slotten have noted, the FRC reorganized frequencies into clear, regional, and local assignments with General Order 40 in 1928, under the auspice of providing reliable radio coverage for listeners. The problem was that there were significantly more applications than AM channels. The FRC was advised to deliberate with "public interest, convenience, and necessity," a phrase never quite defined by the Dill-White Bill. The one area in which different sectors seemed to agree was that adjudication based upon technical requirements set by radio engineers was less controversial than awarding channels based upon genre, cultural belief, or affiliation.

This decision immediately favored applicants who had the funds to not only build a station that met the technical requirements set by radio engineers,[90] but continuously maintain costly equipment for license renewal. As Susan Smulyan has written, this encouraged and hastened the institutionalization of the American advertising model.[91] The second more hegemonic consequence of deferring to technical requirements was that discussions around media policy began to reflect technocratic language in every area—beginning with station maintenance but also in defining audiences in standardized terms.

When the Communications Act was passed, the "public interest, convenience, and necessity" mandate remained a central logic of the bill. In Pursuant to the Act, the newly constituted Federal Communications Commission (FCC) was tasked with reallocating station licenses based upon the FRC's technical language but for a much larger pool of applications. In preparation for the 1934 FCC hearings, ACUBS wondered if a standard frequency allocation range could be recommended to regulators. Instead of requesting a blanket percentage of assignments per area, could a moderately desirable place on the dial—but perhaps not the most economically competitive range—be set aside for universities and school districts? Carl Menzer at the University of Iowa and Harold Ingham at KFKU Kansas University wrote several internal ACUBS memos that frequencies between the 550 and 590 AM range were undesirable enough to commercial stations that educational stations might lobby to receive a permanent "medium space" there.[92] In a September letter to Ingham, another member speculated that "regional channels of low or medium frequency" might be achievable for educators if the stations could fill an 18-hour day.[93] Filling such a long period of time with limited staff would be possible, they posited, if educators could find a way to connect each station to a "controlled federal educational chain subsidized by the government, education department, and department of interior."[94]

Missing from previous accounts of the Communications Act, educators were temporarily successful with their inquiry. ACUBS members were provided with an opportunity to claim special frequencies just before the passage of the Communications Act. ACUBS President Josef Wright reported that educators were offered frequencies in the 1500 to 1600 AM range.[95] However, educators decided that this part of the spectrum was too weak to sustain large regional broadcasts.[96] Most radio tuners had not yet been built to "get frequencies higher than 1500."[97] Since educational stations would have to serve relatively focused constituencies in comparison to commercial stations, they turned down the offer, hoping that the FRC would counteroffer with more desirable frequencies. B.B. Brackett at South Dakota, often the most vociferous critic of the FRC previous to the Act, disagreed with the ACUBS counter proposal. He argued that they should take the frequency allocations because "disadvantages would be overbalanced by advantages"[98]—ACUBS members would no longer have to compete with commercial stations for frequencies and, possibly, several years into the future such frequencies might be tenable for new radios. Unfortunately he was right, the ACUBS' rejection of special frequencies was a huge tactical mistake. Carl Menzer reported that instead of a counteroffer, the FRC cut off further negotiation.

"The FRC takes the attitude that 'you are always yelling for more facilities and you don't use the ones you have. Come forth with a plan that is really practical and we'll see what we think of it.' Yet no plan has ever been submitted officially because they hadn't [sic] been proposed properly. The question isn't, necessarily more time but more power and better frequency allocations."[99]

The entire history of American broadcasting and media reform might have taken a different trajectory had ACUBS officials responded affirmatively to the FRC offer for allocated frequency assignments in the AM band.

From Lobby to Institution Building: The Federal Radio Education Committee (FREC)

After 1934 the Office of Education connected with the FCC to explore how educational broadcasting might be stabilized despite the Communication Act's focus on technical expertise. Formed on December 18, 1935, the Federal Radio Education Committee was organized as a group of forty members who met in various subcommittees for the specialized study of educational radio.[100] Its governance consisted of federal officials, educational, and commercial representatives. Commissioner John Studebaker served as chair, and other notable members of the executive committee included James W. Baldwin of the National Association of Broadcasters (NAB); A. D. Ring, Assistant Chief Engineer of the FCC; Levering Tyson of the National Advisory Council on Radio in Education (NACRE); and R. C. Higgy of the ACUBS and Ohio State University. A research subcommittee of FREC was appointed to "refine the outlines of proposed study projects" consisting of W. W. Charters of the Payne Fund and Ohio State, Hadley Cantril of Princeton University, Robert Lynd of Columbia University, and John Karol of CBS.[101] A third and tertiary subcommittee designed to examine conflicts between member interests included A. G. Crane of the University of Wyoming, Harold McCarty of the University of Wisconsin, George Porter of the FCC, and administrators from NBC and CBS.

In advance of the Act Levering Tyson of the National Advisory Council on Radio in Education (NACRE) warned educators that the networks were too well situated, and that educators should find ways to work with commercial interests if they intended to survive emerging regulatory trends in Washington, DC. It was unclear how educators would proceed with such limited funds, but practitioners decisively insisted upon keeping university stations separate from commercial interests.

From Activism to Advocacy: Shifts in Strategy and Practice by NCER, NACRE, and ACUBS after the Communications Act

As McChesney details, the first media reformers began as activists who lobbied legislators to set aside protected frequencies for educators. But after 1934, the work of media activists evolved in response to the Communications Act to become something more like a media advocacy. Loosely defined, the history of media activism clarified, made visible, and activated adherents around issues in media policy, representation, and access. Activism conducted by the NCER before 1934 successfully raised awareness about the issue of educational radio experiments yet was tactically behind commercial broadcasters in seizing authority among technical debates.[102] It was not enough to work as an extension service of the Office of Education; activists did not yet understand the technical, aesthetic, or distributive infrastructure of radio technology. Despite early policy defeats, NCER activism made a foundational contribution to the history of the political economy of communication research by articulating the first coherent logic of noncommercial media.[103] The distinctions made by Armstrong Perry and Tracy Tyler between for-profit and nonprofit media between 1930 and 1934 continue to resonate today.

After 1934, NCER continued its philanthropically funded lobby work but also began to study and implement system-building strategies in accordance with the public interest mandate of the Communications Act. Its advocacy period consisted of expanding its alliance base; working with federal, grass-roots, and state-based institutions; and implementing best practices in an alternative media system. Reform was structured to take calculated steps and implement tactical benchmarks.[104]

The NACRE after 1934

Levering Tyson remained a prominent advocate of the post-1934 Act. As an appointed member at FREC, Tyson's "moderate" position endeared him to Studebaker, who faced a commercial-friendly playing field. Tyson's connections became a major factor in the Rockefeller Foundation's willingness to fund educational broadcasting research. Upon his appointment in 1930 Tyson wrote a piece that piqued the Rockefeller Foundation's David Stevens's interest in radio. Tyson argued that a "fundamental organization" needed to be created to provide a "clearing house of information" about educational undertakings to advise local councils in broadcasting and enlist any interested agency that was available.[105] The original NACRE board only consisted of seven members and served mainly as a platform for Tyson to meet with stakeholders, including reportedly John Dewey and the commercial networks. Tyson predicted the 1934 outcome. As early as 1931 Tyson wrote to the ACUBS that practitioners needed to "advance from a state of isolation."[106]

But Tyson stuck with educational radio after the Act and was responsible for several pivotal shifts in reform strategy. Returning to the 15 percent protected frequency concept, Tyson received a $7000 grant from David Stevens at the Rockefeller General Education Board to run a conference on whether the original proposal might meet the mandate of "mutual cooperation" declared in a new FCC "*Pursuant (307)*" legislation document.[107] New York University Chancellor H.W. Chase reported on April 2, 1935 that presenters agreed that "active cooperation between the industry and educational forces in the country" would be a "milestone"; the NACRE conference should intimate a sense of the "techniques" that needed to be examined by educators and networks, which, he believed, would serve as common ground between each interest.[108] The conference influenced FREC to release a 16-point initiative to explore opportunities for research and collaboration. Tyson was tasked with evaluating "anticipated outcomes" for broadcasting experimentation: 1) practical determination of ways in which broadcasting can be educationally and culturally effective, 2) recruitment and practical training of personnel with requisite educational and cultural qualifications, and 3) development of interest in educational and cultural broadcasting on the part of cooperating agencies.[109] His conference also became instrumental in attracting the Rockefeller Foundation to take a second look at radio.

Tyson often wrote educators regarding developments at FREC, and before the Act he encouraged practitioners to pay attention to the types of projects that were being underwritten by Carnegie.[110] Tying station practices to federal mandates, Tyson believed, increased opportunities for growth.

"As long ago as 1921 enormous hopes were voiced that the then entire new phenomenon of broadcasting would revolutionize American education. Radio has become more powerful and more generally available. Radio has its uses and liabilities with difficulties pedagogically. Radio reaches many objects and audiences with enormous implications. Educators have lagged behind in developing uses for the new device, and the demagogue and the propagandist has seized it for his own. But there are huge untapped resources to draw upon."[111]

In a 1936 piece titled "What is Educational Broadcasting? An Urgent Need," Tyson wrote to colleagues that when educational broadcasting was imagined "for programs for the school extension, it is erroneously considered boring."[112] According to the Act nearly all programming could henceforth be considered educational by regulators "because most programs influence the listener in one way or another, so it can be good or bad, the radio medium is neither until it is inscripted."[113]

His influence further encouraged the Rockefeller Foundation to examine the BBC, which led to the first transnational exchange in 1936.[114] The Rockefeller Foundation's BBC initiative began with the question of how to improve content delivery. Listeners regularly complained about the educational broadcasting approach, and David Stevens appealed to the BBC to send a representative to address this problem. The BBC response in November of 1935 was to send Professor A. Lloyd James of the London School of Oriental Studies and the "Spoken English Committee" of the BBC to consult with American representatives, beginning with The World Wide Broadcasting Federation in Boston. For some years Lloyd James had advised the BBC on educational broadcast development.[115]

James was a significant figure for the BBC to send the US—he was one of the first to promote radio speech as important for its clarity and "intelligibility."[116] After he arrived James expressed interest in the development of US educational broadcasting but noted that such an endeavor had to begin with basic patterns of style such as enunciation, articulation, and clarity. "Learned Englishmen do not consider American speech dreadful," nor was English the "prerogative" of one country by any means, James proclaimed in one newspaper interview.[117] But at the same time, "they (Americans) must see to it that English language varieties that are not intelligible shall not be encouraged."[118] Due to his influence, speech practices grew increasingly to reflect an Anglophone pattern and concept due to his belief that radio required a commonly accepted mode of intelligibility.

The Rockefeller Foundation wrote that NBC and CBS invited James to speak live on their network broadcasts and were eager to "impress him" with the quality of their content.[119] James, for his part, wrote that he approached the commercial endeavor with "apprehension" but that he was most invested in noncommercial media. "Never have I been engaged on a mission that was nearer to my heart than that of fostering educational broadcasting."[120] By the time he returned to the UK in April of 1936, he had taken part in three speech programs at NBC, consulted with the development of WWBF speech standardization, given talks on linguistic theory in broadcasting, and worked with CBS about creating a method of "standard" English for press speech. This initiative included two early-1936 lunches with a young Edward R. Murrow, who expressed "manifest desire to do all that he could to promote cultural and educational broadcasting," and who apparently was quite influenced by James's concept that educational broadcasting must be reliant upon "execution."[121]

James's success gave the Rockefeller Foundation an idea. What if a qualified BBC agent were able to come to the United States and objectively evaluate educational station practices? After consulting with James about possible candidates, they settled on the BBC's Director of Regional Broadcasting since 1932, Charles Siepmann. Siepmann had joined the BBC in 1927 and was one of its most vocal and open proponents of noncommercial ideology. He was also known to be critical and was thought capable of offering "disinterested" reports toward the betterment of educational approaches to broadcasting. David Stevens and his assistant John Marshall had briefly met Siepmann on a fact-finding trip to Britain in 1936 that was designed to initiate internships for educators at the BBC.[122] Siepmann arrived in 1936 and conducted the first comprehensive review of educational stations.

For better or worse, Tyson's vision of a pragmatic educational advocacy in which practitioners interacted with commercial interests became central to educational broadcasting's transition into public media subsequent to the Act. To secure funding from the Rockefeller Foundation a project had to feature "cooperation" across broadcasting institutions. Cross-sector collaboration became such a necessity that by the late 1930s the foundation decided that future grants in aid had to meet Tyson's path dependency for connected research, in case philanthropic funds "dry up."[123] Funding decisions became based on the prospect that an application could guarantee that it would be able to continue after a grant was disseminated. Within eighteen months of the Act Tyson had helped to influence the government, BBC, and Rockefeller Foundation to invest in educational radio research.

The NCER after 1934

After the Act the NCER initially held out hope that they might continue with Cooper's vision for set-aside frequencies. But once it was revealed that the reserved channel lobby strategy was not only defeated in the Act, but that it had been inadvertently undermined by ACUBS university practitioners rejecting the 1500–1600 band frequencies, Joy Elmer Morgan and Armstrong Perry left the NCER. After the Act Senators Robert Wagner of New York and Henry Hatfield of West Virginia proposed an amendment to nullify existing licenses, start deliberations over, and set aside 25 percent of future radio frequencies for noncommercial broadcasters, including religious stations, but it was defeated by the Senate.[124] Though Armstrong Perry left the NCER, his work inspired reformers to stick to the nonprofit vision of the 1920s. Before the Act they believed that since the business world's profit motive would promote a false conception about the "function of broadcasting systems," it had to be countered with a vision for public access and public good over short-term profits. Businesses, Perry argued, simply had different objectives. An educational philosophy of radio should in contrast follow from an internally consistent concept of educational broadcasting as a public service.

After 1934 the NCER team grew despondent about the prospect of motivating the government to support university stations. Tyler wrote that the FCC had behaved "essentially as a straddle, a defense for killing time while commercial interests become more firmly entrenched."[125] Universities almost uniformly lacked the funding of commercial-quality stations. Tracy Tyler argued that educational stations should not "give in and embrace a commercial model" but should fight back to secure licenses by retaining an attorney, through the development of data that might support new education-friendly regulation. But once the Act was passed a new strategy became necessary.

In 1935 Bolton appointed A.G. Crane and Payne Fund administrator Howard Evans as new co-chairs. Evans made several adjustments to the NCER's central office.[126] After reviewing Morgan's pre-1934 lobby strategies, Evans concluded that the set-aside frequency strategy had failed due to both lack of coordination with the ACUBS and lack of data to support protected assignments. Crane and Evans believed that the public interest mandate had to be reinterpreted by universities and public agencies or face a situation in which "histories of radio control" would become "so entrenched that there is no possibility of successfully challenging them." Instead of lobbying Congress to set aside protected frequencies, they decided that the NCER would "proceed forthwith to assume leadership and cooperation with the industry in order to set up standards of performance which can be utilized by all as a yardstick."[127] In his communications with educational practitioners after passage of the act, Evans recommended that they build their own clear channel and provide cross-state broadcasts at a central university such as Ohio State. He suggested that educators request "high band" frequencies offered by the FRC before the Act, which still were not in use, to conduct relay broadcasts between stations. Co-chair A.G. Crane concurred with Evans's recommendations that the mission of the next phase of the NCER should be to assist in the promotion and protection of educational broadcasters and to encourage and monitor the growth of educational stations, and Crane conceived an additional step. He believed that a continued investment in noncommercial media as a "service of democracy" would hold the reform movement together. Since private media tended to "bar minority access and representation from the air, due to the "relative size" of minority populations," Crane determined that noncommercial media should be differentiated from not only commercial broadcasters but also from third-party noncommercial broadcasters, such as religious or service groups,[128] due to educators' intention to serve every type of audience regardless of size.

Crane wrote that "when it became clear that its original proposal for the safeguarding of education by radio was not to be accepted, the committee began the search for a constructive plan by which the integrity and independence of educational and cultural broadcasting could be established and preserved under the conditions which have come to characterize the American system."[129] Crane's first concept was the development of a "democratic regional plan for an American Public Broadcasting Service,"[130] which he hoped would create a working organization through which educational institutions and agencies, service departments, and citizen groups could mobilize their broadcasting resources, raise the standards of radio presentations, and demonstrate a cooperative method of maintaining working relationships between broadcasting stations and representatives of public bodies.

The Communications Act set a precedent that required educators to understand their utilization of the airwaves in terms of legality, finance, and technics, alongside competition for frequencies that favored private interests. These technocratic parameters permitted regulators to easily identify inconsistencies in applications by noncommercial groups—universities almost uniformly lacked funding for commercial-quality stations, and the FCC recommended against what would, under the terms given, be preferential treatment against those lacking capitalistic versions of competition.

Tracy Tyler believed that a dramatic change in the entire orientation of the movement was necessary. What educators really needed "was not to give in and embrace a commercial model," but fight back to secure licenses by retaining an attorney and continue their activism on behalf of educators by providing information about educational policy decisions and related bills.[131]

A piece co-written by the NCER staff argued:

"Radio is the greatest instrument since the inventing of printing for entertainment, info, and education. It talks to millions of homes both far and near. It calls the whole nation instantly into conference. It transforms America into one great town hall meeting. It is the most powerful instrument ever invented for effective teamwork by a whole nation. It can give all the people in America the best in thought and entertainment or it can broadcast the inferior and the poorest. The life of all America can be elevated or debased by the use made of radio. It is a public instrument for the public good. Radio should be guided and controlled to insure this nation the greatest possible social values. The needs and desires of listeners should govern the character, content, and relative extent and frequency of broadcast programs. Material detrimental to the welfare of listener groups should be eliminated regardless of commercial profit."[132]

Further, the NCER argued, educators needed to retain their vision because the purpose of education by radio—the encouragement of social equity through access to universal public education—required a vision distinct from the networks. The networks simply did not care about social parity, though they did believe in a vision in which program access and diversity of content served consumers. But the populist nature of commercial radio also tended to "bar minority access and representation from the air," due to the "relative size" of minority populations.[133]

Crane came to believe that the creation of a network-like infrastructure would increase demand for an alternative to entertainment alone. An efficient counterpoint needed to be imagined that still nonetheless met the criteria set by Congress. In one letter Crane wrote to the ACUBS that "radio should sell itself" (as in promote) so it would be "vital yet subordinate and incidental to consciousness."[134] While aggressiveness in "business fields" had overshadowed social welfare as a goal in broadcast development, in truth the "new instrument" was still little understood, unappreciated, and experimental. Faculties at various universities had failed to appreciate the limitations of the new medium "to hold an unseen audience." The remaining universities had demonstrated strong public service possibilities, but what was needed was a plan to "conserve radio for public services" among national, regional, and state boards. A "public system" would need to involve multiple affiliated associations and work in such a way that it would cause the "least disturbance to the present system." Crane believed that a public system should emulate a private system, and be controlled privately, by those with public interests.

Crane proposed a plan in 1935 that would "parallel the present private commercial system" as a "government system chain to supplement and not replace the present system, not create any undue interference, not jeopardize investments, but give programs of public interest." Since educational radio had insufficient money or material to challenge dominant interests, all programs would be created overtly for public welfare and stimulate public service initiatives. Crane worried that the ACUBS would not be up to the task of developing an alternative, sustainable approach. In a 1936 letter Crane wrote that the ACUBS still had not settled on a permanent constitution, and he worried that the group was still too unfocused, as they had decided to "subordinate the acquisition of educational broadcasting provisions" as a central merit of their endeavor.[135] Though the ACUBS had moved toward improvement of broadcasts in line with public interest stipulations, their careful and slow evaluation of future steps irritated remaining NCER members.

The NCER dissolved in the early 1940s. Before disbanding Evans lobbied Senator Burton Wheeler that "no right on the part of the broadcasters to determine what listeners should receive or not over radio,"[136] which favored the current network approach. Owners wanted "complete authority" and other wings of the government realized that programs that determined standards for future content selection by the industry had power over vital influence over public opinion. Evans wrote a final piece titled "Toward a More Democratic Radio" that argued that "speculation on the future of broadcasting must consider deliberations conducted by the federal government through its legislative, administrative, and judicial agencies." The industry had invested in talent and improvement of programs in the early days of radio, which had "done so much to give radio its present technical perfection."[137] But an alternative to strict governmental control or the kind of industrial control which had been lax enough to permit objectionable "commercial announcements and over stimulating children's programs" was still necessary. Evans believed that Studebaker had shown that members of the listing audience would respond to a system in which they could also have some say in determining program policies.

After 1936: The ACUBS changes its name to the NAEB and Considers how to Reinvigorate Educational Broadcasting

Practitioners remained behind their public advocates in strategic thinking until the late 1940s. By the late 1930s educational broadcasting had begun to train a second generation, who quickly learned from the mistakes of the 1920s and early 1930s. Over the course of dozens of ledgers, conferences, and interactions with other broadcasting institutions, the ACUBS transformed into something like a strategic sponge, observing and notating every point of progress across federal, advocacy, and commercial broadcasting interests.

In 1934 the ACUBS changed its name to the National Association of Educational Broadcasters (NAEB) in hope of unifying as a national practitioner movement. Part of the conference included the drafting of a new constitution. In the preamble, members wrote:

> "Believing that radio is in its nature one of the most important factors in our national and international welfare, we, the representatives of institutions of higher learning, engaged in educational broadcasting, do associate ourselves together to promote, by mutual cooperation and united effort, the dissemination of knowledge to the end that both the technical and educational features of broadcasting may be extended to all."[138]

Consequently, proceeding the September 1934 ACUBS/NAEB conference, several committees were organized to work on educational broadcasting problems. The committee for "Federal Chain Education Program Development," chaired by Frank Schooley at the University of Illinois, was put in charge of finding federal support for state-based broadcasters. Another committee on "Short Wave Transmission Between Stations," headed by Carl Menzer of the University Iowa, examined methods of distribution outside of rented network wires, especially for rebroadcasts of better shows by NAEB members. Menzer's committee attempted several approaches to program distribution before settling on distributing recorded programs, called "transcriptions," by mail. A committee on "Proposed Recorded Programs," headed by T. M. Beaird at Oklahoma and Harold McCarty at Wisconsin, was charged with looking into how to produce high quality transcription programs, though this committee's function was ultimately folded into Menzer's.

While a step in the right direction, NAEB initiatives started too late to persuade policymakers. 1934 ended as a disastrous year for educators. A *Radio Guide* editorial from September 15, 1934, described the prevailing state of confusion in educational broadcasting. If few educational broadcasts attracted audiences, the piece queried, "do radio listeners in the U.S. want 25 percent of all stations broadcasting educational material?"[139] These stations had not justified their existence, the article stated, because they had not made broadcasting compelling. "If they can make broadcasting interesting then they can have all the time they want on the air, right now. No one thinks that making stations educational will overcome the lure of good radio drama, broadcast of symphony, or good popular music."[140] *The Guide* was a NAB publication, but from the perspective of most regulators and listeners the piece was accurate. Josef Wright, who had warned educators in 1931 that their methods had not been up to par with commercial broadcasts, circulated a new FCC *Pursuant* (*307*) to other members. And educational stations underwent an introspective and slow rebound period between 1935 and 1946.

Infrastructural steps were implemented during this time. The University of Kentucky equipped school centers with radio sets to enable individuals to go to local schools to tune into educational programs.[141] One educator at the University of Washington wrote that the university was engaging in a vigorous campaign to encourage use of radio broadcasting to schools in the state. Contributing to Washington State's place in journalistic history as having trained Edward R. Murrow, the university became the first NAEB member to feature cooperation between educational radio and national press. "Most editors think a radio is just a radio and are unwilling to discriminate between broadcasting stations that help them and those that hurt them."[142] Iowa State "circulated 26,000 volumes in 5 years, with 1800 members" and was by 1935 planning to supplement library facilities with listening stations.[143] In early 1935 New York agricultural and home economics departments developed single programs for airing on 24 separate stations, with 125 brief "talks" developed each month. This may have been the first state-wide distribution format, though it was only based around 2–3 programs that were repeated. Treasurer of the NAEB Ted Beaird of Oklahoma started the first educational rendition of what he called the "man with the travelling mic" format—a show dedicated to "going around and asking questions about stuff."[144] Schools focused more intently on show availability, transparency of schedule, and interconnectivity with other state institutions and listeners, and stations began to develop standards that could be followed with oversight by related institutional interests.

Harold McCarty of the University of Wisconsin, and one of the Rockefeller Foundation fellows who interned at the BBC, wrote to NAEB members that they must in the future convince voters that publicly supported broadcasting would "give them something they can get in no other way."[145] Arguing that not many understood the quiet conflict between education and entertainment, a competition in which education was generally if not always the loser, the larger populace had failed to see the importance of safeguarding educational interests. This included, according to McCarty, a lack of interest from university presidents and "mildly interested" faculty at universities. Four basic questions would need to be addressed by members of the NAEB, which he called the "four problems of radio": 1) facilities, 2) finances, 3) programs, and 4) promotion. Education, he joked, had "come too late to the banquet of radio and must feast on crumbs, or lack thereof."[146] But he remained optimistic that there was "rich talent" for educational broadcasting, should they be given training and provided with standards.

In 1936 the NAEB devised a future plan for their affiliates. The organization would henceforth "serve as spokesman for united organized education," which involved assistance in the protection and extension of privileges of educational broadcasters, promotion of broadcasting to organized schools of all kinds and ranks, and stimulation and coordinated cooperative experimentation and research.[147] Such attention would stimulate the formation of state and regional boards to promote educational broadcasting and assist in the securing of time and facilities for such services. Initiatives in these areas could then collect, publish, and distribute information conducive to the advancement of "public welfare broadcasting." And through increased experimentation, consolidation, and communication over how to best streamline education by radio, standards could be formulated to "appraise the quality and values" of radio programs, thus improving techniques of broadcasting.[148]

A subsequent NCER pamphlet titled "Radio Education through Public and Institutionally Owned Stations" proposed several FREC-inspired investigations into program and script exchange, a proposed recording service, analysis of local audiences, a better organized educational force within distinct service areas, and reaction surveys to instructional lectures.[149] W. I. Griffith at Iowa State wrote a memo stating that radio had passed its experimental stage and advanced to "being recognized as an important agency of education" with "great influence on the listener depending on the material."[150] The next phase of educational broadcasting should offer instruction, but also entertain and have "worthy" programming.[151] Broadcasters would have to envision who intended audiences might be, for example (Griffith offered misogynistically): "Mrs. Thrifty housewife enjoys stories more on radio because she can listen while doing other tasks such as sewing, mending, or preparing vegetables."[152] Further, proponents acknowledged that networks like NBC had offered regular educational features that were well received and even supported by the NEA, and that CBS's American School of the Air had produced quality educational broadcasting since 1929 on literature, history, geography, music, stories, foreign affairs, and vocational guidance. "Scripts are prepared by staff of ten authors specializing in particular subjects and supplemented by weekly issuances containing suggestions for utilization of particular programs."[153] The difference, and the challenge for educational broadcasters, would be to match the networks' production culture.

Charles Siepmanns warned that educators did not yet understand the logistical requirements of running a radio station, and as a whole lacked "constructive purpose,"[154] comparing the endeavor to an "anomalous assortment of matter." But he wrote a set of suggestions that were distributed among NAEB stations that recommended educational broadcasting to be "adjunct to university activities," as a site of research for psychology and sociology departments.[155] If broadcasting became an extramural activity overseen by faculty committee, set on increasing administrative investment and oversight, radio could become a central university activity and attract more funds. The key to stabilizing the practice would be to find a way to make educational broadcasters both a profession and extension service. Siepmann's presence remained an inspiration for educators for decades,[156] which included composing the widely influential "Blue Book."[157]

These shifts influenced a young Richard Hull at Iowa State, who became determined to transform the NAEB into a professional institution. In a December 1946 letter Richard Hull wrote to Harold Engel at Wisconsin "if I were to be harsh, I should say the attitude of most of our stations is still one of complacency whereas we actually have very little to be complacent about even in several rather favorable situations. We face a situation where we will, like the old soldier, not die, but simply fade away."[158] His plan was for the NAEB to act as a primary "information exchange" in which the "pioneer experience" of Midwest institutions would act as a publicity model for new members, and from which monthly publications, monographs, and personnel was released.[159] To meet this goal Hull solicited universities to build new educational stations. His "pitch" package usually comprised of sending several bulletins regarding "station policy" procedures, with a warning to avoid sharing facilities with commercial stations.[160] Under Hull the NAEB transitioned into providing classroom education services influenced by commercial methods. Should a station decide to join the NAEB, members were provided access to "descriptive sheets on coursework" and the promise that a program transcription service could fill needed hours.[161]

Trained under Griffith at Iowa State, Richard Hull witnessed how educators' unwillingness to work with or learn from commercial broadcasters had led to stunted development by university stations. In January 1948 Richard Hull wrote to E. W. Ziebarth at CBS' Minnesota affiliate WCCO that, unlike past advocates, he had long been "anxious" to construct better relationships with well-run commercial affiliates, and that while financing between educational and network affiliates was distinctly different, the NAEB was no longer categorically opposed to dispensing its programming to interested commercial stations. "I will never forget the remarks that Siepmann made to the effect that educators may have everything to teach commercial broadcasters about good taste, but they have nothing to teach them about technique."[162]

Conclusion

The Radio Act of 1927 and the Communications Act of 1934 unexpectedly inspired a loosely knit coalition of lobby, practitioner, philanthropic, and government agency members, who became galvanized to invest in educational radio as the best hope to increase equal access to education via technology. Trade groups NCER and NACRE lobbied so that educational radio might be utilized as a bureaucratic extension service that provided distance-learning opportunities for listeners. The first incarnation of these groups pulled from agendas set by federal and state governments and conducted activist work to shape emerging public policy. After the Act, both the NCER and NACRE underwent structural shifts in which they continued to advocate and build infrastructure for a sustained noncommercial media production culture that could outlive their original policy lobbies.

Although the NCER and NACRE pursued stark differences in activist approaches, they remained bound by fidelity to their core missions. Even as both groups changed and implemented new strategies to carve out a protected space for noncommercial media, the organizing concept of democratic reform synthesized their labors through the 1930s and influenced how the ACUBS/NAEB understood its post-1934 mission. One takeaway from this history is that media activism history reveals how activists adjust and regroup after setbacks and political shifts. No framing about the definition of "media activism" could be extrapolated from one case study. Yet, looking at the long arc of the formation and evolution of media reform trade groups helps to clarify how conceptual investments have shaped the political economy of media institutions. The logics, practices, and decision processes of commercial and noncommercial media industries and associated trade organizations are closely tied to their stated social goals, be it profit or service. With all of the changes between the 1920s and 1930s, the one through-line of early media activist history remained institutional dedication to educational access.

CHAPTER 2

Funding

The Philanthropic Mandate for Collaboration between Educational and Commercial Broadcasters

Understanding Philanthropic Support for Public Media: Standardized Practice and New Deal Nation-Building

As Michele Hilmes has written,[1] the Rockefeller Foundation served the crucial role of underwriting the development of educational broadcasting experimentation and program development. Directly after the Act, the FCC revisited the question of if special frequencies should be provided for educators. However, due to a lack of available AM channels and the influence of 1920s radio regulation, the FCC was unable provide special points on the dial for a specific content approach. Pursuant to the passing of the Communications Act the National Association of Broadcasters (NAB) worked in partnership with NBC to successfully lobby the FCC that they were producing educational content equal to universities. The NAB determined that if commercial media could lay equal claim to the educational genre, that the FCC had no choice but to observe the original 1927 regulatory language of "public interest, "which maintained that levels of audience listenership and continuous station management were the primary areas of consideration for licensure. This left the FCC with only one option to act on behalf of reformers—to carve out provisions within existing policy by which educators might prove that they would be able to steward a specific genre better than commercial broadcasters.

Within one year of the Act it became clear to all reform groups—educators, activists, and government agencies—that they had to reorganize their lobby within the contours of "public interest." It was under these conditions that the Rockefeller Foundation was invited to underwrite research. Government agencies were not allowed to fund one specific third party institution over another. Between 1935 and 1937 the Office of Education (OOE) teamed with FCC to found the Federal Radio Education Committee (FREC) to 1) identify a middle ground that every stakeholder could agree upon as grounds for frequency allocations, and 2) to locate a means by which educational broadcasting might improve and receive special frequencies. They called upon two major precedents. The first was previous broadcast regulation, which required empirical evidence that stations met certain "standards" for maintenance of license.[2] The second was evaluation standards derived from the educational sector itself.[3] The Rockefeller foundation already happened to be working with educators on strategies to triangulate evidence of effective classroom practice, which made for an unusually efficient transition from classroom to radio education underwriting.

Upon entering collaboration with the FCC and OOE, the Rockefeller Foundation appointed John Marshall to oversee funding of FREC-related reform projects. The influence of Marshall's work cannot be underestimated. Between 1936 and 1941 Marshall supported the development of broadcasting practice, facilities management, and audience research, all following from the strategy that FREC-inspired projects should tackle the public interest problem by working within its precedent. This chapter looks at how Rockefeller underwriting consequently set the precedent for philanthropic funding of noncommercial media.

Radio as Educational Extension: The Eight-Year Study's Influence on New Radio Regionalism

Philanthropic groups and government agencies hoped that radio's ability to transgress vast geographic spaces with immediacy could be put into service of nation-building as early as 1927. Reform activities of the late 1920s and early 1930s were influenced by the Payne and Carnegie Funds. The foundational meetings discussed in Chapter 1 inspired the formation of the National Committee on Education by Radio (NCER) and NACRE, but also introduced the concept that educational broadcasting was an attractive area for philanthropic intervention. Philanthropic funding of educational radio began when Secretary of the Interior Ray Lyman Wilberg called a meeting to investigate how educational radio might be of service to federal education.[4] He obtained financing for arrangements through the Payne Fund with additional support from the Carnegie Fund and J.C. Penney. Encouraged by the meeting, the Payne Fund's Francis Payne Bolton became persuaded that radio would serve as the bridge for interdisciplinary work between speech, psychology, sociology, political science, and education.[5] Bolton founded the Fund to achieve "socially important" goals through research into media literacy, to raise awareness about the role of communication in civic society. She wrote that uncritical reproduction of what one had read, heard, or had seen was a major threat to democratic thought, and promoted a new project which she called "reading the lines."[6] She believed that educational media would produce a higher level of thinking than entertainment, and she hoped that the Fund would promote interpretation and evaluation skills. Though the Payne Fund supported educational radio activism primarily through the NCER, as Brent Malin has written, Bolton also was interested in film, comic books, and classroom tools.[7] The Carnegie Foundation received educational radio as a complement to their work with the American Association for Adult Education. By the time the Communications Act was passed, there were already ample precedents for philanthropic support of noncommercial broadcasting. Funding tended to center on critical literacy practices in places such as localized or agrarian communities. Within philanthropic discourses educational radio was closely associated with curricular goals.[8]

The Rockefeller Foundation convened their program in the humanities in 1926, to research its "significance for creative uses and for critical understanding."[9] In a 1933 report, RF trustees endeavored to underwrite projects responsible for "bringing the humanities from books, seminars, and museums into the current of modern life."[10] The principles of the operation were directed toward three enumerated objectives:

> 1) "Within our own country, the aim of the work in the humanities is the preservation and development of American cultural traditions with a view to their continuing growth, 2) Abroad, the aim is to promote cultural understanding among nations, and 3) If gains resulting from appropriations under old programs are to be conserved, certain continuing obligations should be recognized."

Before RF decided to underwrite radio, the board already voiced concern that humanistic research was too closely tied to theoretical research. "It frankly appears to your committee that a program in the humanities is based on a cloistered kind of research, we have more detailed information about a great number of rather abstruse subjects, but that does not logically mean that the level of artistic and aesthetic appreciation in America has been measurably raised."[11] Just previous to the Communications Act of 1934, the Foundation searched for "direct ways of extending the area of public appreciation [that] called for assistance from persons with intimate knowledge of the ways in which the American public now gains its culture."[12] A study on adult education in public schools revealed that state educational institutions provided a direct service for educational needs. The relative size and dynamism of land-grant universities seemed to provide a fertile area for growth, and radio broadcasts represented the rare middle ground in which educational and vocational value combined community, creativity, and adult education.[13] Due to the media's ability to reach large target demographics with immediacy,[14] as well as its unusual capacity to influence opinion and cultural knowledge through program practices, radio was a logical choice for socially-directed philanthropy.

The Rockefeller Foundation funded its first major research project in 1932 when the Progressive Education Association conducted what became known as the "Eight-Year Study."[15] The study was organized to build relationships between secondary and higher education institutions to clarify methods of student evaluation. The notion that a standardized, triangulated form of educational "measurement" could be discovered was widely influential on the Rockefeller Foundation General Education Board's desire to gauge when benchmarks were met, to identify if funding had been well placed. The difficulty of coordinating between levels of education, different institutions, and varying goals of each state made it necessary to develop a commonly-agreed upon method to identify when necessary adjustments to curriculum succeeded in eliciting changes in behavior, comprehension, and classroom objectives.[16] In 1934 educational researcher Ralph Tyler joined Wilford Aiken to conduct research on instruments to help schools evaluate curriculum.[17] Two of the participants in the study were closely connected to Ralph Tyler: W.W. Charters worked with Ralph Tyler's brother Keith Tyler. Through chance and serendipity, the Tyler Brothers became central figures of early broadcasting research.[18]

Early Educational Programming on Commercial Broadcasting

As philanthropic and federal agencies explored educational radio in the early 1930s, commercial broadcasting was already researching educational content. An internal NBC study revealed that most educational stations were not using the time that had been granted to their stations, and if universities shared channels with commercial stations, that noncommercial time was often rendered as dead air.[19] NBC noted that educators had not produced much variety in genre beyond instruction, and that listeners were by and large bored or confused by the content.[20] In contrast commercially-funded shows such as *Let's Pretend,* the *Music Appreciation Hour with Walter Damrosch,* and *The American School of the Air* were successful at bridging audience interest with educational goals. Commercial broadcasters were specifically interested in two university producers—Ohio State and Wisconsin. Ohio State was a leader in dramatized book content, travel logs of great explorers, early documentaries, and storytelling broadcasts. But commercial researchers otherwise considered educational stations to be the purveyors of awkward programming for an unseen audience.

In one internal report to David Sarnoff about how to compete with universities over the education moniker, an aide wrote that "all things honest with themselves, just under 20 percent of broadcasts might be qualified as an educational."[21] But, with the looming struggle over frequencies, if NBC were to consider adding cultural programming to the list of educational programming, there was at least some overlap with 50 percent of educational content aired by universities and school districts. The addition of live music made it possible to claim that 68 percent of commercial broadcasts were educational.

As the Communications Act deliberations loomed, by October 1934 NBC realized that the most successful strategy to persuade regulators would be to testify that NBC believed that they were conducting better educational programming than universities themselves. Indeed NBC's insight was probably true, at least in terms of percentage of quality broadcasts. Commercial broadcasters were self-sufficient, ran facilities in line with the public interest stipulations of the Radio Act, and compared to lecture-heavy formats the networks produced entertaining educational content.[22] Educators were completely unprepared for commercial broadcasters to take this tack.

Hearings of the Communications Act of 1934 as a Mandate for Access through Infrastructure

Robert McChesney has noted that the final decision to favor the definition of "diversity" in broadcasting as the ability to meet "public interest, convenience, and necessity" was a catastrophic one for educators.[23] The bill favored private enterprise that had already accumulated an advantage thanks to manufacturing and advertising dollars.[24] Even NBC believed that the FRC's definition of diversity benefited a "diversity" of business interests, instead of viewpoints or experience.[25] But a close reading of the hearings reveals that less than a struggle between commercial and educational voices, *both* reformers and the networks hedged their public lobby on defining and occupying the term "education."

After the Act the FCC was tasked with examining the meaning of "public interest, convenience, and necessity," and invited expert testimony. The NCER sent representatives Armstrong Perry, Joy Elmer Morgan, A.G. Crane (Wyoming), H. L. Eubank (Wisconsin), and the ACUBS's Josef Wright (Illinois) to testify. The NCER's defense presented that 11.3 percent of noncommercial broadcasts were in cooperation with commercial stations, accounting for 77,500 hours, with educational broadcasters offering 114,000 hours on their own stations. They argued that the wide range of definitions of the term education in broadcasting showed a thriving diversity of practice that deserved special frequencies.[26]

But the NCER quickly lost credibility when Joy Elmer Morgan confused a crucial policy example during testimony. One of Morgan's arguments called upon a report by the Tennessee Valley Authority (TVA), which he contended showed precedent that special frequencies could be awarded based upon previous regulation that frequencies utilized for government purposes were permissible as long as they fell under the regulation of an oversight administration.[27] However, he interpreted the report backward—and the TVA itself stepped in and clarified that it had argued that radio regulation should be decided based upon "reasonable use of radio facilities," as long as such programs were set under non-government and non-partisan control and direction.[28] Much of the NCER's position assumed that piecemeal support by political representatives, such as Commissioner Cooper, or Senators Fess, Wagner, and Hatfield would be enough. They had not prepared a defense of educational radio that was able to compete with the requirement that stations met technocratic standards.[29]

Morgan's mistake in interpreting precedent opened the door for a commercial trade group, the NAB, to testify that education was in fact a component of public interest broadcasting, and not at all separate from what listeners were already tuning in to daily. In preparation for this testimony, the NAB identified three basic issues in defense of the commercial media lobby. The first was that the term "facilities" was not clearly defined by the Act, meaning that a claim regarding "diversity" of facilities ownership could not be determined based upon genre of content broadcast.[30] Second, the incoming FCC commission did not carry authority to implement recommendations for modifications to existing allocation rules, especially pertaining to differences over broadcaster intention. And third, the NAB argued that commercial broadcasters were already providing the service of facilities for educational broadcasting, despite their internal studies that audiences generally tuned out this type of content.

The networks further consigned a series of testimonials on their behalf, that they were airing educational and public service programming. NAB and NBC built the case that the commercial system was meeting stipulations of public interest, while universities were not, and additionally providing a better civic service for the country than educators. Dr. James Francis Cooke testified to this on NBC's behalf that the "conviction of the American people and the average American prefers for his wife to welcome the chatty, familiar presentation of advertising in connection with programming."[31] Broadcasting companies quite evidently had made a contribution to education and art without government subsidy. To change the airwaves from what audiences were comfortable with would deprive the American people of its present-day blessings.[32] Similar testimonials claimed that commercial broadcasting had been responsible for Studebaker's public forums, which was partly true, breakthroughs in community building, and even the circulation of a diversity of music, such as with jazz.

As the NAB paraded a variety of witnesses, NBC President Merlin Aylesworth discovered that the NCER's testimony could be reversed into the networks' favor. One of NCER witnesses had argued that radio should be used to promote the greatest general welfare of all the people, in the "wholesome needs and desires" and relative extent and frequency of broadcast programs."[33] Aylesworth imitated this argument on behalf of the networks, with the twist that commercial radio did a better job than universities at promoting general welfare because it resembled other media sources that audiences implicitly understood such as popular magazines. Radio advertising was a service similar to newspapers in that commercial sponsorship provided a structure for editorials and public affairs.[34] Like with newspapers, radio advertising never took up the entire page, it simply supported civic content.[35] This meant that the educational character and content of a broadcast always remained intact regardless of interruptions. Broadcast flows were "pieces of the larger paper dedicated to sponsorship." And they were more sustainable than the dead air of university broadcasts because, like newspapers, the advertising model stabilized public welfare while providing an otherwise free service.

As the hearings continued, the FCC's hands were tied regarding how to interpret what types of stations might best represent education. Since the term "facilities" was not clearly defined by the Act, the FCC's best recourse was to consider the previous evidentiary framework of the Radio Act of 1927.

The Act had set a precedent for allocation of frequency, power, time, and use of time, and commercial networks were making the case that they were about to be punished for dutifully following communications regulation.[36] Commercial broadcasters also stayed on message in ways that educational trades did not. Network representatives argued that programs should target large audiences, and that loyal listening could only be maintained through the production of a wide diversity of program services. A successful station, according to an NBC report, typically required eight years of continuous operation, annual operating expenditures of millions of dollars, active cooperation of thousands of trained professional employees.[37] Educational stations were unable to meet any of these criteria.

To make matters worse for educators, when they were asked by the FCC to define education as "instruction" unique to universities and school districts, representatives from the Association of College and University Broadcasting Stations rejected the term as too narrow, and claimed that academic subjects, news reports and commentaries, music and music appreciation, agriculture, home economics, and political discussion were the cornerstones of their work.[38] Unfortunately, instruction was the sole unique domain of universities, commercial broadcasting provided an equal and sometimes better record of educationally-inflected broadcasts. The FCC consequently decided that university stations added little value without an established and maintained audience. Simply allocating frequencies to university broadcasters equated to preferential allocation and supported a single "opinion" framework that was not written into the scope of the commission's power.

Sensing that the 1927 Radio Act had set a path dependency for their argument, commercial broadcasters contended that interpretation of "public interest, convenience, and necessity" could only be implemented for licenses during renewal, not a broader thrust of perspective or style.[39] The FCC wrote that due to the tenebrous landscape of broadcasting, and the impossibility of making distinctions between education and commerce, the new commission was compelled to observe previous policies, which of course had already favored commercial broadcasting's infrastructure ownership. The consequence was that the Communications Act was implemented as it was due to confusion over the definition of "education."

FCC Commissioner E. O. Sykes's Pursuant to the Communications Act: "Public Interest" as Entertainment, Access, and Audience Engagement

Upon passage of the Act, a frustrated FCC Commissioner E. O. Sykes co-presided over a series of hearings between October and November of 1934 in which 1,535 frequency allocation cases were reviewed, in consultation with twenty-one additional overseeing administrators, departments, commissions, and offices of the government.[40] One hundred and thirty-five witnesses testified at the hearings and fourteen thousand pages of testimony were analyzed by the Commission to define the terms of broadcast license assignments. Infamously, close to 70 percent of educational stations were stripped of their frequencies in favor of the basic functional expertise of commercial interests. An under-examined component of these hearings consisted of determining a criterion by which commercial operators gained merit by "showing the service rendered by broadcasters to particular types or kinds of non-profit activities."[41] NAB representatives introduced statistics from 269 active stations showing that over twenty-five million dollars had been spent to ensure consistent and nonprofit programming. And it was asserted by the NAB that if the FCC viewed the term "educational" in its broadest sense, to embrace all programs having a cultural or informative value, a greater percentage of network time might further be considered as educational than at universities.[42] Whether the NAB's rhetoric was specious or not (and it was), the FCC weighed this information as evidence that regulation should not change past precedents. And since only the networks were able to offer data of listener interest in educational broadcasts, while guaranteeing that at least one dependable radio signal would be available to residents, the FCC ruled that commercial networks best met standards of "equal access" to broadcasting.[43]

Shortly after the pursuant hearings, in a document produced by E. O. Sykes titled *Report of the Federal Communications Commission to Congress Pursuant to Section 307 (c) of the Communications Act of 1934*, the FCC argued that its treatment of "nonprofit" broadcasting was in large part based upon the Commission's attempt to meet the criteria of the Act for basic access—which did not include guaranteed access by specific groups.[44] Each group would have to substantiate their allocation by showing how they met stipulations of the act:

> "The Commission shall study the proposal that Congress by statue allocate fixed percentages of radio broadcasting facilities to particular types or

kinds of non-profit radio programs, or to persons identified with particular types or kinds of non-profit activities, and shall report to Congress, not later than February 1, 1935, its recommendations together with the reasons for the same."[45]

The FCC noted that all types of nonprofit stations were represented during the study, but also that "no unanimity of thought or plan on the part of these organizations is apparent from the record."[46] The FCC was charged with the responsibility of licensing stations solely in accordance with "public interest, convenience, and necessity"—and the primary point to be taken from these deliberations was that the Commission interpreted assignments according to what extent "equality" was served in terms of the licensee's ability to provide a basic broadcasting service to listeners. The Act was written with a citizen model of reception access in mind, but little to no evaluative grounds for the quality or content of programming. License holders were sent notice of these requirements by direct mail, and wide newspaper publicity was given to the matter of frequency assignment deliberations. But the Commission lamented that "few definite proposals" for dedicated educational station licenses were made by colleges or universities themselves, beyond lobby groups, and in fact several prominent educators had come out against stand-alone educational stations, hoping to protect "present cooperative efforts being carried on between commercial stations and non-profit organizations."[47]

Further, according to the report, by their own testimony many nonprofit organizations admitted to not being equipped to build and maintain full-time broadcasting stations in accordance with the mandate. Noting limitation in "physical laws" and "number of available frequencies," the FCC wrote that considerations "absolutely prevent any general enlargement of the number of broadcast stations," and that the addition of any appreciable number of new stations would "necessarily result in interference with existing stations and in consequent reduction of service areas with the tendency to limit broadcast service to areas immediately surrounding the location of transmitters." Before undertaking to provide special services through the addition of new stations, Sykes reported that the first requirement for serving the general public under available laws would be fulfilled by providing at least one radio service of general interest and dependable signal quality. The provision was intended to ensure that educational programming would still be available, given the unreliability of exiting nonprofit licensees.[48]

Yet the FCC remained open to educational broadcasting allocations if educational broadcasters were able to meet the basic criteria of operation in the "public interest." On behalf of the FCC Sykes offered a provision for "flexibility" for "growth and development in the art of broadcasting...for the best interests of the public as a whole."[49] Access to airwaves, Sykes contended, would be contingent upon "a certain amount of showmanship, if I may use that term...in presenting programs that will attract and hold radio audiences. The commercial broadcasters have taken great pains to learn this art of attractiveness, and the educators need their help in acquiring this attractiveness in their technique of broadcasting."[50] If noncommercial broadcasters (including labor, education, religion, and civic groups) were able to prepare for consistent, high-quality broadcasting, the Commission felt that "present legislation had the flexibility essential to attain the desired ends without necessitating at this time any changes in the law."[51] Among those who attended the hearings included members of prominent Schools of the Air at Wisconsin, Ohio State, and Iowa State, who did not resist the notion that future assignments would be available to educators if cooperating institutions were able to meet the same FCC standards. Noting that "flexibility in the provisions of the law" would be necessary for future regulatory decisions, coupled with insufficient broadcast facilities and a lack of feasible plan by educators, the FCC concluded that nonprofit stations were also best served by the "use of existing facilities" and that fledgling stations would best be served by cooperation with commercial broadcasters.

The Office of Education and FCC Invite the Rockefeller Foundation to join FREC: John Marshall Attends the First Federal Educational Radio Conferences

Sykes closed his report by summoning Commissioner Cooper's previous attempt to hold a conference to promote "mutual cooperation between broadcasters and nonprofit organizations," and "combine the educational experience of educators with program technique of broadcasters, thereby better to serve the public interest."[52] Sykes planned for a conference as a forum to air grievances, but also to put competing interests into conversation through a new FREC collaboration between the FCC and OOE. Planned in coordination with the Commissioner of the Office of Education of the United States, who had already begun to map how they might develop "secondary service" for large metropolitan areas, Sykes made note to permit appeals by "persons interested in the preservation of broadcasting facilities of educational institutions against the procedure under which licensees are required to defend their assignments." He was resolute—educational stations had to produce quality programming that would attract audiences before any special provisions might be provided, and educational stations also had the opportunity to earn the same standard assignments of commercial stations. "The Commission intends actively to encourage the best minds among broadcasters and educators alike in order to develop a satisfactory technique for presenting educational programs in an attractive manner to the radio listener."[53] Without repurposing the logic of assignments, the FCC hoped to lay groundwork by which future allocations could be provided for educational stations.

During planning for the conference, Congressman Anning Prall developed an interest in educational broadcasting. He had previously served in the Department of Taxes and Assessments. Prall was former head of the New York Board of Education and began to speak publicly about special provisions for educators. In an interview with Martin Codel on NBC, aired March 30, 1935, Prall argued that while the progress of commercial radio as an art and as an industry had wildly eclipsed expectations since broadcasting's inception, he did not think broadcasting had taken the "fullest advantage of its cultural, educational, and public service possibilities."[54] Echoing similar sentiment to the Payne Fund, Prall contended that without an educational wing of radio, broadcasting would have a deleterious effect on children. Echoing Sykes, Prall contended that "good clean adventure programs can be made educational," though as prescribed by Congress the FCC would not be able to exercise direct control promoting one content genre over another. In the interview Prall proposed that educators be trained in radio practices as one outcome of the upcoming conference.

The first FREC conference took place on December 10, 11, and 12, 1936. Several visions of educational broadcasting were articulated at the event, from the perspectives of policymakers, commercial broadcasters, and educational researchers.[55] Over 700 persons registered, with over 1000 in attendance, including 177 from national organizations, 141 from colleges and universities, 109 from governmental agencies, 49 from commercial broadcasting companies, 53 from libraries and museums, and 25 representatives from 17 countries,[56] with keynote speakers David Sarnoff and John Studebaker. In the buildup to the first conference, Sykes contacted Commissioner of Education John Studebaker on the question of planning for increased stability for university stations. Studebaker was convinced that the Department of Education should take up the question of frequency allocations; there was almost no opportunity for Studebaker to expand his public forum concept onto the airwaves under the terms of the recent Act.

Every sector was provided an opportunity to voice their position at the conference. RCA had just enjoyed a wave of major legislative successes, coupled with an unprecedented growth in economic and technical infrastructure. According to Sarnoff's keynote, education went beyond "the narrowing influence of classroom walls and campus boundaries" and did not have to signify classroom practice or completion of a state curriculum. The university concept of education seemed to Sarnoff to be "of a steep and narrow path to some high summit in the mountains of specialized learning."[57] Since radio might never provide an appropriate forum to deliver knowledge and understanding, the acquisition of "useful" knowledge would better serve radio's public interest goals. Channels of information might supply food for thought, but it was asking too much to demand that radio should teach audiences what to think.

> "Radio, in common with other forms of mass communication and entertainment, belongs to the second of these two educational fields. Radio programs can be created to inform the mind and elevate the spirit, but when one seeks to impose upon them the requirements that they also furnish mental training and discipline, one narrows their appeal and risks the dispersion of the inevitable audience, thereby defeating the very purpose for which the program was prepared."

Sarnoff pointed out that programs on NBC and CBS, such as *American Education Forum, The World is Yours, Your Health, The University of Chicago Round Table, America's Town Meeting of the Air,* excelled as educational programs that also attracted loyal audiences.

Further, Sarnoff argued that commercial radio provided an unprecedented public service for the political process by broadcasting campaign information. Twenty-seven million had voted in 1920, but the number grew to forty-five million in 1936 after radio began covering elections. This evidence met the public service obligations of radio as defined in the 1927 Radio Act, and addressed the "public as a whole, that such a universal medium implies universal service, and that radio frequencies which are limited in number must be used in the broad interests of the general body of listeners."[58] The commercial model provided the most democratic vision of all, and commercial broadcasts also carried resources to "spread American democracy" to other countries, encouraging an educated international public.[59]

Secretary of the Interior Harold Ickes followed Sarnoff with a middle-of-the-road review of prospects for educational radio. Though educational broadcasting was still in "its infancy," it was the position of the Department that radio should disseminate content that benefits small community equal to state or nation. The Department of the Interior hoped to develop programs for all ages to constitute a "University of the Air" so that those who participate would be informed and able to "know intimately the subjects with which they were dealing"[60] such as the "cultivation of good English" and the "force of adult education" for those who had been denied equal opportunity. Educational radio was a new and powerful instrument, and new capacities were still being discovered "through the time honored system of trial and error." If cultivated correctly, radio could help to disseminate information from one section of the country, creating a shared sense of responsibility and belonging across the nation.

Commissioner of Education John Studebaker's keynote argued that radio could be utilized to promote knowledge, and a clearer understanding of the "baffling problems of this bewildered world."[61] Contending that broadcasting was "one of the most expensive undertakings of modern business" Studebaker praised the networks for the educational content that they had produced to that point, as well as the network promise to supply facilities, engineering and directorial services, publicity assistance, and good council to educators as they learned their craft. However, he lamented that the OOE was restricted from utilizing a utility that was federally licensed but privately controlled. The OOE was not challenging the ownership policy of the Act, but it was clear that educational broadcasting required intensive study along executive, technical, and administrative subcommittees to "think out" questions of radio's service to education.

Following Studebaker, the head of the OOE's Educational Radio Project, William Boutwell, echoed the FCC that the great problem faced by educators was that their programs were not enjoyable and lacked production values. Until education developed a corps of teachers and supervisors who could write and produce "reasonably good programs," little would be available for educators toward new frequencies. "Proof" needed to be offered regarding competence in using the airwaves.[62] The FCC also provided two representatives with technical and regulatory perspectives—T.A.M. Craven, Chief Engineer of the FCC, and Chairman Anning Prall. Craven was asked to speak about how the evolution of the technology of radio had influenced radio regulation. He noted that the primary problem at hand was "frequency scarcity." The FCC was bombarded with requests for channels from every possible sector, such as aircraft, boats, radiotelephone service between nations, networks, the "use of radio to combat the criminal" and military establishments. From this perspective the "demands of educational groups" for radio facilities were primarily understood by the FCC in terms of one interest group vying for access among other nonprofit groups within a limited spectrum. Craven speculated that if educational districts were all allocated protected radio frequencies that the FCC would have to accommodate 127000 school districts, numbering 15000 stations, and called upon scientists at universities to coordinate for the most economic use of frequency channels that might be devoted to education.

Anning Prall spoke to the FCC's appraisal of the "present status of educational radio" and how it may be improved for public interest. An adequate concept of what radio would do for education demanded a fair consideration and study of the three types of radio systems—the British model without advertising but license fees, and the two American approaches of the advertising-based networks found in most of Europe as well as Turkey, and the largely unfunded public sector educators. While Prall believed that Americans would not stand for a tax on radio receivers or a license fee, he did believe that an educational broadcasting option was crucial, and "wholeheartedly supported" the movement toward the development of a comprehensible plan for education by radio. Echoing Craven's lead-in that the spectrum was limited not just for cultural use of radio but for technical and military use, Prall nonetheless argued that educational institutions had provided many of the foundations of science used by the FCC, and that he had full confidence that the scholars, physicists, and scientists at such institutions would both understand the limitations faced by the FCC, find technical ways to overcome those obstacles. He noted that future frequencies would be available with television, and that a concerted effort by educators to link present broadcast facilities would be both "staggering" and auspicious.

But perhaps the most unintentionally influential talk came from Henry Link, in charge of market research at the Psychological Corporation in New York. He looked at how the Association of National Advertisers had developed surveys for audience response to content, and how Pauline Arnold of Market Research Corporation innovated calling during a program to ask what the listener was tuned into, later popularized by Clark-Hooper. Measuring audience activity would similarly have critical significance for educational broadcasting, such evidence would reveal what audience cared about, and if the audience believed content had value. Link identified a pivotal gap in procedure that he hoped could be taken up by a research body—methods had not revealed how intensively a program was be listened to, or how strong of an impression a program made on an audience. In preparation for the conference Link conducted a cursory study on educational broadcasts, and found audiences were "pitifully small in comparison with the audiences for commercial or sustaining programs, even when the relative power of the stations is borne in mind." Radio was not the same thing as compulsory education, and though it might serve educational purposes, the "situation" of radio meant that educators had to alter traditional models of pedagogy for media presentation, focusing more on radio personality than expertise.

As private, public, and federal sectors speculated about how radio might serve public education, a representative from the Rockefeller Foundation quietly took notes on their speeches. In a December 1935 letter to the Rockefeller Foundation, the OOE and the FCC had invited its president, Raymond D. Fosdick, to attend.[63] In the letter they announced the formation of the FREC for the purpose of: 1) eliminating controversy and misunderstanding between industry and educators, and 2) promoting actual cooperative arrangements between educators and broadcasters on national, regional, and local bases. FREC as constituted represented all organizations having any "conceivable interest" in the question of educational broadcasting. Its creation included a planning committee set to meet weekly for several months, commencing in February 1936. Early meetings had cataloged "difficulties" experienced by educators. Noting that the federal government had not set aside funds for improving media culture, the RF was invited to help "take stock and to determine what can be done."[64]In the buildup to the conference, Studebaker wrote to Dr. Stacy May, Assistant Director of the Social Science division of the Rockefeller Foundation, that the OOE was "vitally" interested in the development of radio as an educational instrument.[65] Since allocations had been entirely commercialized, both the OOE and the NAB agreed that few interests were satisfactorily served by legislation. Educators had little access to broadcasting, and the NAB members were not interested in the prospect of investing in a broadcast structure with little hope for return on investment.

FREC was launched by appropriations under the Emergency Relief Acts of 1935 and 1936, from the same funding lines as science, history, current affairs, and social science projects.[66] But FREC needed additional funds to explore radio as a "scientific" and educational medium, in accordance with the demands of listenership and broadcasting method. Mastery of the "techniques" of radio, Studebaker wrote to May, would aid the OOE in developing radio presentation activities of "modern" government services. They sought to involve collaboration of educational authorities, school students, municipal officials, and local broadcasting stations to improve the instructional value of broadcasts.

Internal memos reveal that the Rockefeller Foundation openly wondered why federal institutions were not funding new research, and Marshall believed that commercial stations held some degree of responsibility to provide funds for academic research into audience. But as an initial gesture, the Foundation granted the FREC a nominal sum of $2500 for an educational scriptwriter, with more to be determined after a representative attended the 1936 educational radio conference.[67] Upon attending the conference, though, John Marshall reflected that "this was the best attended and best planned conference on education in radio" he had yet been to, and that great discussion had ensued after each session. Studebaker and Sarnoff's speeches were of special interest, and Marshall was impressed by the FREC's holistic approach to working toward cooperation between different sectors. Marshall was especially taken by Sarnoff's distinction between "attempting to train the mind through broadcasting and supplying materials which can nourish mental growth and extend appreciation."[68] Marshall concluded that educational broadcast advocates had little sense of how to use radio correctly, and that research was needed into how to create programs that would be educational and compel listeners.[69]

As works by Gary,[70] Hilmes,[71] Buxton,[72] and Tobias[73] have noted, Marshall's participation with FREC would change the course of educational broadcasting. The Second National Conference on Educational Broadcasting, in 1937, followed the first conference by describing new objectives taken up by FREC, such as 1) to provide a national forum where interests concerned with education could exchange ideas, 2) to examine and appraise situation of broadcasting for future public service, 3) to appraise listeners' interest in programs that come under general classification of public service broadcasting, 4) to examine the present and potential resources of education through radio, 5) to examine and appraise the interest of organized education in broadcasting, and 6) to bring to a large audience findings that become available from studies and research conducted.[74] In addition to the previous year's participants, many of who returned, the American Association for the Advancement of Science, the American Association of Museums, the American Federation of the Arts, the American Library Association, the National Council of Parent Education, and the National University Extension Association also participated. Presenters included Prall and Sykes, Studebaker, members of NBC, and William Paley of CBS. Sykes reminded participants that no legal provisions had been set in the Act to provide special privileges for groups and that they weren't favored by Congress, but that this didn't mean that educators should be shut off from future allocations. William Paley's paper argued that the radio industry agreed that educational broadcasting was essential, and that CBS supported FREC. But he believed that more research was needed before educational content would be deemed desirable by the networks.[75]

John Marshall Begins to Fund
Educational Access Projects

Working under David H. Stevens, between 1936 and 1937 John Marshall awarded the first FREC-connected research grants. His work was informed by RF's Humanities Division research, which aimed to "preserve and develop American cultural traditions, promote cultural understanding among nations, and continue with obligations from previous programs in philosophy and education."[76] In his publication, *The Humanities in Theory and Practice,* David Stevens wrote that the function of the humanities was to make "the individual a citizen of the world in matters of the spirit—to create within him his own forms of mental, emotional, and spiritual freedom."[77] This could be accomplished, he posited, by recreating imagination "beyond the ordinary" via the transmission of values, meanings, and critically informed research via radio, film, drama, libraries, and museums. At the program's inception Marshall believed the best way to achieve this would be to disseminate and chronicle "regional life,"[78] in which Native American, urban, and southern experiences could be preserved through recording, and then curated as wide repositories of knowledge that would be available at universities.[79]

Due to Cooper's initiative in the 1920s, the Rockefeller Foundation had already dabbled in radio research underwriting with the Carnegie Fund. Two years before the FREC conferences, in 1934, Marshall commissioned a report by State Assistant Commissioner Dr. George Wiley, of the New York State Education Department, on the prospect of funding radio. Wiley's report argued that experimental work in radio education was distinctly different from the public service programs put out by the networks due to their dedication to instructional programming. While radio had improved as an "instructional instrument," "sufficient data" had not yet been obtained with reference to its value.[80] Wiley recommended that Rockefeller look to the progress of local practitioners, in Rochester in particular, to determine the "value of regular instruction of children by means of the radio."[81]

Wiley further recommended a 2-year period during which student achievement would be "measured before, during, and after a series of broadcasts,"[82] in both control and experimental classrooms, some fitted with a radio, some without. But more importantly for this history, Wiley suggested that the project should begin by contacting the most successful noncommercial and instructional broadcasting practitioners in the world—the BBC. Shortly thereafter, Marshall commissioned a report from the BBC regarding their experience with instructional broadcasting.

In early 1935 Wiley received their report, written by H. A. L. Fisher of the BBC's "Central Council for School Broadcasting," discussing a 3-year experiment carried out in Britain. Wiley conveyed Fisher's primary recommendations to Marshall. It concluded that, for any broadcasting experiment to work, "student reception must be good." This meant that each classroom teacher had to be knowledgeable about the aim and scope of the courses, "and of the part he himself [sic] must necessarily play in making the lessons of permanent value to his class."[83] The BBC experimented with this instructional approach by framing the value of broadcasts in terms of their extant curricula, with "five or six persons, each possessing some special qualification of scholarship, broadcasting technique, or practical knowledge of the school" assigned to broadcasting instruction.

David Stevens was persuaded that investment in radio could contribute to education, which he opined would be similar to how a school architect designs buildings so that "light comes over pupil's left shoulders" for reading.[84] Similar to architecture, radio needed sound design, which required research. Design did not always equate to reform, since modern schools had "miserable acoustics because the new buildings, plaster on tile and the like, do not absorb sound and because by their design modern school buildings produce disturbing echoes."[85] But design was a necessary first step for reaching audiences. He encouraged Marshall to keep an eye open for research that would streamline "present practices" in school broadcasting.[86]

Marshall noted in an April 10, 1935, report that the foundation had an opportunity to "render valuable intermediary service in promoting co-operative endeavor of commercial and educational interests."[87] Noting that, since the Act, both educators and commercial broadcasters were "coming to recognize how extensive their common interests are," Marshall believed that helping educators produce better programs would be key to its future. The committee put aside roughly $200000 for radio projects in conjunction with the General Education Board and sought an external committee to "reduce routine work and give more adequate selection on a nation-wide scale than is possible with present staff."[88]

After FREC convened, Marshall poured money into the project. Within the first eighteen months Marshall spent $288870 on educational efforts. This covered internships for educators at networks, support of facilities experiments and consulting. By 1937, due to the influence of educational evaluation, the conference, and recent communications regulation, Marshall determined that media reform would benefit from the development of evidentiary practices. Marshall believed that the logistics of educational broadcasting, such as recruiting and training personnel with qualifications, and exploring the best methods of developing interest in educational and cultural broadcasting on the part of cooperative agencies, was the future of noncommercial radio.

While Marshall funded education radio projects, the NAB noted that the loss of educational stations had increased the expectation for commercial stations to produce public service broadcasts. Now that commercial broadcasters had laid claim to being the best educational source, it was their responsibility to serve as a university extension service, beyond managing the economy of scale of advertising, talent development, and related practices. They had been tasked with producing "sustaining" programs, which originally referred to any program that aired without a sponsor.[89] Commercial networks and stations originally developed an advertising system to fund program development without manufacturer support,[90] and over the 1920s this led to mastery of production techniques for effective and popular programming,[91] which buttressed their aggressive lobbying to obtain frequency assignments. But they had also now inadvertently taken the mantle of declaring themselves to be the country's civic center, and this came into conflict with some of their programming plans, which relied on advertising.

The consequence was, now that the landscape had been defined in their favor, they saw value in helping educators improve their craft, to potentially regain a small number of stations and reduce the NAB burden for public service programming. Their approach to their frequency lobby significantly changed over a series of post-Act testimonies at the FCC. In one case they argued that "recognition by Congress, by the commission, and by the public, that since the air belonged to the people, it belongs to all the people and no group, party, click, or even administration,"[92] and that public interest programming should become the "voice of minority groups as well as majority groups, because their responsibility in the post-Act environment was to elevate the cultural level of US broadcasting by the "slow projection of new technique and new ideas." Adding to Marshall's mandate, commercial radio gestured that educators were learning how to use radio as a means of education that was not "dry as dust," and perhaps there were grounds to help educators hone their craft and regain future channels.[93]

The Rockefeller Foundation's Grant Model Exerts Limits and Pressures upon Proposals and Practice

While commercial broadcasters navigated their role as the new default educational public, John Marshall funded several of the most important precursory projects to public media. FREC proposed a budget of $168620 for comprehensive study of educational broadcasting, so that "definite remedial steps could be taken or even suggested."[94] Within two years RF had far exceeded that number, and after the 1937 conference FREC conceived of sixteen projects designed to answer: 1) the general question of how cooperation between educators and broadcasters could be furthered, and 2) the groundwork for future developments in educational broadcasting theory and practice. Their main concern was how to meet the requirements of legislation when educators knew "little of the listener interests on which broadcasting has to build."[95]

FREC suggested that the Rockefeller Foundation support four primary areas: 1) as an instrument to distribute civic programs to an "impressively large audience," 2) coordination of the efforts of 400 participating broadcasting organizations to promote educational programs in the fields of science, history, current affairs, social studies, and mathematics, and help to develop techniques of distribution, 3) facilities and funds for directing the organization of such a project under the oversight of the Social Science Research Council and other public officials, and 4) studies aimed at increasing the circulation of programs and the quality of educational programming.[96] Side projects were devised to explore avenues of cooperation between local agencies, broadcasting stations, and state-based institutions, and to measure the role of teachers and school principals in evaluating the effectiveness of school broadcasts.

As FREC conducted its work, Studebaker circulated a document regarding "services which the OOE can contribute to the plan for a script service to aid school and other producing groups." The proposal, simply titled *What the Office of Education Can Do*, was based upon what the OOE already offered to school districts, with recommendations such as assembling checking committees, arranging for cooperation of the NAEB, school officials, and school groups, and Parent-Teacher Congress groups, mimeographing sample copies of scripts, and carrying necessary overhead, such as renting telephones, telegraph, supplying heat, light, stationary, etc.[97]

FREC's Project #15, the "Study of Radio Influence Upon Children and Adults," intended to "discover the effect of radio broadcasts upon the acquiring of information, the changing of attitudes and the modification of conduct of children and youth" and proposed to employ "first-rate" scholars in the fields of psychology, sociology, and education, to bring their expertise to bear on radio, to undertake research studies in their field, and eventually to organize a series of conferences about their findings. The committee proposing this project included Hadley Cantril of Columbia, Edgar Dale of the Payne Fund, and the well-known sociologist Robert Lynd, and is the subject of Chapter 4. Proposal 15 piqued John Marshall's interest. The notion that information acquisition was related to attitude changes, which included "the modification of conduct of children and young people," might be of interest to educators, psychologists, and sociologists.

> "To what extent the project could go beyond establishing that broadcasting is influential in the ways enumerated, to how it gains those effects, is not yet clear. But it is clear that broadcasting could be materially bettered for young children and young people only if its effects on them were directly related to the elements in broadcasting that produced them. Certainly the influence of an authoritative and well-planned study that established such relations would be such as to warrant a considerable expenditure. If the broadcasters cannot feel such expenditures commercially justifiable, a project of this character perhaps has a special claim on funds from other sources, in promising a measure of external control in the public interest for a part of broadcasting important for society's future."[98]

Project 15 was renamed the Princeton Radio Research Project.

The First Economy of Scale of Public Media Industries Takes Shape: Standardized Approaches to Production, Research, Aesthetics, and Broadcast Facility Maintenance

The Rockefeller Foundation's investment in FREC projects consolidated the requirement for public interest as technical expertise, but also served the valuable role of synthesizing humanities research and goals with technical benchmarks for civic media. The entry of philanthropic funding into US noncommercial media industries was directly influenced by the limits and pressures placed by federal agencies and previous legislation from the radio conferences. The consequence was that instructional broadcasting, which began as lectures into a microphone, shifted to a broader exploratory terrain that looked to become an alternative radio industry dedicated to education.

In the process the commercial lobby, which had overplayed its hand in relativizing educational media approaches, became a new partner for media reform work. Though the NCER had failed in defining educational broadcasting as special and deserving of protected frequencies, it was almost immediately shown to be in every stakeholder's interest to locate a compromise for Schools of the Air based at universities. Every purposive and accidental agent now participating with philanthropically funded advocacy moved to follow Sykes's Pursuant. The nexus of regulation, aspiration by reformers, government organized collaboration, and philanthropic vision, influenced how noncommercial institutions were built, and how information emanating from those institutions was coded.

The Rockefeller Foundation's entry into reform work guided strategies for reform. Grants also inspired new exploration into educational infrastructure. Marshall accepted that educational broadcasters would maintain their vision that educational broadcasting should be advertisement free. This meant that a program could be less focused on obtaining the largest audience to please an external interest from the station itself. Universities were able to broadcast to an expected audience of one hundred for a language class, or one thousand for local farm report. This provided, at least in theory, more opportunities to reach diverse audiences, and to explore peripheries of cultural expression beyond the popular. After the Act, reformers turned their attention toward more educationally sound approaches to developing standards, evaluation, and evidence about what media practice achieved.

Conclusion

Thanks to increased attention from FREC conferences, educational radio was given the veneer of rebounding, even if the grass roots university stations had not yet reorganized after the Act. By the end of the 1930s it had become clear from Rockefeller's work that the only path forward for educators was to shift from activist lobby to building a media industry. As soon as competition was introduced for radio frequencies, philanthropy stepped into the equivalent role of advertising as noncommercial media income. Their role as a granting agency allowed them to mediate and build relationships between commercial and educational broadcasters, while adding prestige to the educational ranks.

Crucial to understanding the idiosyncratic contours of US media, no history of commercial or noncommercial broadcasting can be told without gesturing to the engagement between federal educational, regional, and state educational interests and FREC participants in the 1930s. One outcome of this dynamic is that grant models associated with philanthropic groups played a deeply influential role on the educational radio practices, advocacy strategies, and noncommercial genres implemented during the New Deal. Considering the dynamic collaborative atmosphere of 1936, a broader discussion can be broached about the role of granting institutions in the standardization of practice, content, and technics that left an indelible mark on research and development models of both public and commercial media industries. Looking at the origins of the philanthropic wing of public media helps to inform discourses in media economics in two ways. It clarifies how funding sources play a role in determining an institution's economy of scale. And neither reform or commercial media history can be understood without an examination of how cross-sector, collaborative advocacy between public and private media formularized and defined standardized practices across logistical, listenership, and production divisions in American media institutions.

CHAPTER 3

Distribution and Facilities

America's Public Media Industry:
From the Rocky Mountain Radio Council
to the National Bicycle Network

Public Media's Economy of Scale: Public Media as a Civic Alternative to for-profit Media Industries

After the Communications Act educational broadcasters designed programs to respond to regulatory changes, pressures exerted by government agencies, commercial media, and philanthropic groups. No longer satisfied to discuss principle alone, between the 1930s and early 1950s instructional radio transformed into a reform movement that was focused on innovating strategies to make advertising-free media a sustainable approach in broadcasting. In 1935 the National Association of Educational Broadcasters (NAEB) had been whittled down to less than three-dozen stations. The major broadcasting entities Wisconsin, Ohio State, and Iowa State remained. It became clear to educators that they had to pay more attention to the craft of broadcasting. Subsequent to the Federal Radio Education Committee (FREC) conferences of 1936 and 1937, the NAEB placed emphasis on development of best practices that could be replicated across the country. Compelled by the lure of Rockefeller Foundation funding and new FREC suggestions, educators looked to the models of distribution employed by national and regional networks.[1]

Educators pulled from three major concurrent models. The first was commercial broadcasting distribution methods, training, standards for live performance, and facilities management.[2] The networks had initiated a strong industrial workflow that was sustainable and met with audience enthusiasm. Second, it was clear that lobbying for special frequencies based upon a perceived public service contribution could not persuade regulators under conditions of frequency scarcity. The public interest mandate favored the established, moneyed system, but it nonetheless presented a benchmark for educational broadcasters. Over the mid to late 1930s and into the postwar era, educational broadcasters realized that to maintain their unique service mission they must emulate the technical and aesthetics characteristics that audiences had grown accustomed to. Third, the Rockefeller Foundation introduced external consultants. John Marshall brought Charles Siepmann from the BBC. In what might be described as one of the more eccentric exchanges of media history, he wrote devastating and cutting criticisms that impugned upon the provincial nature of early educators, while at the same time providing sound advice for how they might approach their craft.[3] Somehow by the end of his consultation he became a beloved figure, to the point where the NAEB regarded him as an early founder of public media.

The final institutional structure that educators settled on in 1949 was a synthetic mix of previous influences: making do with limited resources while calling upon external examples of successful broadcasting practices. Pulling from Rockefeller Foundation funds, two major experiments between 1935 and 1940 pointed to how the NAEB might network educational station broadcasts. The University Broadcasting Council of Chicago (UBC) targeted adult listeners and instituted the first public/private collaboration between NBC and local universities. It was a city-specific initiative that attempted to solve many of the problems of educational broadcasting. The Rocky Mountain Radio Council (RMRC) represented the transformation of National Committee on Education by Radio's (NCER) strategic approach from lobby to system building.[4] Working from a Rockefeller grant, A. G. Crane of the NCER and President of the University of Wyoming carefully modeled the first successful educational network plan to reach rural populations. Meanwhile, John Studebaker and the Office of Education set up the first clearinghouse of scripts, setting a precedent for the NAEB distribution network.[5]

By 1948, under the supervision of President Richard Hull of Iowa State, the NAEB centered on day-to-day operations of radio stations, content measurement, and training of radio practitioners. The Allerton House Seminars of 1949 and 1950 united universities as a "network" of universities and school districts, with the NAEB serving as the official umbrella organization. Instead of a centralized profit-based model, the NAEB planned a decentralized, nonprofit consortium dedicated to civic concepts and free public education. The result was that after eighteen years the NAEB founded the auspices of what became public media in the 1960s. The NAEB set up a lobby division like the one pioneered by the NCER and set up a clearinghouse like the Office of Education.

The early idealism of educational broadcasting was short-lived, and the 1930s represented a time in which stations looked to established aesthetic models to hone their craft. As Amanda Keeler has written, perhaps the most influential early figure in all of educational broadcasting was Judith Waller of NBC Chicago.[6] She worked with local Chicago public schools, DJed on a regular basis, and was perhaps the first to frame how to make educational content palatable to a broad audience.[7] Harold McCarty of the University of Wisconsin was reportedly so inspired by Waller's broadcasts that he transitioned from theater to found WHA, University of Wisconsin's School of the Air.[8] Under NBC's Franklin Dunham, Waller and NBC's John Royal worked closely with the FREC board. After 1934 commercial radio temporarily became the default broadcasting voice of US media, but the advertising-first model was not without internal critics. An internal note by Waller and Royal openly questioned the purpose of saturating the airwaves with one economic model. "Was it solely to make profit? Render public service first, with hope of making a profit? Make a profit with home of rendering public service? Careful perusal of schedules to decide the proportion of time available for both services?"[9] Claiming to be the best radio educators came with certain pratfalls. Commercial broadcasters were now saddled with the responsibility to produce unprofitable programming for small audiences. Numbers dipped when airing content—especially instructional programs.

By 1938 NBC's John Royal openly opined that it was impossible to "draw a sharp line between programs which are educational and those which are not, for any program—whatever its purpose—may have educational consequences."[10] By the end of the pursuant period of the Act, NBC had successfully persuaded regulators—and itself—that sustained interest in any genre of broadcast was synonymous with a civic contribution. One internal report waxed that an "American and his wife in the average American home welcome the chatty, familiar presentation of advertising in connection with some programs," and the rapport between host and audience satisfied conditions of public interest.[11] Commercial broadcasters clearly saw the benefit of providing educational content, "to increase knowledge, to stimulate thinking, to teach techniques and methods, to cultivate discernment, appreciate and taste, to enrich character by sensitizing emotion and by inspiring socialized ideas that may issue in constructive conduct."[12] After 1934 NBC endeavored to develop programs "built primarily for the 15% but interesting enough to win the 85%."

From a media industry perspective, it might have been in their interest to steer the debate away from tenets of public service and promote profitable content. Yet, internal records show that NBC put significant research into educational radio between 1934 and 1938, including analyses of how to provide direct service to schools and colleges, develop adult education programs covering "multiple intellectual themes," and air public roundtable discussions concerned with "ethical and religious problems."[13] After educational content still ranked among the lowest listenership NBC decided to push sustaining programming to undesirable time slots such as Sunday morning.

After the 1935 FCC frequency allocation hearings, commercial broadcasting's windfall was so considerable that nearly any program could be claimed as educational for yearly license renewal. A barn-dance program was educational because it showcased local culture. Drama was educational, NBC argued, because it encouraged problem solving and attention to the arts. It was a difficult argument to rebut, since educational stations aired the same content, typically with worse production values. But the thorny issue of low engagement persisted, and by the end of 1938 NBC decided to take a second look at how it might help university broadcasters to ease their own burden.[14] NBC began by feeding commercial stations educational content during school hours. They then distributed free program transcriptions[15] to university stations produced by top talent. But universities were unable to attract new listenership.

While the networks deliberated about how to handle their role as educational stewards, NAEB members plotted next steps to improve the quality of their programs. B. B. Brackett wrote to NAEB President Harold McCarty that "nearly everything that we are now using will almost certainly be condemned."[16] Stations did not have funds to pay for equipment and by and large listeners were unhappy with university-produced programs. But the NAEB was optimistic that close study of the Act itself would help stations to rebound and grow.

Defining Public Media Industries: Strategies for Development, Distribution, and Administration based on Civic Principles

Five trends emerged directly after the Act. First, educational broadcasters never wavered in their myopic focus that noncommercial media should remain nonprofit.[17] In a way commercial media industries were far more complicated entities, balancing manufacturing, advertising, entertainment, civic outreach, and national interests into a programming schedule that had to reach repeating listeners. Nonprofit broadcasting never intended to reach the largest audience. Second, educational broadcasters had to answer to the needs of academic departments and state mandates for adult education. Third, educational content was comprised of a mix of new, repeating, and syndicated material divided by academic discipline, more than entertainment genre.

Fourth, the division of labor at university stations grew to closely resemble commercial broadcasting. However, similarities ended there, and administrative educational broadcasting discourses continued to center on how to serve classrooms. The trajectory between 1935 and 1950 was focused on an ongoing discourse about the relationship between best practices and mission statement. Since no universal charter existed describing the relationship between programming and mission, the NAEB increasingly referred to Syke's Pursuant as a guideline for how to plan next steps. The Act articulated conditions by which research and development could be conducted toward the end of better educating audiences. The emergence of the first educational broadcasting networks synthesized a philosophical mission with the technical expertise designated by the Act. The Radio Act of 1927 placed an artificial burden on evidentiary practices to meet criteria for diversity of licenses. Yet, the public interest mandate unexpectedly helped to clarify what direction reform work would take. Emergent advocacy strategies included testing of technology, imagining a new division of labor, and a coalitional framework dedicated to the common cause of equal access to education in the postwar era.[18]

The NAEB's Carl Menzer and the Origins of Public Media's Decentralized Distribution: Shortwave Rebroadcasting, Program Transcriptions, and Script Exchange

As early as 1932 Carl Menzer and T. M. Beaird of the Association of College and University Broadcasting Stations (renamed the NAEB after 1934) concluded that the best way for the group to reconcile the problem of poor program quality might simply be to exchange broadcasts. Menzer faced an especially difficult situation at the University of Iowa. The university was only supporting educational broadcasting on the barest terms, and his immediate supervisor did not understand the ramifications of producing efficient extension services the radio.[19]

Menzer dreamed of a mechanism by which different independent stations might begin to share examples of their best programs. Between the 1930s and late 1940s he was responsible for exploring different technologies of relay and exchange. His work continued until he helped to found the University of Iowa's television station,[20] completing an important trajectory that began with the basic question of meeting regulatory standards by testing and reporting relay technologies on behalf of the NAEB consortium. In 1934, Menzer designed the first economy of scale for NAEB distribution with two experiments. The first was that he attempted to utilize shortwave radio to exchange content across state lines. The second was an experiment with "rebroadcasting." The NAEB settled on "program transcriptions," or the pressing of vinyl records, as the preferred choice of the organization. Where stations lacked funds to produce quality content, recorded programs could fill station schedules.

In 1936 Menzer purchased and tested equipment with NAEB funds. Line rental was too expensive for live broadcasting. Well-funded stations would be the only ones able obtain new frequency assignments, and a larger network was impossible because educational stations would remain in the domain of universities. Menzer wrote to Harold McCarty in December 1936 that if each station invested in an "HRO Receiver," programs could hypothetically be rebroadcast from station to station by shortwave, circumventing telephone line rental. Menzer believed this could "tie-up" a new network of stations from Kansas to South Dakota. "I can visualize an educational chain which would extend over the United States with contributing stations at any desirable location."[21] The idea was plausible as along as stations were willing to buy shortwave devices, and experiment over a trial-and-error period. Menzer's plan gained interest from NAEB brass Wright at the University of Illinois and Griffith at Iowa State. Titled the "Educational Broadcasting System," Menzer planned for a central school to broadcast a program by shortwave, first to the University of Illinois, which would then broadcast it to Chicago, and so on. Though no physical "EBS" would actually exist, Wright joked in response, the official moniker would sound impressive to listeners.[22] Menzer determined that a minimum power of 5000 watts would be necessary to convene the project.

EBS's first tests seemed to make it a workable idea. Iowa relayed programs to Iowa State by shortwave, and they planned to create a rebroadcast network of "Iowa Educational Stations." A report from Illinois found "satisfactory listening conditions" for rebroadcasts within the state itself, and it was speculated that educational stations could fill up to 3.5 hours per day with rebroadcasts.[23] However, once a signal had been rebroadcast further than a couple hundred miles, "unsatisfactory" overlaps with commercial stations occurred and the quality of transmissions depleted. Menzer suggested that stations might record relays and then broadcast them from transcriptions for other regional stations to rebroadcast on frequencies that wouldn't interfere with commercial stations.[24] But once top of the hour station identifications were replayed at other stations, the NAEB realize that they had broken FCC rules and confused audiences. Purdue located a grant to "tie together conventional lines in the middle-western educational stations to facilitate exchange of programs during the day," but this only lasted a brief time due to ongoing expense and the unrenewable nature of the grant.[25]

By the late 1930s Menzer's team settled on transforming the NAEB into a consortium that would record and distribute programs through a clearing-house to association members, without call letters, on an as-needed basis, which eliminated the use of wires or shortwaves. As Susan Douglas and Alexander Russo have written, this form of syndication was already proven to be successful for the BBC and the Mutual Broadcasting Service of regional radio stations.[26] All Menzer's plan required was that stations put forward a unified front and buy efficient record recording equipment. Menzer tested several models in preparation for this, to "determine the feasibility of using present day recording equipment for producing electrical transcriptions."[27] Menzer tested metal, duraltone, and acetate transcriptions, as reported on the difference between 78rpm and 33.3rpm players in NAEB newsletters. Subsequently all NAEB stations began to purchase Universals for record pressing.[28] A backlog of drama, civics, home economics, music appreciation, and other shows rapidly began to accumulate, but the NAEB lacked a home base for distribution. Ohio State and Wisconsin were well funded enough to capitalize on Menzer's concept, and by 1938 both universities offered NAEB members the opportunity to purchase program transcriptions for $2 per record.[29]

Within five years of the Act Carl Menzer and the NAEB had shifted course to focus on technical strategies to maintain quality broadcasts. They produced multiple reports on topics from transcription tests to new equipment for frequency response, noise level, turntable stability, dubbing tests, and mechanical construction.[30] By 1939, the auspice of an efficient program distribution network already seemed possible. A program could be produced at one station, recorded onto a transcription disc, be archived, and then be sent out to requesting stations for rebroadcast. While Menzer attended to best practices in program reproduction, the NAEB worked on its administrative structure.

The American Council on Education (ACE) held a conference on educational broadcasting in 1936, and attendees across educational sectors decided to work together on discussing "means by which radio may become a more effective instrument for education, both formal and informal."[31] After the conference ACE agreed to work with the NAEB to set up a clearinghouse for information and scripts. At a 1936 Ohio State conference, NAEB members decided that they needed a central headquarters with personnel who would work on increasing the number of educational programs, improving their quality, and "stimulating leadership" through understanding of the fundamentals of broadcasting. Internal discussions turned from the "character" of noncommercial broadcasting philosophy to discussions by which radio "may become a more effective instrument" and "enable all phases of subjects" so that listeners could become acquainted with their educational station and "exchange ideas and experiences."[32] Over a series of memos and correspondences, NAEB members turned to "stimulate the formation" of advisory boards to improve programming techniques of educational broadcasters by formulating standards.[33] T. M. Beaird, treasurer of the NAEB, posited in a letter to W. I. Griffith at Iowa State that the NAEB needed a facility capable of providing an adequate script writing bureau that would conduct all program distribution on behalf of the organization, and find ways to procure funds to maintain a clearing house.[34] Under the NAEB's core leadership, three "Projects in Educational Broadcasting" were named between 1934 and 1936.

The first initiative, headed by Frank Schooley at the University of Illinois, located potential allies in the federal government. John Studebaker presented himself as an ally of university stations, but also informed them that their main difficulty was that they were not agreed upon what they wanted from radio.[35] Studebaker assured Schooley that the OOE was interested not just in a federal educational extension, but promotion of licenses for local, state, and regional educational stations, and from there they began a regular correspondence regimen.[36] Studebaker advised the NAEB to assemble a vita of accomplishments to distribute to legislative and regulatory bodies. Many of Studebaker's letters to Schooley concerned questions about craft, training of radio personnel, and improvement of technical standards.[37] Schooley followed Studebaker's prompt and wrote to the FCC to notify them that university radio workshops would engender "ferment" to solving practical problems of production.[38] Over the next several years Schooley's correspondence with Studebaker helped the NAEB to frame their educational agenda in line with national movements in education: "I would say we are representatives of institutions of higher learning, engaged in educational broadcasting to promote dissemination of knowledge to the end that both the technical and educational features of broadcasting may be extended to all (from preamble)."[39] From correspondence with Studebaker, the NAEB generated technical recommendations to the FCC, and wrote continuous letters to Congress about the services universities provided to their states.[40]

The Office of Education Builds the first National Clearinghouse for Educational Radio

While the NAEB slowly organized, Studebaker built strong momentum for educational reform. Studebaker was convinced that experimentation in the classroom, studio, and university radio workshops would help to solve the practical problems of broadcasting production.[41] He used his perch to promote educational broadcasting practice, and hatched plans to promote research and testing. Studebaker voiced the first persuasive rhetorical case for a diverse national radio spectrum—that radio was exerting a powerful educational force whether broadcasters intended it to or not.[42] An authoritative body (such as Congress), he posited, should institute safeguards to ensure that radio genuinely serve public interest. Educators had admittedly failed to meet public interest standards in the past, but oversight from governmental institutions quickly streamlining practices, and civic-based public interest programming was immanently plausible. On this he wrote:

> "While entirely sympathetic with the basic aims of educators, broadcasters were cognizant too, of the practical problems with the question involved. Limited funds, lack of training personnel, and the natural preoccupation of educators with education made it improbable, in the opinion of broadcasters, that educators alone could successfully establish and operate stations in the public interests, convenience and necessity, as provided in section B of the Communications Act."[43]

Educators previously lacked the production facilities or formal system of training of commercial broadcasters and suffered 'impairment' in productive and economic means; but now that the FCC had delineated clear standards for obtainment of broadcast licenses, if such standards were met there should be space for educational broadcasts to function within the dominant model. Besides classroom use, Studebaker imagined radio as a naturally educational medium that could be used to discuss current affairs. Between 1936 and 1937 the Office of Education sponsored nineteen experimental public forum demonstration center experiments, investing over $500000.[44] In that time several thousand meetings had been conducted with nearly a million attending. Several hundred 'forum-leaders' had been trained, and the Department of Education developed standard publications, exhibit materials, and the like.

In 1936 President Roosevelt endorsed a plan called the *Educational Radio Project*[45] to fund three educational radio programs over network facilities, titled *Struggle for Freedom*, *Let Freedom Ring*, and *Work of the Government*, and granted $75000 for an 8-month production window.[46] With war in Europe looming, and hoping to maintain nearly complete ownership of the airwaves, the networks decided to produce an additional swath of educational programs. Between 1936 and 1937, due to pressure and funding from Studebaker and the government, the networks produced 342 total public service and educational programs (though with many as short as 5 minutes) and 8 ongoing series, in facilities from coast to coast.[47]

Much to everyone's surprise, the shows received over 400000 letters of support in response, with only 100 of those letters being negative in sentiment. And the project began to snowball—by the end of 1937 the government had contributed $262700 to the networks, or roughly 20 percent of a production budget, with additional help from the Rockefeller Foundation and the Smithsonian. However, this brief period of commercial educational broadcasting was, as Studebaker reflected in a piece titled *The Educational Radio Project and the Office of Education*, a "delicate" relationship.[48] Networks were predictably skeptical that educational programs could continuously attract any number of listeners, but for public relation purposes they repeatedly stated that they would gladly present educational programs as long as they could attract mass audiences implicit to the network broadcast agenda. The Office of Education agreed to allow networks to choose their own staff, with notable advisors that included Edward R. Murrow, Franklin Dunham of NBC, and Studebaker himself. The Department of Education, upon completion of a broadcast, would archive all materials, and the department set up a research center to adapt educational programming for civic and "defense"-related purposes.

One amenity provided by the OOE included offering more than 30000 visual aids to listeners in advance of broadcasts, an effort that was quickly noted to have advanced the "educative influence" from the broadcast.[49] A show called "Answer Me This" challenged audiences with a single fact or question that became the guiding theme of the rest of the show.[50] By 1938 the Educational Script Exchange employed more than 100 workers in Washington and New York, and each member eventually went to work for school districts as a specialist in interpretation of educational script production or classroom management of radio education.[51] The script exchange further devised methods for assessment of the quality of scripts on hand. The Exchange held meetings and supply suggestions regarding what scripts were strong and why, which led to a standardized list of 100 model scripts by which newer scripts would be devised in reference to.

Among productions that aired on the commercial networks, *Democracy in Action, I'm an American, Freedom on the March*, and the seminal program *Americans All, Immigrants All* were produced in conjunction between network and FREC input. *Americans All, Immigrants All*, as chronicled by Barbara Savage,[52] was a particularly successful program with a staff that included W. E. B. Du Bois, Gilbert Seldes, and Alain Locke. By the end of 1938, Studebaker constituted an Educational Script Exchange made available to schools, colleges, and radio stations, distributing more than 80000 copies in just a couple of years, laying a model for educational broadcasting organization in the postwar era.[53]

Educational Media's Best Practices: Rockefeller Foundation Invites the BBC's Charles Siepmann to America to Evaluate the NAEB's Educational Experiments

Paralleling the work of the Office of Education, the Rockefeller Foundation funded apprenticeship and internship programs for educators. John Marshall invited Charles Siepmann to come to the States in 1936 based upon the recommendation of John Reith and Edward R. Murrow, to address "insuperable difficulties in education on a national scale."[54] Marshall observed that Siepmann was regarded as one of the "ablest members" of the BBC, and had been with the organization since its creation, working directly under Reith himself. According to Marshall's personal notes, Siepmann confided that Reith was "thoroughly able but personally difficult," and had exercised "almost magnetic control over members of staff."[55] He had unwittingly infringed upon Reith's power by publicly challenging him, and Reith was "inclined to view personal prominence of individual staff members unfavorably."[56] In a letter with the Rockefeller Foundation's David Stevens regarding possible travel funds, Marshall wrote that Siepmann's "liberal position in the BBC resulted in his being out of favor for some time," and this had led to Siepmann being transferred from Director of Talks to Regional Director. Siepmann's interpersonal tensions with Reith had eroded enough that he was almost sent to the States qualified as an independent consultant. But both Marshall and Stevens were impressed with Siepmann's grasp of nonprofit broadcasting. Marshall wrote, "I think we have a real chance of doing something of international importance" through Siepmann's visit. Siepmann was sent to the United States with some degree of coronation. Part of the agreement for Siepmann's consultation included, on Reith's insistence, that "senior officials travel (only) first class or cabin on the transatlantic passage."[57] In March 1937 Charles Siepmann came to the United States to aid educational broadcasters in the development of broadcasting practice.[58]

Marshall's plan for Siepmann included travel from New York to the Pacific coast and a return, including scheduled evaluations at Ohio State, the UBC, Wisconsin, Minnesota, Iowa City, Portland, San Francisco, Wyoming, and other locations. Siepmann had missed so few days of service at the BBC over ten years that he continued to receive paychecks at the BBC during his excursion and was paid an additional three months of vacation time. At the conclusion of his tour, Siepmann was asked to prepare and submit a report characterizing the "accomplishment and opportunities of each station visited" for the purpose of "better understanding of the needs of regional broadcasting in this country."[59] He was scheduled to arrive roughly March 24 on the Queen Mary and consult on a rigorous schedule that saw him going to Ohio State between March 26 and 31, the University Broadcasting Council in Chicago April 1 to 4, the University of Illinois April 5 and 6, the University of Wisconsin April 7 to 11, and so on every few days until he reached Portland on May 21, just to return to NY by train on May 25 with a planned departure to London on June 9.[60]

Siepmann reviewed every station in detail. With cutting wit, he pointed to the deficiencies of educational broadcasting practice. His visit to the University of Iowa produced a document that observed that station manager Carl Menzer had "qualities I all but overlooked...an engineer, but with a difference. He understands and cares about broadcasting."[61] Yet Iowa's staff was "woefully inadequate" for its 12-hour service license. Menzer had run the station singlehandedly in 1932 as engineer, announcer, and program organizer and often filled time by playing the violin himself, alternating with a limited repertoire of records. Noting that Menzer was dedicated yet discouraged, Siepmann pointed out how far the station had improved under his stewardship. Menzer "took heart. He needs all the courage and patience he can muster."[62] The problem, Siepmann noted, was not Menzer but conditions at the University of Iowa, "a most depressing situation," with the radio station part of an extension learning department that had no agents in the field. Menzer's boss "Dr. Mahan" had "no mind for education, and no fundamental question about objectives." Mahan was at best "a chatterer, controlling a routine, uncritical, specious, preoccupied with arbitrary exercise of his own power." Mahan was, Siepmann wrote, a "bad man...his influence is fatal, obstructing all progress." Menzer consequently "looked crushed," but was supported by a small group of "enthusiast" volunteer amateurs "up to some mischief." Until radio ceased to work under the current administration, it would remain an ineffective department.

Though one of the most important founding stations of US educational broadcasting, Siepmann described Iowa State University in similarly dire terms.[63] It had a broadcasting range of nearly 300 miles, reaching far beyond state boundaries. But the studio was reported to be "poor and démodé" with a detuned piano. The audience was reputably huge among educational broadcasters, with 138417 pieces of correspondence received between 1935 and 1936. Its primary service consisted of market information for farmers with occasional gramophone recitals and a radio book club. But the station had a "pathetically limited staff," who, to their credit, had achieved a better "and more practical realization of programme possibilities than I have found elsewhere."[64] On station manager W. I. Griffith, Siepmann found him to be "shrewd, practical," though "a rather heavy uncongenial type with a rather subnormal culture." Yet Griffith had a first-rate business head and an eye for methods. His staff was described as "rough cut, pitiable, poor down at the heel people, who strangely and ironically carry with them the patient vision of the true possibilities of broadcasting." He was "pretty sure this man deserves encouragement."

Charles Siepmann's 1937's report on Wisconsin's WHA was equally harsh. While it began with a discussion of how well equipped the station was compared to other stations, especially in terms of studio construct, when it came to management Siepmann went right for the throat.

> McCarty is a disappointment. He speaks the right language but his values seem to me to be derivative. He has a somewhat sensitive vanity and his conception of broadcasting is emotional rather than intellectual. He is not professional in his control and direction of his staff. His judgment of persons is not, I think, altogether reliable. He protests too much, and considering the potentialities open to him at this university, less has been achieved than I should have thought was possible, even within the pitiable restrictions of finance and staff that obtain here.[65]

Siepmann wrote that McCarty had put so much of a personal stamp on the station that he inhibited its development. "I heard a performance which was not bad at an amateur level, but I reckon there is some danger of this student having his head quite turned by McCarty's excessive praise and lack of critical guidance."[66] Further, Siepmann felt that staff were not sufficiently professional, and the station was unable to pay speakers, rehearse correctly, and classroom lectures had been conducted in an unsound manner. But, if "regional broadcasting" was to be developed in the Midwest, Wisconsin offered the best opportunity.

Upon visiting Ohio State's WOSU, widely received as the best educational station of its time, Siepmann reported that the staff was nonetheless "quite inadequate in quality and quantity."[67] Station manager R. Higgy was an engineer by training and, while a very nice man, "lacked the ability and imagination to conceive of the dynamic possibilities of broadcasting."[68] His primary staff were described as "keen, cheerful striplings" who lacked "necessary qualifications." Standards of effective broadcasting were not "yet anywhere above the horizon." WOSU's studio was acoustically poor, ill equipped, and not soundproof, and the station carried very little funding. Most programs, by design, were classroom instruction by professors and visiting speakers, with almost no heed to broadcasting aesthetics. This approach, Siepmann worried, had "disregarded" the difference in audience needs in form, style, length of broadcast, and content. More so, Ohio State seemed to exhibit a "confusion of thought about main educational objectives and the distinctive field of service through broadcasting." Staff had been most concerned with public relations for the university, perhaps to gain more attention and funding. Shows consequently lacked interest in "good controversy," as well as educational research about poverty, problems of industry, and activities of the state. The station lacked focus and functioned with a "primitive understanding of broadcasting technique" that was likely to prove a "fatal limitation" to development.

Of the University of Illinois station, run by Josef Wright and Frank Schooley, Siepmann noted that programs were planned on a semester basis with 25 percent consisting of records or transcriptions, and many classroom lectures. The station now reached "90% of the state," but had an audience "limited to women at home, unemployed men, the sick, and possibly including farmers in the lunch hour." Studio equipment was "rather poor and space is limited." Wright was reported as a nice, provincial type with great loyalty to the University and a competent public relations officer, but wholly lacking in "constructive educational ideas." This "defect in leadership has unhappy consequences." There was no plan or purpose about programs, subordinate staff were poor, and Schooley struck Siepmann as "an efficient clerk of a rather rough sort, but he doesn't begin to understand broadcasting as an art or education as a science."[69] Schooley was further reported as an "insensitive and not very intelligent" man who had produced "odd" programs.

In contrast to these Midwest stations, on the West Coast NBC-west (Blue network) had set up collaborative activities with the 50000-member California Teachers' Association, the State Department of Education, Stanford University, and Berkeley. They were producing four hours of educational broadcasting a week. Compared to university stations, NBC had achieved "a great deal of good will by contact" with local institutions, and shows were notably better than many universities.[70] Further, NBC had integrated 3–4000 schools into their listenership. But Siepmann was similarly miffed by their educational content. Their practice was "based on the theory that in broadcasting continuous listening involves too great a strain for ordinary people and that these interludes of music are justified by rest periods. I think it a dreadful theory."[71] Scripts were presented more professionally, but programs "lacked personality or any sense of intimate contact with the class." The station manager (unnamed in the report) lived in "immanent fear of losing his work" to an East Coast administration that did not appreciate inroads made out West, and Siepmann speculated it was because people "might easily dismiss him as a vague dreamer." In contrast to the educators NBC was a "credible if not remarkable" broadcaster, but still fell short of anything "one might call educationally significant."

Siepmann concluded that educational infrastructure was so poor that it was liable to "endanger the reputation of educators and encourage belief of commercial chains that educators had little to offer."[72] The root of the problem, Siepmann argued, was the educators themselves, who featured "nowhere any general appreciation of the responsibility which educators carry to make effective in their field and for their own ends a medium of revolutionary potentialities." Over and over the failure to secure "intelligent and dynamic direction of the service" had been compounded by inadequate and subordinate staff.[73] Programs lacked constructive purpose even within a restricted field of opportunity.

Broadcasting was costly and such limited resources and the burden of "filling time" prevented the development of "special skills in matters of technique and forms of presentation that might result" in the goodwill for a university.[74] The dearth of talent was evident to the extent that students and amateurs worked for free, and at best educational broadcasting in the US in 1937 could be described as a "great misfortune."[75] The future of the enterprise would necessarily require "difficult technique," a constant liaison between broadcaster and teacher, advisory committees, and trained administration. "A bad talk kills more interest than a dozen good talks can sustain," Siepmann concluded. In his final assessment, he wrote that "the above critique, while no means exhaustive, is sufficiently destructive to warrant the impression of unfriendliness." Brutal and frank, Siepmann's report ironically turned out to be a milestone in educational broadcasting history. Its tone was curiously well received by every station, advocate, and federal committee. The content of the report was pragmatic, critical, and dedicated to educational broadcasting improvement. Marshall called Siepmann's report "unusually forceful of the point in question."[76]

Yet in the epilogue of his report Siepmann provided guidance to educators about how to translate their purpose into action. Siepmann wrote that a study of listener capacity and "readiness to hear" was central to understanding information. The primary concern of broadcasting should be the determination of priority of interests that correspond to "urgent needs as a human being and citizen."[77] Educational radio had to instill a culture that valued acquisition of knowledge, relevance of broadcasts, and the relationship between information and the prospect of survival until "intermediate needs of men are intelligently provided for." Siepmann suggested that best practices would have to be organized with administrative guidance through rehearsal, standards, pooled resources, elimination of redundancy of broadcast style, and cooperative planning between university interests. But Siepmann did not believe that the "present distribution of activities on radio, where associated with universities, is sound."[78] The NAEB was not yet in a position, Siepmann believed, to strengthen their service. Even if an "unimaginable" increase in staff and finance was procured, the university stations were not prepared to provide daily 12-hour service in line with FCC regulation, and if they were able to create such broadcasts, they would not be useful to the public.

He advised supporting two "parallel developments" instead of investing in NAEB stations. First, a federal commission should be set up to determine basic principles of policy and "a concerted scheme of action similar" to the BBC.[79] The commission would take "variant resources" of radio technique as applicable to education and create a report to crystallize what may be necessary to create an alternate BBC-like broadcaster to ensure legislative measures necessary to implement "the scheme." If it was politically feasible, a parallel development in controlled broadcasting experiments would then be centered in the universities to develop services under experimental direction "appropriate to the medium and relevant to education." The allocation of a special wavelength by the FCC would be necessary for universities to direct their experiments with some focus. "The tragedy of what is being done at present at universities throughout the country seems to derive from the fact that little is demonstrated beyond the incapacity of educators to realize the significance of what they attempt or to achieve work that has demonstrable value."[80] Universities could be a strong center for responsive research, but not for broadcasting leadership. Siepmann settled in the United States and became a citizen in 1942.

The University Broadcasting Council, Educational Broadcasting's First Network: NBC, University of Chicago, and Northwestern University

The inconsistencies in best practices described in Siepmann's report were already the subject of wide discussion among NAEB affiliates. As the Rockefeller Foundation surveyed the educational broadcasting landscape, John Marshall identified a promising early experiment that sought to professionalize the trade. According to an application by the University Broadcasting Council (UBC), the city of Chicago provided the Rockefeller Foundation with an unusually rich opportunity to test cross-institutional collaboration, with its local universities, museums, researchers, and commercial interests all dedicated to radio's improvement.[81] Allen Miller of the Radio Department at the University of Chicago hoped to stimulate the production of "radio programs of cultural and educational value to strengthen the development of a regional center and to promote cooperation between radio stations and educational institutions in the Chicago area."[82] Miller formed a consortium composed of the University of Chicago, Northwestern University, and DePaul University with a board of trustees consisting of two representatives from each participating university and Judith Waller of NBC.

Provisions had already been made. Universities set up studios and agreed to pay the salaries of a staff that included a director, publicity director, office manager, secretaries, and technical and engineering personnel. The UBC devised a procedure for measuring the effectiveness of programs through correspondence with listeners, and a system for payment to performers rendering service.[83] The goal of the UBC, in contrast to regional rural stations as well as commercial broadcasters, was to pool distinct nonprofit entities into an advisory committee to meet civic needs of the community, in line with public interest stipulations of the Act.

Marshall supported the project after a commissioned report by Allen Miller titled *The Problem of Educational Broadcasting and a Plan for Its Solution*. Due to the "increased complexity and variability of modern society," Miller argued in the report that continuing education "throughout life" had become a need of paramount importance.[84] Radio held the unique potential to be the most economical and powerful medium for dissemination of information and education to a large and widely scattered adult audience. The UBC could aggregate intellectual talent to speak to a built-in audience. A recent study had shown that nearly fifty percent of all radio homes listened to University of Chicago radio features at some point in the week, amounting to nearly 250000 potential listeners.[85] Such an experiment, based in a large diverse city such as Chicago, would address the basic problem facing educational radio: Miller argued that only a small fraction of educational radio's potential had been realized because educators had previously been "ignorant" of the techniques that would make curricular broadcasting viable.

Noting that the strengths of personality and technical ability seemed to be "far more important considerations in educational broadcasting than academic reputations"[86] to the radio audience, Marshall pressed Miller to reflect commercial aesthetics in instructional content to improve its reception. Miller replied that he believed that educators could develop reputations not only as scholars but as entertainers. The best way to develop new techniques would be under the supervision of experts in overlapping departments dedicated to selection of talent, choice of subject matter, and perfection of presentation techniques. Previous experiments had been poorly designed, especially classroom lecture formats. A student registered for such a course often had no pre-training for "technical jargon of a specialized subject" and no way to engage with the classroom to find out.[87] New instructional techniques included talks, but also interviews, roundtable discussions, dramatizations, and lectures with "illustrative inserts." Miller met with networks to discuss his idea, including Merlin Aylesworth at NBC, Fred Willis at CBS, and Phil Loucks at the NAB, and all had agreed to contribute to the UBC. A subsequent meeting with Anning Prall at the FCC and John Studebaker of OOE further strengthened early support.

Miller planned to broadcast over a 200-mile listening radius and to cover subjects such as social studies, drama, music, and many more. The group aimed to provide eighteen broadcasts a week at first, ramping up to sixty broadcasts a week over time. The consortium hoped to pool funds for the training of new educational radio practitioners, using studio equipment that "will not be elaborate or expensive."[88] They predicted they could set up one central location connected by telephone wires to several campuses, which could be supported by roughly $55000 a year. To reach wider audiences and school districts, a shortwave rebroadcast could supplement local Chicago broadcasts. The coordination of various programs of the universities in the area would eliminate needless duplication and make inroads toward securing sympathetic support of newspapers as contributors and publicists.[89] The UBC was able to secure the cooperation of five stations in the Chicago area, and to purchase the use of transmission wires from Bell Telephone.[90]

Miller spent time thinking through what it would take to develop educational "talent." He introduced a conversational element to broadcasts, and emphasized the use of simple vocabulary by its participants, instructing hosts to speak in "short and simple words in common usage" even for complex ideas, and the utilization of non-technical vocabulary.[91] Miller felt that much educational radio was "dull," leading to "walk out" on programs due to its inability to utilize the medium correctly, so a friendly, personal, and democratic attitude was more stimulating than a simple classroom lecture. By the end of the first year the output was impressive, including 912 broadcasts, for 333 hours of time that equated to $303231 of "commercial value."[92] Shows had been broadcast on a mix of local superstations, independents, and networks, including 92 on the NBC affiliate WMAQ, 195 on the powerful clear-channel independent station WGN, 25 on WBBM (CBS), 568 on WJJD, and 37 on WLS (NBC). Miller gained collaborative support of other educational institutions such as the Field Museum, the Museum of Science and Industry, the Chicago Public Library, and the American Medical Association. Within a short period of time an impressive consortium had been constituted that was able to take advantage of the best in education and commercial methods in the Chicago area.

If Miller's experiment was successful, John Marshall wrote, there might be an opportunity to reproduce the model in New York City. Chancellor Chase of NYU was interested in the possibility, and David Sarnoff had agreed that a New York experiment would be possible, offering NBC's Merrill Denison as a consultant should such a project get off the ground.[93] The goal of the experiment, Marshall believed, was to see if education could be combined with entertainment provided that adequate staff, writers, and production managers were available. One show, "The Old Judge," introduced legal problems in a dramatic form. Its central character was a judge who had retired from the bench but continued to give legal advice to countless clients with a philosophical demeanor.[94] Other shows focused on extemporaneous book reviews in American literature, dramatic biographical sketches of great scientists culminating in their discoveries, "non-technical" discussion of business practices and events, and so on. Airtime was provided to parent-teacher organizations, the Illinois League of Women Voters, the National Congress of Parents and Teachers, various musical performers, and a curiously popular show based at the University of Chicago called the Round Table, in which three speakers discussed controversial topics and contemporary news items on Sunday afternoons.[95]

Yet, however promising such widespread support from major institutions initially appeared, Miller was not provided with a working cooperative as good as he and Marshall had hoped. Viewing the initiative as a peripheral experiment instead of a sustainable project, administrators at the major universities were unwilling to grant their faculty course releases to concentrate on programming and development. Worse for Miller, existing faculty had little understanding or interest in learning the sophisticated techniques that sustained media industry production. Quality programming by academics with no prior experience proved to be a nearly impossible task, and a series of documents point to the difficulty Miller had in coordinating basic functions that commercial broadcasters had long ago streamlined.[96]

One musical education show run by a local school district was staffed by hosts and an engineer prone to technical flaws and resistance to educational goals, reportedly calling recommended pedagogical techniques "high falutin' notions."[97] Yet Miller had no replacement on hand for the hosts so the show continued. One result of such difficulties was an increased reliance on transcriptions, or recordings of programs. which, as Miller claimed, could be played "100 times" before the needle wore out the record.[98] Yet live broadcasting was the gold standard of early radio; transcriptions were regarded as second-best and a poor substitute for live.

The *Chicago Tribune* wrote a positive review of the experiment in early 1937:

> Organized less than two years ago by Allen Miller, who now directs its activities, the council is constantly demonstrating that Nobel Prize winners prove as exhilarating as Alexander Woolcoott; that so-called absent minded professors are as agile in ad libbing as Fred Allen; that savants are more effective word slingers than senators, and that the night skies are at least as mystifying as night life. In short the council is proving every day that there is entertainment in erudition.[99]

Problems aside, by the beginning of 1937 the UBC was providing an average weekly output of eight hours comprising talks, discussions, music, and dramatization. The UBC was praised by Marshall for its ability to be independent from both universities and networks yet able to "initiate ideas and to execute programs which are true to properly considered educational objectives and, in themselves, illustrate the integrity of academic standards."[100] Cooperation with commercial companies, as difficult as they may have been, had assured hours of transmission over the networks.

In his 1937 assessment, Miller wrote that such problems were helpful for improving the UBC's overall awareness of best practices in radio broadcasting, and by the end of the UBC's first two-year experiment, both Miller and Marshall felt that they had made some progress. The first year was, according to a letter from Miller to Marshall, one of initial organization in which assembling a staff and balancing educational quotients with commercial aesthetics led to a high turnover of participants.[101] The second year helped to develop the scaffolding of an educational approach to mass-audience programming and was deemed one of "active production."[102] The exploratory qualities of the UBC were repeatedly broached in letters to Marshall in lieu of excuses or apologies for execution. "The Board feels strongly that the UBC is in almost all respects experimental in character. Not only is our organization an innovation in cooperative effort but our day-to-day activities are distinctly experimental in character."[103] The first two years, Miller estimated, were 85 percent directed to activities other than broadcasting.

An experimental show produced by the Field Museum called "From the Ends of the Earth" aired an anthropological program with live background music to enhance content. More work was needed on editing and alteration of the manuscript before the show, and the museum staff, when faced with continuous changes to the script "were shocked by the level of elements which would have been modified, to the extent that the entire field of reconstruction is now taboo with them."[104] Museum curators were so detail-minded that small shifts in dramatic quality seemed to appear to undermine scientific accuracy, leading to two to three rewrites before broadcasts when little time was available in the first place. The result was an "unusually heavy mortality rate among writers and would-be writers."[105]

By the third year Miller was receiving "less and less help from members of the faculty except for the few who serve on Council committees and take part in the Council's programs."[106] Universities began to balk at high expenses, and the Carnegie Corporation was enlisted to help fund development. By the end of 1937 the UBC had spent nearly $1.2-million dollars.[107] Miller's bosses at the University of Chicago—Robert Hutchins and William Benton—wrote to Marshall that such a large uncooperative consortium of local broadcasters was simply too difficult to execute, and that the university no longer wanted to support the project. Benton was, Marshall wrote, "determined to bring about an early disbandment" of the experiment.[108] The Council, Benton argued to Marshall, was not proving successful and was taking funds and faculty time from the University of Chicago. Hutchins stipulated that if the project were to continue, the Rockefeller Foundation should not have to fund it so dramatically, providing more oversight by the university for future decisions.

However, Benton wrote in another letter that one program showed a great deal of promise: the *University of Chicago Round Table*. While he felt that the UBC signaled a "fledgling approach," Benton remained optimistic that in spite of the general propensity for UBC programs to be "of mediocre quality due to lackadaisical faculty interest," the *Round Table* presented a new educational genre in which experts discussed "world events and the specificities of their findings."[109] The *Round Table* ultimately ran for twenty-two years and became the standard format for later political shows, as well as public broadcasting news interview formats. Further, Robert Hutchins and William Benton's interest in radio had been piqued by Miller's wide-scale attempt and the success of the new public affairs genre format.

William Benton, who got his start in advertising, became interested in the notion that a "quality" form of educational broadcasting could be developed. Due to interpersonal problems with Miller and the UBC's employee turnover problem, and after a meeting in which general faculty discussed which programs should be culled from the schedule based upon their quality, Benton decided to end the experiment. Benton had been persuaded that more could be accomplished for the future of educational broadcasting if a limited number of high-quality programs were proliferated outside of a single network. Quite a few experimental programs had been produced—three hundred and seventeen over two years—but the UC faculty told Benton that they were pleased with only a small fraction of them and that the university should spend less energy on such a project.[110]

The UBC was, in its way, the first substantial experiment in educational broadcasting. A final report was written by Marshall in 1941, nearly three years after the UBC had been dismantled. Due to the UBC, commercial companies had begun to take this work more seriously. While the UBC had failed to create a sustainable alternative to the networks on a regional scale, it "undoubtedly set standards for educational broadcasting both in the companies and more generally throughout the country" by realizing new educational possibilities that compared favorably to other stations.[111]

The National Committee on Education by Radio Builds the First Regional Educational Network: The Rocky Mountain Radio Council

The University Broadcasting Council opened a path for philanthropic groups to fund noncommercial infrastructure. After the Act one of NCER's members, University of Wyoming President A.G. Crane, proposed a project like the University Broadcast Council of Chicago.[112] He envisioned a wider scope for broadcasting than local stations, and proposed a consortium centered in Colorado and Wyoming that would provide free education for students in the Rocky Mountains. He noted that the UBC had served a small but populous area and hoped that the RMRC might extend the same concept to a wider, less populous region with more need for such an initiative.

Marshall recorded that Crane complained of initially being "omitted" from FREC projects, but the RMRC proposal was submitted in line with FREC recommendations, and due to "the feasibility of state-wide or regional organization for educational broadcasting."[113] In an April 1937 letter Marshall worried that Crane was too ambitious and not practical enough to reach such a wide audience, as no technical infrastructure had yet been built, and commercial telephone wire rentals were few and far between in that area. "Crane tended to assume that educators are already prepared for effective work in broadcasting."[114] However, that Crane had already gained the confidence of state institutions in Wyoming and Colorado led Marshall to give the concept a chance. It was an ambitious initiative. Crane not only proposed an experiment in educational radio regionalism in line with the public interest facilities mandate of the 1934 Act, but also intended to increase the technological development of radio technology itself. The radius of broadcasts would cover Colorado and Wyoming and parts of Nebraska, Kansas, and New Mexico.[115]

Charles Siepmann was sent to survey the RMRC in 1937 as part of his analyses. He agreed with Crane that individual universities were too small to provide a base for educational broadcasting, and that a regional broadcasting approach was preferable. But Siepmann's review was mixed. "Dr. Crane has, I think, a proper understanding of the importance of professional standards," Siepmann wrote. But the RMRC would "achieve nothing effective if it becomes a mart for ineffective salesmanship of the wares which the different adult educational associations have to offer."[116] In early 1938 Crane nonetheless went ahead with plans for his project. He had limited but stable finances to pull from at the University of Wyoming and a working relationship with Colorado educators.[117] Marshall kept tabs on the experiment and reported in his diaries that "preliminary conversations have enlisted the interest of about 30 organizations active in the area," and that Crane's efforts had "stimulated the feeling of local broadcasters that some such organization of this kind is in order."[118] His initial plan was "closely analogous" to the UBC, in that it proposed a central production agency responsible for producing and airing broadcasts over local stations.[119] To begin Crane secured the cooperation of ten commercial stations in the region. By February 1939 Crane enlisted the support of twenty-six institutions in the region, including every Colorado state university and local adult education group, parents and teachers' organization, women's club, medical society, public library, schools of theology, farmer cooperative, and most significantly the Wyoming Department of Education. The RMRC wrote a constitution and by-laws, scheduled visits of the director or staff to each participating agency once a month, selected a "place for central office and studios," and purchased recording and technical equipment.[120] Further, unlike the UBC, the RMRC proposed four-to-six-month training periods for educational radio directors and staff. Trained staff was placed at different broadcasting nodes to run day-by-day operations, oversee equipment function, and maintain contact with the central unit. And RMRC was the first educational network to propose to chronicle "evidence" of success based in agency and listener response. Early program experiments included titles such as "Makers of the West," "The Story of Regional Products: Sugar Beets," "What is a University?," and "Dude Ranching," as well as programming on history, geography, English literature, language, astronomy, music, vocational guidance, botany, art, health, and geology.

The Payne Fund was excited enough about Crane's project that it named Crane's concept one of the NCER's primary public projects.[121] Crane's work also piqued the interest of the NAEB. In 1938 he consulted with the University of Minnesota station, suggesting that it create programming as a "socially desirable service that must be useful, attractive, and acceptable. It must successfully meet the standards of the better grade of commercial programs. Your plan for thirty hours of broadcasting per week is a stupendous task. Most in the field are inexperienced amateur producers."[122] He was credited for the eventual NAEB decision to recommend a standard of two rehearsals for each broadcast, instead of the usual zero. "This means forty rehearsals or equivalent attention in script editing, program planning, for twenty unit broadcasts per day."[123] He was aware of Menzer's vision for a decentralized distribution network, but believed that "to maintain a program of this magnitude day after day demands very definite and extensive plans be made to establish training centers and to furnish all needed facilities."[124] Crane advised the NAEB that a centralized organization was needed to oversee general management, script editing, general program planning, recording, supervision of school service, clerical work and correspondence, testing listener response, evaluating programs, providing listener services, interregional services, publicity, and training broadcasts.

Crane hired broadcast announcers from local commercial stations to both announce for the RMRC and train younger broadcasters. In an August letter to Marshall at Rockefeller Foundation, Crane wrote that "our program for training local and institutional broadcasters is vitally dependent on recording studios which we hope will eventually be established in each of the major institutions or communities. In the establishment of these local recording studios, we shall need expert advice and counsel or there will be many mistakes or money wasted."[125] RMRC planned to broadcast its programs on commercial stations by renting airtime and wired connections. Crane proposed to "establish an organization and facilities for producing cooperatively public radio programs to be known as the Rocky Mountain Public Program. This program of broadcasts is to be made available for transmission to both commercial and educational broadcast stations in the area."[126]

"Listening Schools" were equipped with facilities, technology, teachers qualified to stimulate discussion around broadcasts and textbooks, and attention was paid to "social and economic backgrounds of the community" in development.[127] Time was provided to review broadcasts, secure assistance in the way of musicians and dramatists, and perform rehearsals. To ensure programs remained at a similar caliber, "central radio workshops" were set up for staff.

The RMRC's organizational arrangement was more sophisticated and advanced than the UBC. Crane requested Rockefeller Foundation funds to conduct a "planning period" to "mobilize resources accordingly."[128] The Rocky Mountain region was widely separated, and wire transfers were surprisingly expensive between institutions, as was travel back and forth to institutions as "personal contacts and acquaintances with stations."[129] Crane applied for $49150 from RF largely to distribute program transcriptions and strategize rebroadcasts between institutions. Crane's official release regarding the project stated that the "organizational members of the Council will contribute to the project time, talent and publicity which has a market value many times over the amount required for the maintenance of the central organization."[130] RMRC made three proposals to RF: 1) to create a working organization through which educational institutions and agencies, service departments, and citizen groups could mobilize and coordinate broadcasting resources; 2) demonstrate the emphasis and value of radio as an instrument of democracy; 3) demonstrate a cooperative method of maintaining working relationships between broadcasting stations and the producers of noncommercial programs; and an offshoot fourth goal of providing a "wider range of choice" in the area in line with public interest stipulations.[131]

Marshall agreed to fund Crane on one condition—that he hire Robert Hudson of the Adult Education Council of Denver to monitor the quality of programming.[132] Marshall trusted Hudson because he had written evaluations for the Rockefeller Foundation and had professional radio experience. Crane agreed, and Hudson proved to be the right choice. According to Crane, Hudson "adjusted to the work of class instruction easily."[133] However, an early evaluation by Hudson noted that he did not feel that the project was yet sustainable. He speculated that perhaps within two years a basic administrative structure "could" be achieved—which was, Hudson joked, better than a statement like "I hope we can."[134] When this negative review returned, Marshall temporarily cut off funding for the project. Marshall wrote that "I gather from some remarks that he has not yet appreciated the full force of this argument. He feels it inevitable, for example, that information will come from the centers."[135]

Crane appealed to Marshall for a smaller $5000 for continuation in 1939, by which time Marshall looked to Paul Lazarsfeld of the Princeton Radio Research Project for a professional opinion. Lazarsfeld examined the RMRC documents with disapproval, arguing that the RMRC seemed like little more than an organization in "the business of manufacturing educational records and induc[ing] stations to broadcast them." Lazarsfeld was skeptical that a centralized "network" that manufactured educational records and broadcasted through shortwave radio might act as an efficient counterpoint to commercial broadcasting. However, he lauded Crane's unusual ability to successfully coordinate the first operating educational infrastructure to include distribution and production.[136]

Upon receiving a second wave of funding in 1940, Robert Hudson was appointed as full director, and expanded services to include divisions of workshop centers in which studio auditoriums were available for educational listenership. By 1940 the RMRC had produced thirty-two programs in eight continuous series, broadcast one hundred and nine times over its thirteen affiliates.[137] But the most unexpected boost for the RMRC had come in 1939 from the FCC, who anticipated a need to distribute governmental information and propaganda during wartime.[138] Studebaker's public forums went into use by the FCC briefly in the late 1930s, and the RMRC offered its services and institutional connections. Offering a mix of entertainment and government information, the RMRC gained support from federal interests looking for a reliable western connection. Of this Crane wrote to Marshall:

"…our council is nonpartisan, nonpolitical, democratic, organized and operating in accordance with American ideas. The council's organization, procedure, and objectives demonstrate the ideology of democracy as contrasted with the ideology of totalitarianism. I believe war times would give us better hearing in this region than would more peaceful times."[139]

His letter was accompanied by a letter of support from James Fly, now chair of the FCC, who congratulated the RMRC "on the occasion of its initial broadcast of the Rocky Mountain Civic Series," and its "27 educational broadcasting institutions and 17 commercial broadcasting stations coordinating commendable effort." Fly's commission had recently put out a ruling that stated that "just as it may be a powerful instrumentality for public good, so a broadcast station has potentialities of causing great public harm, and it is accordingly imperative that the limited broadcast channels belonging to the public should be entrusted to those who have a sense of public responsibility." Fly believed the RMRC had met such stipulations and promised continued support of frequency allocations.

With a coherent plan and support in place, a report devised by Hudson to John Marshall in 1940 detailed the RMRC's slow development. "The Council plan is basically a plan for machinery to implement the project. It is a plan aiming to provide for cooperation between all elements concerned in civic broadcasting in this region." Specifically, the promotion of workshop centers equipped with control rooms, observation rooms, studios, reception rooms, and business offices had been noticed by the FREC, who had begun to recommend other regional stations go to Denver to learn at such centers. As the NAEB contended, program transcription resulted in the most reliable manner of broadcasting, with well-edited "technique," and excellent quality. Certain shows had been duplicated so many times over within a year that Crane reported "duplicates of duplicates" in the region. The result, Crane excitedly reported, was that while it was still too early to conclusively speak about a "rise in standards," stations were "emphatic in stating that council programs were better than the stations had been receiving from civic broadcasters before."[140]

Crane was responsible for implementation of the first organized use of transcriptions in noncommercial broadcasting, predating even the bicycle network.[141] Due to the initiative's regional nature, placement among public land-grant institutions, and attempt to qualify educational broadcasting as "public interest" programming, Crane began using variations of the term "public broadcasting"[142] to describe the RMRC's plan, including "public radio" and "public service broadcasting" This appears to be the first institutional usage of the term in the United States, mentioned multiple times in letters to Marshall.

By 1940 the Council accumulated active participation from twenty-seven institutions including all of the regional universities and was successfully broadcasting over fourteen distinct radio stations.[143] Crane was in part successful because he began logistics so crucial to sustainable administration. By 1941 Marshall was convinced that Crane's experiment had made a contribution under Hudson's supervision. He wrote:

> "…the council is equipped to offer an unusual degree of leadership. Its programs already have a finish which is unusual for programs originating outside the industry. Furthermore, its offers have a well-defined program of leadership for the Council. They propose, for example, as a next step to undertake a careful appraisal of the problems of the region and to base their future program policy on that appraisal, on the assumption that such problems involve matters of direct concern to a majority of their listeners."[144]

Rockefeller subsequently provided a three-year grant. Following a catastrophic policy defeat, the NCER had rebounded and contributed an example of an efficient economy of scale for a noncommercial network, while transforming the strategic design of New Deal media activism into a set of system and coalition-building procedures.

The Allerton House Seminars: Institutionalization of Best Practices in Production and Distribution

In 1941 attention turned to the war. Multiple educational broadcasting practitioners went to fight overseas, worked with the OWI,[145] and continued with streamlining day-to-day practices without much growth until 1946. Upon returning from the war, educational broadcasters were even more convinced that civic use of radio, and now television, would be an important part of maintaining democratic discourse. The previous decade of media reform had emphasized several necessities: the need to work with multiple sectors to implement a vision of education by radio, learn the craft of broadcasting itself, and to align a vision of collaboration that included strengthening the consortium of stations. After WWII the NAEB was the last standing association or trade group. NAEB members had participated in, and studied, many of the strategies implemented during the New Deal. Two new leaders—Richard Hull of Iowa State, and Wilbur Schramm of the University of Illinois—played a major role in consolidating all the different influences of the past into one infrastructure. The NAEB had rallied after the Act to connect remaining stations, the Office of Education had set up a national clearinghouse and advised educational stations on how to frame their work for legislators, Charles Siepmann brought BBC discipline in program development to land-grant universities, and two experiments in Chicago and the Rockies had shown that educational broadcasting was feasible.

On December 6, 1945, educators were granted six protected FM channels, and another two-dozen applications went under review.[146] In 1948 the "TV Freeze" began.[147] The specter of a new medium reduced institutional anxieties about frequency scarcity. NAEB President Richard Hull sought to parlay their progress into a winning formula in upcoming television channel applications. Hull's planned expansion, the NAEB's successful protection of their FM frequencies, and the serendipity of the freeze motivated members to prepare for a new advocacy push. NAEB membership bounced back in the 1940s and neared 100 member stations in 1949.[148] However, the expectations required for FM frequency holders—well-funded facilities, a full day of filled airtime, and public service contributions to schools and the larger community—were difficult to supervise across the board. Many of the same problems from before 1934 continued. The organization had not received philanthropic funding since before the war and sought a way to reconnect with John Marshall at the Rockefeller Foundation. Marshall had not been in touch with practitioners for at least five years.

Hull's first pitch to Marshall was to see if they might be willing to fund training of university students to become commercial broadcasting practitioners. In anticipation of the forthcoming television regulation, Hull wanted to find a way to display cooperation with commercial broadcasters. Barclay Leathem, one of Hull's colleagues at Iowa State, applied to the RF for $77500 per year for three years to build a "communications department" training division for television production. Marshall gave the application serious consideration but concluded that such an institute "would appear to be practical only if industry is prepared to contribute substantially to its capital and current costs," since many of the students would go on to work in commercial broadcasting.[149] Leathem spoke with the networks and made progress in securing an agreement for future funding, but only if the program was already shown to be effective. Marshall wrote that he knew of only "very few instances" in which experimentation outside the industry had influenced production practices internally; the most noteworthy examples were the Chicago Roundtable and the RMRC.[150]

Other NAEB member stations also solicited Marshall. A letter from the President of the University of Illinois, George Stoddard, highlighted the NAEB's new institutional base in Champaign-Urbana. "The situation is once again as fluid as it was when educational stations first came into the field in the early 1920s. This is therefore a second chance for educational stations to take the leadership they have let slip from them."[151] Founding Chair of the Institute for Communications Research Wilbur Schramm at the University of Illinois wrote Marshall that he understood that during the 1930s the foundation had granted a series of fellowships to key personnel at NAEB stations, only to be disappointed with the NAEB's results. "The most favorable comments on the experience which we get from them are on the informal seminar which we held fortnightly while a group of them were in NY."[152] But Schramm had secured support from previous Rockefeller and FREC participants to build an educational broadcasting wing of the new communications research institute. He urged Marshall to take a second look at noncommercial media.

Between 1946 and 1950 Illinois hired specialists in every subfield connected to the development of public media advocacy—Dallas Smythe of the FCC for communications policy research,[153] Robert Hudson of the RMRC (and a stint at CBS), and of course Wilbur Schramm, who previously worked with Harold Lasswell on propaganda research during WWII and founded the Iowa Writer's Workshop. Schramm oversaw the research side of the Institute and "hoped to assemble a good team for research of mass communications" centered around the study of the "flow of communication in the Midwest."[154] Marshall was inclined to listen to Schramm due to his relationship with Lasswell, as well as his decision to hire RMRC administrator Robert Hudson as a founding faculty member. Based upon the past success of the FREC conferences, Schramm was able to convince Marshall to revisit the collaborative conference format of the 1930s but applied to the question of how to obtain television frequencies.

Schramm wrote that the NAEB had previously "stood pretty still while the industry has walked around them, because of swift changes they are now at a put-up-or-shut-up place."[155] But stations "now realize that their programs are, by professional standards, not attractive and that their audiences are, by professional standards, puny,"[156] and it was time to make use of research and administrative lessons toward consolidating the vision articulated during the 1930s. Schramm believed that a conference was needed to discuss "the nature of public service radio" including the "procedure...centered around problems and consultants."[157] Marshall noted that new NAEB members were indeed calling upon many of his findings during FREC, and saw one last opportunity to promote training in measurement, production values, and political advocacy.

On April 11, 1949, Marshall authorized a grant for a three-week summer conference at which the University of Illinois agreed to host fifteen consultants and twenty educational broadcast institutions.[158] According to Schramm, educational broadcasters needed "a philosophy before a practicum. Furthermore, it is about time they begin to make use of research as a tool in planning."[159] Among invited participants were Richard Hull of Ohio State, Dallas Smythe, Ralph Steetle of Louisiana State, soon to be appointed to the Joint Committee for Educational Television, as well as Paul Lazarsfeld and Charles Siepmann.

Lazarsfeld spoke at the conference about the "inhibitions that prevail in noncommercial broadcasting including many programs never tried."[160] Charles Siepmann, now a widely influential figure for the NAEB Executive Committee, spoke about the "important function in supplying elements in the broadcasting diet that the commercials did not supply."[161] Siepmann argued that universities had to function as commercial broadcasters in practice and an educator in concept. Educators had a need for skills and services offered by commercial broadcasters, a responsibility to serve community stations, and, most centrally according to Siepmann, educational broadcasters had to attend to "conditional factors with practical implications," such as regional tradition and community need.[162]

Hull argued that if educational broadcasters were to widen its listenership, advocates would first need "knowledge of capacities and resources and obligations, working knowledge of the radio audience for the radio educator, and a picture of what radio education can do and should be in the 20th century."[163] Irving Merrill at KUSD, South Dakota, B.B. Brackett's old position, wrote: "I left the conference feeling that I had participated in a meeting of historic significance...in a sense it proves educational broadcasting does have an obvious objective which readily distinguishes it from other types of broadcasting."[164] After two weeks of discussions attendees found that they agreed on most strategies and principles. George Probst of the University of Chicago Roundtable wrote to Schramm immediately after the conference, saying that he had been treated to "a week for philosophizing on the problem to begin with, and then a second week for some more philosophizing to spill over into, with about three or four days at the end devoted to analysis of proposals for action."[165]

The conclusion of the conference led to a series of letters between Marshall and Schramm that discussed a need for "intelligence" regarding policy and practice in the field, with six points of value:

1. "Our own research, and that of the few other units who are doing anything closely pertinent to educational radio.
2. An extensive correspondence with persons who have ears to the ground.
3. Questionnaire-type reports on such topics as the policies of educational stations in handling politics and religion; the technical equipment of stations; the kinds of tape-recorders available at stations for handing exchanged programs; the programs of educational stations; the financing of educational radio.
4. Evaluation and translation of printed research from journals and survey reports.
5. Evaluation of trade press news, FCC actions, etc.
6. Exchange of semi-confidential information among educational stations—information which could not go into the NAEB bulletin."[166]

John Marshall's interested was again piqued, and for the first time since the 1930s he reappraised NAEB stations.[167] He concluded that the RMRC had become a foundational example of noncommercial radio due to its combination of administrative and content production. Marshall anticipated that television would take over the job of mass entertainment. He considered "modest assistance" to "consolidate their (NAEB) broadcasting on FM networks and by an exchange of recordings, turn them from local educational effort to more general public service."[168] Marshall wrote that the conference had provided a pathway for four improvements to educational broadcasting practice: 1) practitioners would have a unified front of standards to seek assistance to pioneer work in television including funds sufficient for construction and equipment, 2) this would in turn lead to the possibility for future fellowships for educational broadcasters, 3) the conference consolidated the interest to establish a national educational transcription service for the educational stations, and 4) the NAEB would institute much-needed administrative offices.[169]

In an October 26, 1949, letter, Marshall wrote to the Lily Endowment fund that for some time he had been skeptical about what educational broadcasters could accomplish as an alternative to network programming. To the best of his knowledge, the NAEB had done "little more than hold an annual meeting, publish a newsletter, and etc...but the seminar had provided him with (p) retty tangible evidence that these people were beginning to take themselves [*sic*] serious."[170] To that point, Marshall noted, the work of noncommercial broadcasters had been too narrowly educational and had missed opportunities to experiment with "programs of a serious character."[171] But Marshall reported that seminar attendees had finally admitted that most programs on air were "not suitable for repetition, too locally based, and worthy of a wider hearing," but that with a "traffic center to route programs, a national office, and a basis of useful function for program production, that momentum would be immanently plausible." In one of the last of Marshall's grants to educators before losing his charge of the Rockefeller Fund, he underwrote a study called "Radio Programming in Colleges and Universities," which took statistical analysis of available educational nodes to connect through production, script exchange, and research.[172] In assessment of data, the report further recommended a laundry list for each educational institution, such as hire directors who were individual specialists in radio with attention to showmanship, discover means for adequate budget allotments, create degree programs, increase attention to audience measurement, and provide a way to receive and exchange scripts among institutions.[173]

In a consequent letter, Schramm wrote that the Allerton Seminar "proved" that a clear course of action had been broached to answer the question "what is the job of educational broadcasters?"[174] Schramm proposed a follow-up conference. Schramm argued that educators would first and foremost have to learn to make and present programs, "how to translate educational resources into imaginative and effect broadcasting, for the audiences which can make use of them."[175] To do this, they would need to learn to effectively "share program resources so that the strength of all educational broadcasting will be reflected in each educational broadcasting operation."[176] Part of this problem, Schramm wrote, was administrative, financial, and technical. But another large part of it concerned the concept of program-making itself. "If we are to share programs, what kinds of programs? What quality of programs? How can the intellectual resources of American universities, considered as a unit, best be utilized for broadcasting?"[177]

Schramm posited that the next "logical step" was to build a strong educational broadcasting service. A second conference, Schramm posited, could address how to translate educational resources, especially in the humanities, into effective radio. The best way to do so was to "challenge the imagination and ingenuities of young men who have opportunities to broadcast substantive materials, directed at 'small' audiences, and subject qualitative standards in measurement." A second conference would be smaller and focused upon "central intelligence service into the realm of operation."[178] But Marshall was not convinced that the NAEB was a good home institution for a new and potentially expensive investment. In a January 1950 document titled "Possible Program in Radio" Marshall reviewed an internal report by Robert Hudson on the state of public service programming on the commercial networks.[179] Hudson concluded that networks were producing less educational content than they had before the war. So Marshall agreed to fund a second conference on methods of educational broadcasting practice.

With Marshall back on board, Richard Hull attempted to procure funds from the Lincoln Foundation."[180] In his application Hull wrote that the NAEB hoped to provide daily access to broadcasts, produced with the best techniques available to inform audiences of "facts and ideas in the arts and sciences," as well as daily events. The present structure of educational broadcasting had limited educators from pursuing these standards, and there was little likelihood for any marked change without external support. Yet educational radio was undergoing a "renaissance not only in the establishment of new facilities but in training and acquiring personnel and in development of workable philosophies and techniques."[181] Funding would consolidate and coordinate the activities of noncommercial stations, which to that point had been "isolated and for the most part working independently." The NAEB planned to program sources and build a central administrative office to coordinate engineering data, program advice, and comprehensive information for new stations, and found a central production and distribution center. Without funds, the NAEB would find it difficult to survive, and "might well spell the death knell for any nationwide, consolidated, or coordinated activity for educational radio and restrict it to token activity only, confined largely to a state or regional basis."[182] These initiatives were already underway, the letter stated, with Dallas Smythe at the University of Illinois conducting a preliminary program study, and Harry Skornia developing budget and facility studies at the University of Indiana.

The Lincoln Foundation did not fund the new initiative, but Hull's framework resonated across the NAEB. Lee De Forest reviewed the plan, and wrote to Hull that it seemed "most thoughtfully worked out, and forcefully presented."[183] Dallas Smythe reported to the NAEB Executive Committee in a confidential letter that by November 1949 the Allerton report was printed and received by over 1000 educational institutions, and was under review by "the top men" in university administrations.[184] Smythe's "Future Basis for Research" detailed next steps that NAEB administrators planned to take, including: study of training and qualifications necessary to be a program director, survey and comparison of programs, audience measurement policies, public relations, students' educational radio program experience, teaching techniques used successfully in the broadcast of classroom instruction for college credit, and of manuals, study guides, and aids."[185]

Schramm and Marshall corresponded in the buildup to the second conference. Schramm contended that the Allerton Seminars inspired educators to plan educational initiatives in a "cooperative, group, sharing situation."[186] The first conference asked "what is the job of educational broadcasters?" A second proposed conference would cover how to do the job. Schramm was especially concerned that without a second conference the NAEB would remain unsure what steps to take for how to make and present programs and share program resources "so that the strength of all educational broadcasting will be reflected in each educational broadcasting operation."[187] Schramm was convinced that an educational network would be inevitable, built around administrative, financial, and technical precedents set by previous Rockefeller Foundation initiatives. "The next logical step in building a strong noncommercial and educational broadcasting service would be a seminar on the planning and production of programs. All production would be local, and then strategies to gather resources and distribute was necessary."[188]

Marshall wrote to Schramm in a February 6, 1950 letter that the first seminar was "admirably conceived" but wondered if it would be wise to pursue the title "educational broadcasting," in favor of Lazarsfeld's proposed moniker of "serious broadcasting."[189] Educational broadcasting had taken on a negative connotation of amateurism, and a strong public relations campaign would need to distinguish noncommercial from commercial forms. A modest $7200 was requested for a second conference and was approved.

In the brief time between the two conferences, Schramm configured the University of Illinois curriculum to include divisions such as a school of journalism, broadcasting, library, facsimile, university press, an institute of communications research, continuation center, visual communications, and "all the other units on campus chiefly concerned with the use of mass communications."[190] Part of the program's anticipated growth included planned construction of a television station that would produce content under the supervision of communications research.[191] The invitation to join the seminar invited participants to ask not just "what" is educational broadcasting, but "how to do it" as well as an attempt to politically formulate "what our society needs from broadcasting" for advocacy purposes.[192] The conference centered on logistical underpinnings of local broadcasting efforts and how to expand its network.

After the conference participants circulated a co-written final document internally titled "Educational Broadcasting: Its Aims and Responsibilities," which argued that while educational broadcasters had to admit that they had not achieved their full potential, for the first time they possessed a resolute sense of how to move forward. Though radio stations were required by federal regulation to operate in the public interest, convenience, and necessity, the policy lacked a well-defined notion of public "necessity," a civic obligation only an educator could fulfill.

Educators planned to devise an approach to programming that informed, stimulated the individual to organize and give meaning to information, contributed to understanding that makes for better human relations and adjustment, and broadened participation in the culture of society.[193] Educational stations would act as an outlet for varied expressions of a community and provide a variety of experience that permits and encourages the development of tastes and interests. The document represented the first unified analysis of how conceptual goals would be translated into infrastructural development."[194] The success of educational broadcasters would be measured not by number of spectators or economic results, but by achievement in fulfilling educational objectives. Noncommercial broadcasters had to attend to financing, skills, techniques, knowledge of their audience,[195] and there were limitations to utilizing the medium, but the NAEB would not remain limited in pursuing their purposes and goals.[196] While some institutions maintained their own facilities and others bought time on commercial lines, educational institutions planned to meet professional standards of production, with the additional responsibility of translating educational philosophies into institutional practices.

> Whereas the commercial station in its daily program design must emphasize the common denominators of public taste, and reflect in many of its programs the widespread popular desire for relaxation and escape, the educational station operator can aim his programs at the wide variety of special needs and interests in his audience. He can program for unserved segments of the universal audience, for special areas or special needs. He can offer a service flexible enough to meet individual differences, and can reflect the total resources of education in terms that will appeal, at different times, to all segments of the audience.[197]

Standards of efficient production were already available with the application of audience and technical research to program development, especially in psychological and sociological effects of broadcasting on listeners.[198] For this reason, the report recommended the creation of communication research departments to support educational broadcasting. As such, the future of educational broadcasting should include the creation of academic programs for training for future production and measurement including programming, audience building, radio research, and radio in the curriculum.

The announcement signified one of the watershed moments of the discipline of communication studies. NAEB members marveled just how serendipitously previous institutional movements had synthesized into a coherent concept. Robert Hudson articulated this perspective in a widely read piece titled *Allerton House 1949, 1950* that followed the conference:

> "The Allerton seminar asserted that…educational broadcasting has been most clearly distinguished by its high concern for integrity in the selection and handling of materials, and by its consistent dedication to social purpose. This purposeful activity has taken several forms, among which are: (1) informing, (2) stimulating the individual to organize and give meaning to information, (3) contributing to the understandings that make for better human relations and adjustment, (4) broadening participation in the culture of our society, (5) acting as an outlet for the varied expressions of the community which the station serves, and acting as a force within the community to help it solve its problems, and (6) leading the way, by experiment, toward new forms and activities of broadcasting."[199]

Members decided to improve national distribution by founding a program transcription service. And stations were encouraged to expand community outreach and build audience loyalty. Educational broadcasting was free from having to observe "commercial schedule commitments, and ability to vary control factors." Because of this, there was no reason that the NAEB should hold back from attempting to build a fourth network. Programs could air and then be sent to other stations to address similar demographic and community needs."[200]

The corresponding document suggested that universities provide career development for personnel in audience building, research and teaching, as well as publicity. Resulting from these discussions, a twelve-point prescription was broached for future activities by educational broadcasters:

> "1) assess community needs and resources, 2) develop new program techniques, 3) build audiences, 4) develop appropriate areas of research and pilot plant experiments, 5) further the preparation of competent personnel, 6) make the possibilities of educational broadcasting known, 7) establish a central service for sharing programs by tape or transcription, 8) establish

one or more regional FM educational networks, 9) establish a national educational transcription service for planning, producing, and distributing programs to educational stations on a particular schedule, 10) establish a central and permanent administrative office to serve as a repository for educational station data, a central program for engineering advice, and editorial headquarters for an expanded and regular publication on educational broadcasting, 11) cooperate with the rest of the industry (as equals instead of antagonists), and finally, 12) consider whether the situation does not call for bold steps."[201]

Hudson wrote to NAEB members that the second seminar set in motion research on how to construct university subjects that would support an educational network, including training in critical analysis of recorded programs, "mechanical aspects," and the need for program exchange.[202] The NAEB solicited advice for how to organize such an initiative, contacting, for example, longtime educational supporter Judith Waller of NBC Chicago. Hull explained in a letter to her that the new function of the NAEB after Allerton was to foster and encourage universities, as "in a sense the trade organization for educational broadcasting."[203] Hull requested information about how Waller had attended to questions of copyright, program availabilities, station operation, and finance.

The Bicycle Network Public Media's Decentralized Economy of Scale at the NAEB, University of Illinois, and WYNC

In July 1950 FREC was defunded after commercial broadcasters rescinded their promise of grants.[204] The NCER and NACRE had long been dissolved, and the NAEB was the last remaining advocacy group with institutional memory of previous initiatives. But by 1950 the NAEB was setting its sights on becoming a "network," that might compete with but carry a very different mission statement than CBS or NBC. Hull described their plan as exploring the "basic advantages to be gained from working to get these various organizations together into somewhat more unified group."[205]

Originally titled the "round robin" network, the NAEB renamed the initiative the "bicycle network" to encapsulate the process of production, program pressing, and distribution, where transcriptions were literally "pedaled" from regional station to regional station.[206] In 1950 thirty stations joined. Illinois secured funds from George Stoddard for duplicating equipment, making Illinois the official headquarters for the NAEB. Richard Rider, who oversaw program distribution under Robert Hudson, wrote of the service: "in essence, what we are trying to do is provide educational stations, on a mutual basis, programs which they would be unable to acquire individually."[207] In another internal memo Rider described the Tape Network as the major service of the organization into the future. "The NAEB is a national organization of stations, and broadcasters interested primarily in the educational and social aspects of broadcasting…in effect the network acquires outstanding programs, duplicates them, and circulates them among the member stations."[208] Allen Miller, early pioneer of the University Broadcasting Council of Chicago, was not a supporter of a decentralized approach. "The bicycle experiment, which I believe in most instances has worked out well, is merely a temporary expedient."[209] Miller had invested a great amount of effort to organize a centralized equivalent to the commercial networks. His position led to intense debate among the executive committee. Among topics discussed, the committee was concerned that distributing records and tapes required an alternative economy of scale much larger than they had anticipated, including a need for prorated costs, membership fees for minimum services, standards for distribution time and program length, and a stable and permanently funded library of broadcasting.

But the distribution plan worked, and the NAEB stuck with the Tape Network for the next seventeen years, becoming the National Educational Radio Network (NERN), which survived even past the Public Broadcasting Act of 1967. The NAEB grew to be a major political force as an umbrella organization for administration, policy analysis, and content standards and distribution by consolidating the previous 15 years of initiatives into a unified institutional focus as a decentralized network." The effort in no small part succeeded due to the forward thinking planning of a December 1950 subcommittee founded by Seymour Siegel at WNYC, who was voted president of the NAEB in 1951.[210] The board included luminaries such as Gilbert Seldes, Charles Siepmann (now at NYU), University of Chicago alumni Robert Hutchins (soon to be of the Ford Foundation) and William Benton (now a senator from Connecticut and later with UNESCO).[211] At least initially, a steady stream of funds supported the network thanks to a popular journal on children's programming, endorsed by parent-teacher organizations and women's clubs.[212]

Perhaps more importantly, the FCC took note of the NAEB's progress thanks to persuasive advocacy for FM frequencies and a letter writing campaign by Richard Hull and Dallas Smythe. Paul Walker of the FCC wrote to Smythe in 1952 that his continuous reporting of standards-based research had endeared the organization to legislators. "Intensive research in a local area provides a good basis on which to make an objective evaluation on program service. A study of this kind enables us to see what stations are actually doing and gives us an overall picture of program service."[213] In consultation with Richard Hull, a student at UCLA wrote a sociological dissertation on "successful" tactics the NAEB had recently pursued.[214]

The Allerton House Seminars culminated the period of system building and advocacy that followed the Communications Act. Ultimately the seminar was successful in synthesizing four major intertwined rubrics of American cultural history—the media reform movement, public broadcasting, educational technology, and communications policy and research—into one institutional formation. The conference reflected the moment at which the media reform movement crystallized residual strategies as an institutional structure. The NAEB took its place at the center of a consortium of university and community stations.[215] Through the bicycle network, the NAEB replicated the content output of commercial networks, with new stations able to mine NAEB clearinghouse resources for programming to meet public interest requirements.

Conclusion

Why did advocates put so much work into developing noncommercial media industries when there was no specific economic benefit and considering the many difficult technical and regulatory hurdles that they faced?[216] It's a difficult question to answer, but one of the ways to look at the origins of public media is as an attempt to scaffold democratic goals as a technical infrastructure. In this way the bicycle network became a unique American project; one that indirectly set a legacy for future experiments in democratic technology. Noncommercial media industries experimented with standardized practices of technical, distribution, and genre, with fidelity to compulsory education principles for decades. Early models began local, but the aspiration to compete with the free market ideological and technical framework of the commercial networks, without advertising income, became an almost myopic endeavor for public education.

The noncommercial production infrastructure remained deeply indebted to experts from the commercial sector and the influence of Rockefeller Foundation grant funds. But at the same time, reform experiments provided a novel and resonating example of an alternative use for mass media. Educational media differentiated itself from commercial media in its insistence that media be rooted in a mission statement situated in public service. The material construction of educational radio networks evolved to be synonymous with principles of democratic access, and technical strategies to expose as many listeners as possible to learning content.

CHAPTER 4

Research and Development

The Emergence of Communication Studies: Reception Research as a Strategic Tool of Media Reform

In 1927 the Federal Radio Commission (FRC) set a precedent that media regulation would follow metric-based, technocratic evidence in determining frequency allocations, which created a path dependency that discourses around ownership "diversity" were subject to technocratic and standardized models of evaluation. Judge E. O. Sykes, who sat on the original FRC deliberations and was unable to pass a post-Communications Act amendment for educators to receive reserved channels, discovered that his colleagues at the Office of Education also sought evidentiary methods for classroom assessment. Reformers received the FCC's decision as a concession to free market principles that blocked implementation of an equitable playing field for noncommercial broadcasters in 1935. Yet administrative pressures set by the FCC and Office of Education exerted a positive influence upon subsequent educational advocacy. Sykes advised reformers that their future success would be contingent upon careful mastery of the institutional and logistical strategies of broadcasting, within the standards set by "public interest."

The term "standard" was widely interpreted across categories, including technology, grant applications, and even radio enunciation practices. Beginning in 1936 the Rockefeller Foundation funded "standards" based research projects in a range of areas from equipment testing to program distribution. The confluence of regulatory precedent, grant funds, and genuine confusion over how students received information via radio effectively consolidated a new epistemic regime in the nexus between education and mass media. By 1937 reformers and public agencies had come to an implicit agreement that identifying an adjudicative "middle ground" would benefit every interested stakeholder. Each sector explored how a taxonomic system might contribute needed clarity to help educators frame the effectiveness of their broadcasts to legislators. A belief emerged that if educators, regulators, and commercial broadcasters agreed upon a shared discourse of fair "assessment," that a clear path could be forged so that reformers might regain licenses.

John Marshall wrote that in making staff appointments, that he hoped to "secure the services of men of caliber equal to those working on Ralph Tyler's evaluation study."[1] Commercial broadcasters had already developed basic methods of audience outreach and assessment from which to begin, but their audience categories were limited and entirely focused on contributing to advertising demography. It was under these conditions that early communications researchers were assigned to investigate evidentiary methods in line with the public interest mandate. By 1937 regulatory, university, and reform sentiment had discursively aligned, in part based upon the impulse to set an equal playing field through the establishment of standardized practices. Communications research did not have an official academic home, so to understand the phenomenon of audience reception, Marshall-funded projects looked to available models such as listener surveys, classroom assessment methods, and social psychological measurement.

During the Federal Radio Education Committee (FREC) conferences the FCC and Office of Education organized sixteen research projects to better understand if and how curricular broadcasts were received by students. FREC tasked educational researchers to strengthen the regulatory standing of educational stations, improve the quality of broadcasts, and increase cooperation between sectors. Supported by John Marshall at the Rockefeller Foundation, every one of the sixteen projects green-lit by FREC's "Committee of Six" required evidence-based results for reporting purposes. In 1936 John Marshall received inquiries from two of the members of Committee of Six: W. W. Charters of Ohio State and Hadley Cantril of Princeton University. Charters worked with the General Education Board (GEB) on the Eight Year Study, and Cantril had just coauthored the first social psychological study of radio with Gordon Allport.[2] Harold McCarty, who sat on one of FREC's subcommittees on behalf of the National Association for Educational Broadcasters (NAEB) submitted a third proposal.[3] The Rockefeller Foundation funded all three projects. Harold McCarty and Wisconsin looked at the relationship between their broadcasts and state audiences, to streamline the craft of educational programs. W.W. Charters and Ohio State attempted to determine comprehensive psychological categories for types of listeners. But it was Committee of Six member Hadley Cantril's Princeton Radio Research Project that made the biggest and unexpected impact.[4] Due to his unusual access to commercial and educational broadcasting records through

FREC, the Princeton Radio Research Project (PRRP) was able to synthesize methodologies found in both academic and private sectors, in the process laying the groundwork for media effects research. The PRRP interrogated the relationship between demographic affiliation and content reception. The PRRP method was designed so that broadcasters could quickly aggregate and apply findings to change content, write educator reports, and support research and development divisions.

The PRRP's capacity to understand a diverse body of listeners opened a new methodological space that far exceeded the mandate of the project. The PRRP also curiously participated in two major cultural events—the *War of the Worlds* broadcast, and Adorno's relocation to America. Already accounted for by scholarship, Adorno was fired from the project for his refusal to abandon humanistic analysis.[5] He conflicted with his fellow researchers who resolutely stuck to FREC's instruction to streamline empirical methods. But it's important to revisit the context in which Adorno left the project. Adorno's engagement was framed under the context of which direction to take with national education and communication policy. FREC's PRRP not only met the mandate of identifying which subgroups understood radio content in what way by 1940—between 1937 and 1941, the team of Paul Lazarsfeld, Frank Stanton, Hadley Cantril, and Herta Herzog developed what became an internationally appropriated methodology to account for trends in psychological reception of content. As the infrastructure for noncommercial media took shape in the 1930s, one of the most unexpectedly successful reform strategies was the innovation of new approaches to studying classroom audiences.

Educational Broadcasting as a Standardized Practice with Measurable Results

Paul Lazarsfeld's early "administrative research" focused on providing tools for public policy work, understanding perception to social events and product assessment, and conducting policy analysis through the lens of group perception. Lazarsfeld's approach was in part informed by logical positivist philosophy, and in part designed to satisfy the grant expectations of specific government agencies to interpret the reception to information and messaging. In the 1930s some social scientists made it their goal to develop models of measurement to account for types of survey respondents.[6] Coming up with such a system held the practical application of fitting individuals into associated categories so that government agencies might consolidate formularized demographic profiles, to streamline administrative procedures.[7]

Upon the passing of the Communications Act reformers searched for a way to maintain their public service mission while identifying a way to appeal to government agencies. Because early broadcasting experiments were met with mixed results, in 1936 it was not self-evident that educational broadcasting would make the social contribution that its proponents aspired to provide.[8] The public interest mandate provided a context for how to move forward, with its attention to standardized criteria for judging the effectiveness of a broadcast. FREC discovered that no one had yet devised an accepted, unilateral technique to understand audiences. This presented a major opportunity for educators, not only to account for audience satisfaction with broadcasts, but to gauge what listeners learned from the content of broadcasts to report to the FREC consortium. There were indications that educational research might take a role in media reform in the early 1930s. The National Committee on Education by Radio (NCER) was keenly interested in how they might develop evidence-based language to substantiate state funding for educational networks after the Act.[9] Activist groups worked to accumulate evidence of the effectiveness of educational broadcasts to support broader moral and civic claims about noncommercial media.

In 1936 FREC approved sixteen projects, with Rockefeller funding totaling $168620. Researchers were asked to commit to comprehensive studies before "definite remedial steps could be taken or even suggested" in national policy.[10] The projects worked under two main headings: 1) the general question of how cooperation between educators and broadcasters could be furthered, and 2) the laying of the groundwork for future developments in educational broadcasting theory and practice. FREC initiatives were asked to work within the confines of new legislation, promote distance-learning initiatives, and help educators with their craft, even though most believed that they knew "little of the listener interests on which broadcasting has to build."[11]

The major educational precedent for audience research came from Payne Fund work at Ohio State, where W.W. Charters had pioneered evaluation techniques with colleague Ralph Tyler. Just previous to early communications research, distance-learning educators experimented with evaluation that they believed created a curricular "unifying function" between classrooms. Upon reception of Rockefeller funds for the Eight Year Study, Ralph Tyler and W.W. Charters analyzed evaluative techniques that could maintain curricular goals yet reflexively adjust to the needs of classrooms. They settled on standardized testing as the most promising equalizing mechanism to gauge classroom success. One consequent outcome of educational measurement's influence on communications research was that Ralph Tyler's work on "evaluation" led his brother Keith Tyler, who happened to be an educational technologist at Ohio

State, to set about developing the first evaluation model of radio classroom research through a Rockefeller Foundation grant.

Legitimating Educational Broadcasting with Empirical Evidence, Ohio State: Instruction by Radio and Early Communications Research

Ohio State's FREC project ambitiously sought to define the methods and procedures of audience research that combined educational broadcasts and facilitating classroom radio study.[12] By applying new evaluation techniques of classroom listeners to radio audiences, OSU believed that they could combine classroom management strategies with sound learning, to support "objectives of general education in a democracy."[13] The development of a method that would unite broadcaster, administrator, teacher, and pupil concerns into one measurable phenomenon was highly desired by classroom educators. If possible, Ohio State hoped that they might further persuade the FCC that educational broadcasters had assembled a coherent system to rival the networks that additionally served state education requirements.

Ohio State was one of the earliest educational media research institutions. Thanks to the work of B. F. Darrow and R. C. Higgy in the 1920s, by the early 1930s Ohio State had expanded its research docket to cover visual instruction and broadcasting. Visual instruction was handled by Payne Fund liaison Edgar Dale.[14] Ohio State's Keith Tyler was a 'true believer' in the promise of educational instruction as classroom extension. He was so invested in the classroom dimensions of radio that when public broadcasting finally gained federal support in the late 1960s, Tyler was reportedly disappointed by its journalistic, cultural, and less instructional tone. By the Public Broadcasting Act, Tyler had already put forty years of work into the creation of equal access to universal public education through technology, spearheading the major Midwest Airborne project in the early 1960s.[15] Tyler was invited to participate with FREC along with W. W. Charters in 1936, due to Charters' connection to the Eight Year Study.[16]

Ohio State was unique among educational stations in that they had already determined that educational broadcasting had been "hindered by lack of evidence" as to what may be expected to gain from pedagogical broadcasts.[17] "This lack of evidence has not only stood in the way of a widespread acceptance of the radio but it has also made the task of the educational broadcaster difficult if not impossible."[18] Programs were planned, Ohio State conceded, without adequate knowledge of the results, and a study would need to be constructed to "make a possible number of generalizations regarding results to be expected from certain types of school broadcast programs." Such a study would furnish guidance to teachers in selecting and utilizing broadcasts and inform the larger national movement in determining criteria for building new programs.

In 1937 Ohio State proposed to evaluate school programs to provide FREC with "abundant evidence as to the effectiveness of specific selected broadcasts."[19] They titled their project "Guiding Principles Related to Research and Service Activities." Charters and Tyler proposed that their study would produce useful "generalizations" about audiences, similar to standardized test reports, which could then be applied to local, national, and regional programs. They framed evidentiary practices as an opportunity to increase cooperation between broadcasters and teachers, which they detailed in five objectives:

1. "Acquisition of important information and concepts in various fields of human knowledge through objective tests, written examinations, and records of oral discussion.
2. Application of important facts and principles extrapolated from group discussions, interviews with pupils, parents, and follow-up examinations.
3. Development of interests through voluntary activities, records of free reading, choices of movies and culture, and recording of chosen leisure-time activities through diaries, interviews, and questionnaires.
4. Development of social sensitivities through analysis of group discussions, interviews, and tests on awareness of social problems.
5. Development of attitudes toward significant issues in modern life in terms of scales of belief measured by group discussions, interviews, questionnaires, and samples of writing."[20]

John Marshall asked Levering Tyson of the NACRE to review their application. While Tyson had some interpersonal disagreements with the Payne-funded NCER, he responded on behalf of the Committee of Six that the OSU project represented a contribution to radio research. Keith Tyler made a special personal trip to discuss the proposal with the Committee and made clear to the Committee of Six that he intended to apply Ralph Tyler's methods of classroom evaluation to radio classroom practice.[21] OSU's project was approved for a five-year period to evaluate listener response to "on the air" content through a cooperative of teachers, broadcasters, and staff, who were selected to sift through the difference between "potentiality" and "relative importance" of broadcasting data. Tyler persuaded FREC that

Ohio State's new "instruments and techniques in collecting evidence" would help to conceptualize the relationship between audience research methods and broadcast objectives, streamline inferences, and "formulate criteria and generalizations" regarding the effectiveness of educational broadcasting, methods of utilization, and place of broadcast.[22]

The project was planned in seven phases. The first phase consisted of gathering and clarifying educational objectives by listing, classifying, and revising objectives until unnecessary "duplications" were removed. The second phase tentatively selected broadcast content objectives that they believed would contribute to classroom learning. This process included committee discussions about the veracity of program information and how it met classroom objectives. The third phase collected, organized, and interpreted numerous examples of "pupil behavior" that the team felt best represented achievement of objectives, which they gauged through the administration of tests, instruments, measurements, anecdotal records, and examined pupil diaries. The fifth phase conducted comparative analysis of broadcast methods, which OSU logged as a clearinghouse to exchange among teachers. The sixth phase constructed instruments to help collect evidence of pupil achievement to validate committee adjudication of the utility of specific instruments. And the seventh phase refined instruments and techniques to continuously improve validity, reliability, objectivity, and practicability.[23]

As a preeminent educational broadcasting institution, Ohio State was the first university to consider how audience research might fit in to radio production, distribution, assessment, and adjustment practices. Ohio State promised the Committee of Six to produce "specific generalizations felt to be true and important," with the unique capacity for results to inform future production of programs.[24] Research was designed to evaluate: 1) attitudes and appreciations, 2) interests and self-motivation, 3) critical thinking and discrimination, 4) creative expression, 5) social behavior and personal social integration, 6) skills and techniques, and 7) informational background, for the purpose of synthesizing educational broadcast practice with audience techniques and curricular goals. Ohio State noted that previous studies on the effectiveness of radio programs had been based upon "information alone" and that it was probable that the "distinct contribution of radio programs is to fields other than information" would additionally help to supplement disciplinary work conducted on radio—from public policy research stated in their application, to mathematics education and language acquisition.[25]

Ohio State developed a "dictionary" of radio behavior to define types of listeners. To deal with the relatively limited scope of attributes considered during audience evaluation, they sought to define and list a comprehensive set of categories to describe every type of learner, curricular goal, and possible listener reaction. Charters and Tyler believed that their radio dictionary could provide an annotated list of suggestions for how to improve audience listenership. For example, if a goal of an English lecture was to "develop a purposeful interest in current social problems," their list of audience categories would prescribe a procedure that named modern novels dealing with those social problems.[26] The dictionary delimited the set of instructional possibilities an instructor might take, like a lesson plan, but additionally listed possible demographic reactions. By today's standard the dictionary only considered a limited diversity of students and pre-formularized curricular outcomes without consideration of positionality or learning style. If a goal for a lesson was to "enjoy all forms of literature, including radio programs," the report provided up to two-hundred possible outcomes of the project.[27] The dictionary then predicted "expected" curricular outcomes in line with specific student types. While previous to the study educational broadcasters produced broadcasts based upon assumptions of moral or cultural value, the Ohio State approach applied measurement to include additional variables contingent to the broadcast itself such as "developing interest," "shifting attitudes," "shifting interests," "effects between," and perhaps most influentially for later research, the "effectiveness in achieving educational objectives."[28] This last goal can to some extent be tied to Ralph Tyler's evaluation research.

By identifying "peculiar characteristics" of educational audiences, especially in rural areas, the project presumed to locate strategies to connect reception of a program with "integrated and closely knit school populations."[29] Methodologically Ohio State was the first to envision the relationship between standardized curriculum, audience preference, and reception during a listening context. In many ways their attempt reflected the immediacy of their goals—to streamline educational broadcasting methods. In spite of its many flaws, the study set a precedent to understand the relationship between demographic groups and anticipated behavior and response to programs.

University of Wisconsin, WHA, and Educational Broadcasting Method

There is so much to say about Wisconsin's place in noncommercial broadcasting history between 1917 and the Public Broadcasting Act of 1967 that Jack Mitchell's book on the station should be required reading for any media history course.[30] As Hugh Slotten has pointed out[31] Wisconsin was first to experiment with classroom extension courses, adult education, and aesthetic methods of civic broadcasting. And especially in the post-Act era, they stood out from other broadcasters for their financial stability, program continuity, and trained staff. Along with Ohio State, WHA was also one of the first state-based broadcasters to design courses with curricular measurement in mind. This led to a high level of interconnectivity between the station and state institutions.

WHA served an unusually wide and consistent audience compared to other NAEB stations. They operated at 5000 watts, reaching a roughly 100-mile radius, and their satellite station at Stevens Point broadcast to a similar range. The School of the Air, founded by Harold McCarty in 1931 already registered an impressive 43000 students by the time they applied for Rockefeller funds. Combined with a supportive Wisconsin Education Association that consisted of 20000 teacher members and an active Committee on School Broadcasting, WHA persuaded the Wisconsin legislature that radio education complemented state agriculture, conservation, and rural public school education initiatives.[32] If the station proved that radio curriculum was as effective as a textbook, the state was prepared to divert money into station programming.

After Rockefeller put out its call, WHA applied to explore needs of the state through "direct inquiry" in consultation with teachers.[33] The grant committee included McCarty, the Wisconsin State Superintendent, the Dean of UW-Madison's School of Education, and Wisconsin Educational Association members. More focused on classroom strategies than audience methods, McCarty's application promised "practical experimentation" with radio classrooms, which included persistent check-ins with teachers and students themselves regarding perceived effectiveness of programs, for the benefit of the station.[34] To tabulate results WHA developed "informal tests" to elicit "controlled experimentation," so that the station could report the effectiveness of a broadcast as "accurately as possible."[35] WHA's Rockefeller Foundation application was conceived not only to meet FREC's goals, but to model how a state-based station might work with educational institutions while meeting curricular goals. Compared to Ohio State, their approach to "data" was geared toward standardizing reporting more than innovation of listener categories. In spite of Charles Siepmann's take on the University of Wisconsin, John Marshall nominated McCarty as a Rockefeller BBC fellow based upon the application.

This experiential learning model required different funding distribution than the other Rockefeller Foundation experiments, for station infrastructure and personnel travel. They requested a grant to hire an educational director, a production director, and a script editor who would also travel to various schools to conduct the equivalent of focus groups about content with students. At the time of application WHA devoted roughly 40 percent of its airtime to music and 60 percent to news, farm reports, and classroom instruction, with subject matter heavy on homemaking, literature, agriculture, and politics. Wisconsin planned to address some of the problems being reported by NAEB participants, especially how to devise and test successful testing programs. In "Research Project in School Broadcasting" they envisioned the station as a laboratory for an experiment on the qualities of educational broadcasting, with audience research as secondary to meeting the needs of School of the Air listeners. Courses were written and prepared with signposts where edits might be made after student evaluation, which they then retested to determine a broadcast's "educational value," to share with other NAEB stations.[36] The application stated that it would also be the first to formulate objectives that would consequently be applied to actual production and be the first to publish reports on the relationship between educational philosophy, psychology, and radio teaching methods. Information derived from research would be applied to script production, vocabulary choice, and teacher training to increase standards of "presentation in general."

WHA discovered that talk, dialogue, roundtable, and dramatization all evoked different learning success rates, experienced varying listener recidivism, and measured different types of academic performance.[37] They examined aesthetic practices from rate of delivery to which subjects might be better by sound than textbook learning.[38] The project was conceived as a two-year study in which the first year would consist of evaluating their existing curriculum and devising new methods to measure "educational significance." In the second year WHA designed experimental courses to take "objective measurements" of audience response.[39]

After John Marshall requested defined roles for the research team, WHA devised a taxonomy that described "Workers and their Functions in Educational Broadcasting."[40] They designated a "Radio Education Specialist" to survey the field, formulate projects in terms of academic research, oversee procedural adaptations, observe schools, stimulate adaptation to evidence, and write a final project report. And WHA hired an early version of an educational script writer, who would study network scripts and then apply those techniques to "effective presentation of learnable content." The script writer was complemented by a "Production Man" who was tasked with experimenting with production and presentation techniques dependent on the grade level, training casts for dramatizations and roundtables, and devising a "standard of presentation" that made educational aesthetic content recognizable.[41] University researchers administered tests before filing with project secretaries. And, in what might have been the project's major innovation,

WHA combined the project with "graduate study in education toward a degree, institutionalizing educational broadcasting research and degree accumulation."[42]

Unlike the commercial broadcasting approach, WHA was resolute that their production purpose was "to develop proper attitudes" and provide skills to "develop the ability to interpret and evaluate facts regarding" intended curriculum. Broadcasts were planned from a choice of topics, and a designated editor oversaw script preparation. Once the concept, intended outcomes, and script were complete teacher aid materials were prepared for use with broadcasts, general directions for using broadcasts in the classroom, detailed suggestions for each topic such as follow-up activities, and a bibliography for further reading.

To understand audience reception to a broadcast, WHA provided students with pre-tests, which were then measured against final tests, given after last broadcasts. The tests were measured against what McCarty described as a "mimeographed bulletin" that described series objectives and listening topics. He applied what he called "control testing" by asking teachers to teach and test with and without the radio broadcast. After the radio broadcast version of the lesson, students were observed for changes knowledge, attitude, interest, and behavior modification. Teachers submitted observation records, a list of activities, books read, and observational records to consider as many variables as possible. Teachers were further assigned to prepare observations and test scores for research staff, who translated findings into statistical data regarding each classroom and school. Budget distribution was flexible to which programs seemed to need the most adjustment, improvement, and attention.

The WHA study was the first to demarcate the number of hours per week needed for educational radio instruction (transmitter, staff, talent), number and kinds of audience to be reached (publicity, census research, visiting delegates to cities), kinds of personnel involved (recruitment, training), and costs of radio instruction as a model for a national group. These factors, WHA realized, were also useful for expanding "station relations," which took time, effort, diplomacy, knowledge of a community, and rehearsal scheduling.[43] The procedure for experimental testing was based around one thirty-five-minute class period each week dedicated to a broadcast including preparation five minutes before, fifteen-minute broadcasts, and fifteen-minute follow-ups.

The project strongly interested the Wisconsin legislature, and a "Statement of Policy Relative to the Use of the Radio Broadcasting Channels Licensed to Agencies of the State" report was released that announced a State Radio Council. The council was formed on December 6, 1938, under Order 21 as a transfer and "vest" to the board of regents at the University of Wisconsin to control and operate the radio station.[44] Noting the station's "inspiring record of the constructive and beneficent possibilities of this new agency of mass communication," the board's mission statement identified the civic dimensions of broadcasting as a means to prevent misinformation or "rousing of passions of their fellows"—a clear reference to concerns over rising fascism.[45] A fear of "domination by a factional central government through controls of instruments of coercion, and the determination to safeguard local freedom of expression and a degree of local economy" placed radio as a significant tool for cultural gatekeeping.[46]

The State of Wisconsin released funding for WHA based upon the Rockefeller project, with the expectation that the station would act in accordance with "educational implications of school broadcasting."[47] The purpose, as stated, was to supplement and enrich classroom education instead of replacing it and be so designed that objectives be stated explicitly and devised by experts. The Wisconsin Research Project in School Broadcasting experiment set scaffolding for other NAEB stations to create early methods for educational broadcasting methods. But as the project progressed among state politicians, Marshall felt that their experimental data had yielded mixed results not persuasive enough to be statistically significant.[48] Attitude changes had been statistically positive, but most cases had unexpectedly favored control broadcasts or simple classroom teaching of the same material over radio broadcasts.

From the Federal Radio Education Committee's "Project 15" to the Princeton Radio Project: Collaboration between CBS, Social Psychologists, and the Office of Education

While Wisconsin and Ohio State developed projects to improve NAEB stations, the Committee of Six tested its own research plan. The principle researcher of FREC's "Project 15"—Hadley Cantril—was on the Committee's board, and his pitch framed the question of educational "information" as a "subject of general radio inquiry."[49] Cantril proposed to discover the effect of radio broadcasts upon the acquisition of information, and to what extent radio content influenced "attitudes and the modification of conduct of children and youth."[50] After several meetings FREC realized that a mass public study on the relationship between broadcasts and public opinion had never been employed. They decided that FREC provided an unusual opportunity to put different sectors into conversation, and combine relatively new methods of demographic research into a single project that would concentrate on the "basic psychological and social factors involved in radio broadcasting as they affected children and youth," with the goal of defining "specific and observable effects of radio to be properly interpreted."[51] In contrast to the commercial broadcaster model, the committee set out to understand the multiple situations that affected the ways in which radio was received, including social and economic status, learning, and general cultural background.[52]

The final formulation of the project proposed to expand demographic categories, which they believed would help to understand the experience of radio as an affective medium, as well as shed light on listening habits and preferences, attitudes, conduct, tastes and skills, fantasy and dream life, and auditory habits.[53] Project 15 was renamed the *Study of Radio Influence Upon Children and Adults*, and Cantril wrote that his team aimed to discover how radio affected patterns of information acquisition, attitude change, and the modification of conduct by defining a method that could answer "certain questions of basic interest to both educators and broadcasters" through "systematic investigation."[54] The PRRP's first team was approved on September 1, 1936, with Cantril, Edgar Dale of Ohio State and the Payne Fund, and well-known sociologist Robert Lynd, with Levering Tyson of the NACRE named as a project consultant.[55] Cantril completed the team with the recruitment of Frank Stanton of CBS,[56] a recent graduate of Ohio State, to oversee audience measurement, Paul Lazarsfeld, a researcher in the Newark City School System, and Herta Herzog.

The timing was opportune, as educators and commercial broadcasters had been simultaneously but separately exploring survey methods. The study aimed to be the first to establish valuable middle ground between advertisers and public education.[57] In May 1937 John Marshall brought the study's proposal before the Rockefeller Foundation's General Education Board, and changed the name to the Princeton Radio Research Project.[58] In his memos, Marshall noted that even though federal and commercial interests did not agree to contribute funds to research, Cantril's work was of high interest due to his stated goal of addressing fundamental cross-disciplinary questions such as radio's effectiveness in "cultural diffusion" and general listening publics. Cantril and his team framed the study in line with Syke's Pursuant, as "who listens, where listening took place, when listening took place, and what was listened to." If successful, the study would make headway in describing how listeners understood what they heard, and what if any effects radio had on memory and learning.[59] The PRRP's goal of defining the relationship between radio listenership and taste would benefit the broader reform project. "Though the Project is to be administered and carried through by the Princeton School of Public Affairs, it is an integral part of a plan of a larger program of research which will be sponsored by the Federal Radio Education Committee."[60] This met the criteria of FREC's project mandate, and the Committee was satisfied that Cantril would advance research about radio per se. If the project innovated techniques reproducible across control experiments, any broadcaster would be able to apply the method to evaluate a target listenership. The GEB committee unanimously approved the proposal and hoped that the study would be of additional use for training future investigators as to when and why a broadcast was effective.[61] Marshall received special approval to cultivate the PRRP project for an indeterminate amount of time, to satisfy the intriguing goal of defining triangulable audience data.

Hadley Cantril, A Forgotten Founder of Communication Research

Cantril's appointment was an auspicious decision. He had just coauthored The Psychology of Radio in 1935 with Gordon Allport. They argued that radio provided psychologists with a new opportunity to locate "wider intellectual, social, and political referents and ramifications" of social disputes that took place in the public arena. In the book, Cantril argued for a robust public radio system, "removed from the dictatorship of private profits."[62] As the project got underway Hadley Cantril's memos repeatedly stated fidelity to noncommercial media, and surprise at the lack of previous research. Why had universities not taken media more seriously as a research topic? How could social sciences have studied information without thinking about reception? Before the Communications Act, Cantril noted that the only support universities typically provided for educational broadcasters was a space to work. "Educators too often felt that the sole remedy for an improved use of radio was to give educators more time on air."[63] Universities assumed educational broadcasting's civic intent was sufficient for a program to have made a public contribution. Cantril understood that empirical proof would help to establish media research as a fundable discipline. Cantril agreed with Sykes that there was a lack of understanding about how to "properly use the time already allowed since they did not understand the art of showmanship,"[64] and it was past time for educators to conceptualize and define media as a phenomenon of study. The tendency for pre-Act educational broadcasters to refuse to engage with commercial broadcasters had left them in a position in which they were "unwilling to profit" from the experience of the networks. This meant that educational researchers missed out on learning research and development practices.

Cantril marveled that while commercial radio programs reached a mature stage of aesthetic practice by the 1930s, they had done so with skeletal research tools and had consequently not fully understood the effects of their programs upon different belief sets. Commercial sponsors were primarily concerned with sales, and beyond that limited purview they had little insight into how their work contributed to social scientific research into radio "as a social force."[65] Because networks had not asked contextual or cultural questions that produced data beyond basic demographics, commercial broadcasters did not carry knowledge regarding why programs were liked or disliked, or why audiences held certain opinions about a show's content,.[66]

The PRRP began with an unprecedented level of access to audience research records. Thanks to FREC Cantril was given access to industry reports from 1927 and 1934. The PRRP began by examining data from Crosley Survey and Clark Hooper that included 32000 personal interviews, in which researchers had divided listeners by income, size of city, and time zones.[67] But Crosley had not considered core questions such as age, sex, education, occupation, location, or cultural background, nor why listeners tuned into one broadcast over another. CBS turned over early Starch Surveys that looked at preliminary information on age and sex, but they only conducted 2500 inquiries.[68] In 1936 CBS research planned to investigate the difference between home and automobile listening, and how the spaces affected preference and capacity to understand a broadcast. But again, these divisions only worked in the context of expanding sales models.[69] Commercial broadcasters asked survey questions related to consumer habits. The same information, Cantril believed, could be applied to schools, listening groups, and public conveyances.

Lamenting that "all of the industry's activities" were governed by commercial considerations, Cantril wrote that the industry had only been concerned with the listener as a "prospective purchaser." The focus on audiences as consumers had artificially delimited knowledge of listener characteristics. His plan for his team to review audience demography developed by the networks, for the purpose "in principle" of improving "broadcasting as an instrument of public service," with the broader goal of improving the methods themselves.[70] The industry was already on the precipice of expanding questionnaires to include multiple variables, and new information collected by "broadcasting and advertising agencies" pointed to where progress might be made in developing an "experimental method involving segregated and controlled groups."[71]

Cantril set out to provide empirical evidence of radio's influence upon attitudes, conduct, taste, language, and listening habits[72] by defining who was listening and in what way. But the study also endeavored to ask questions about the relationship between context in which information was received, the perspectives of those who received information, and how the basic formal characteristics of programs (voice, volume, speed, sound effects, music) influenced student behavior. Identifying the correlation between listeners among groups, subgroups, and preferences, would reveal "ambitions, attitudes, repressions, capacities, temperament, responsibilities, and overcoming environmental handicaps/limitations for social participation."[73]

Educational broadcasting presented a uniquely effective opportunity because of its national attention, opportunity to fund researchers, and the consensus that "its present effectiveness" was not "nearly as great as it should be."[74] The study was designed to provide "both educators and professional broadcasters" with "assistance" from psychological research to answer basic questions about the medium. Cantril thought that clearer methods of classification would help define a psychological schema that would help practitioners prepare a "shorter and more manageable list of topics at the heart of" educational practice.[75] His schema included categories that included content preferences at different age levels, the number of ideas introduced per program, the spectrum between abstract and factual information, the relationship between fantasy and imagery in appreciation, as well as logistical questions such as sampling size and learning effects. Surveys and questionnaires were of service solving practical problems such as understanding the mental processes of children.[76] And he hoped that tracing adjustments within the "environment" of radio would reveal data that was measurably reproducible, similar to movements in social psychology.[77]

Cantril corresponded widely with John Marshall between 1936 and 1939, and their rapport reveals much about the relationship between FREC's regulatory goals and the emergence of what was to become a new academic field. If successful, they pondered in their letters, the project would delineate the relationship between "techniques and problems," approached from an "educational bias" formulated within "the framework of the FREC."[78]

Frank Stanton's Streamlining of Listener Research Techniques

Cantril received permission from CBS President William Paley to invite Frank Stanton to join the PRRP as Associate Director[79] after Cantril wrote that Stanton "knew practically all of the research men in the large companies and I believe Stanton is without doubt the best man in the field."[80] Stanton made an immediate impact helping Cantril outline a formal structure for survey interview questions reproducible across control experiments. Through close examination of the data submitted to the study by the Cooperative Analysis of Broadcasting, Stanton found that he could standardize demographic categories while at the same time continuously add subcategories, since it was found that interviewees consistently named unchronicled associations. He described this work as the study of "primary characteristics," which when combined with Cantril's research into comparative effects, helped to point to trends in informational preferences.[81]

The primary characteristics model divided audiences into six categories: potential audience, available audience, daily available audience, station audience, daily station audience, and program audience. Based upon these categories, Stanton posited that the size of the audience should be correlated to its composition in socioeconomic status, education, sex, age, and occupation, and then assessed according to the "distribution" of geographic place. Once these compositions were determined, the researcher extrapolated what the audience was doing, besides listening, while the receiver was on. A control group was then gauged for reported attentiveness, co-listening, and location in proximity of a house or public space, through mail, telephone, personal contact, questionnaires, automatic recording devices, and panel techniques.

Rarely discussed in media and advertising history, Stanton was also responsible for streamlining methods of audience data accumulation. Stanton came up with tactics to incentivize respondents to participate with "request mail," such as sending tickets for live broadcasts, information about artists or sponsors, descriptions of impending changes to program content, and samples of items related to broadcasts. He found that there were many advantages to mail-based survey research, including that it was inexpensive and better at eliciting direct response to a specific station or program by providing a longer period to respond. Stanton traced minutia such as the paper used in audience letters, quality of grammar, and signature type infer economic status, educational level, and sex, as well as predicted use of advertised products, regularity of listening, and opinions and reactions to broadcasts. A contemporary reader would note the obvious deficiencies to his model, such as lack of researcher control over the experiment, inability of illiterate audience members to participate, interpretive error, and (most significantly) interpreter bias. But Stanton founded many early methodological strategies for communications data accumulation within the first month of the project.

Stanton additionally consulted with George Gallup to streamline telephone interviews,[82] and together they classified two methods of phone research: incoming and outgoing calls. Incoming calls, or calls solicited over the radio or by mail that encouraged listeners to "call in," were collated under the same category as "mail response," to gauge relative size of the audience. Solicitation for listeners to call in after a program or newscast was inexpensive and so successful at garnering opinion that it's still utilized by talent shows. Outgoing calls reached an intended geographic region and could identify trends in response by asking standardized questions over a short conversation.[83] Stanton divided outgoing calls into four categories: coincidental surveys, recall surveys, immediate recall surveys, and a combination of these categories. Coincidental surveys, first developed by early program ratings analyst C. E. Hooper, asked recipients which station their radio was tuned to, what show they were listening to, and whether they could identify the sponsor. Recall surveys, developed by Hooper's rival, Cooperative Analysis of Broadcasting, asked recipients of phone surveys what they could remember about their past radio listening. Both were useful at establishing trends over the course of a day. Stanton settled on what became known as the "personal contact" approach, a hybrid of coincidental and recall techniques. Stanton believed that the intimacy and time provided by personal interviews further benefited the project by allowing respondents more time and help with remembering what they had heard, which he called "aided recall surveys."[84] Stanton reported that aided recall "eliminated memory loss to a large extent," and added to program interpretive models by eliciting audiences to reflect upon what they had heard.

Stanton discovered that audiences retained and understood more of a show's content than audiences themselves realized. Aided recall questioning helped audiences to remember details they hadn't realized that they had internalized, yet nonetheless had influenced the listener's affective relationship to a broadcast or purchasing habits. Because he was on loan from CBS, methods in data accumulation spread quickly—broadcast stations were applying phone and personal interviews across "diverse markets in just two years." After the PRRP he brought his discoveries to CBS and helped to streamline the "panel technique" of advertising research, for which he contributed several approaches, particularly "sales response" to how content overtly or implicitly promoted a product through pleas and polling of radio editors, theater attendances, studio audience observations, and restaurant patrons. His contributions were archived in a "Listener Research Techniques" report submitted to the Rockefeller Foundation in 1938.

Paul Lazarsfeld's "Informed Hunches" and the Discovery of Accelerated-Result "Administrative Research"

Paul Lazarsfeld's original job description was to investigate if newspaper ownership of radio stations helped or detracted from the public interest?[85] But unlike Stanton, and crucial for the history of communication research, Lazarsfeld was persuaded by Cantril's contention that the "technical aspect alone" would not be enough to achieve media reform goals articulated by FREC. Besides the potential expansion of audience research, Lazarsfeld was immanently interested in questions about how information carried "cultural effects," and is rightly regarded as having innovated a form of demography that avoided schematic categories.[86]

Stanton assigned Lazarsfeld to correlate listener categories to trends in control groups and "formulate factual data."[87] But Lazarsfeld was not satisfied that sorting methods would be enough to understand educational issues. "It would be futile to measure isolated radio programs for their effectiveness," he wrote, unless such information was combined with broadcasting as a whole to "form a chain of influences varying in their strength at different periods of an individual's life."[88] Impressed upon by the plight of educators, he became invested in the PRRP project to provide general information of a psychological character about audiences for reformers, so that educational broadcasting could achieve its ends "more effectively and economically."[89] Lazarsfeld's fidelity to the educational dimensions of the PRRP's mandate deeply influenced the methodological questions that he asked.

In 1936 the PRRP assigned Lazarsfeld to investigate which radio programs were most popular. Participants rated programs and then provided a date for when they listened.[90] The top 25 percent and bottom 25 percent of experimental groups were then asked to take the test a second time to confirm trends in answers. Early phases asked, "who listens and why," and at the end of the initial period of evaluation, over ninety studies had been undertaken, of which forty-five were administered to confirm consistency. Results were analyzed to understand how content was interpreted by each affiliated category. Lazarsfeld oversaw organizing "psychological" groupings, while Stanton streamlined the reliability of statistical analysis. Lazarsfeld impressed upon Cantril and Stanton that this work could indeed be translated back to the FREC mandate, and he soon rose within the project's ranks. Lazarsfeld was keenly able to identify trends in response stimuli and distinguished himself as a researcher able to extrapolate broader cultural significance from each study.

As David Morrison and Hynek Jerabek have noted their foundational research, Lazarsfeld previously studied statistical research methods at the University of Chicago and Vienna Circle.[91] According to Lazarsfeld, he was inspired that the PRRP aspired to an additional methodological dimension of "being directed by psychologists," which he felt made it the first positivist-influenced project with self-reflexive interpretation of evidence to extrapolate "general principles" from empirical data.[92] He had become interested in the strengths and deficiencies of positivism after a Vienna Circle experiment that found that respondents were able to correctly match photographs when hearing playback of voices, through what respondents described as their "intuition." There was nothing in positivism that could point to a direct correlate between matter-of-fact data and interpretive understanding. He hoped to reconcile how personal and cultural intuition might become a method by defining a conclusive "effect." The PRRP was tasked with understanding which groups understood broadcasting content in what way. But Lazarsfeld believed that sorting types of listeners and developing trend analysis was not enough to exhaust the phenomenon of understanding, and that a qualitative dimension was necessary.

Within the first year Lazarsfeld made gains in assessing the relationship between intention, personality, and reception, in line with the "value of the theory" of the project as a whole: toward civic usage of technology, and to find a way that data might be used to encourage democratic participation.[93] The empirical approach of the project was chosen in service of a particular aspiration—to understand educational listening pending new radio legislation. This allowed the project to identify a relationship between "features" and "influences brought to bear upon people" toward tendencies, needs, and desires elicited from different aesthetic decisions.[94] Lazarsfeld shaped his goal around Cantril's project-founding questions "who listens to what, why, and with what effect?"[95]

Like earlier effects research,[96] the PRRP inquired about how groups interpreted information. The project interpreted the public interest mandate to investigate "what was taught in the classroom" with "areas of neglect" in educational broadcasting,[97] but soon evolved into an investigation of how effects might be combined with "gestalt theory and experimental psychology," in which "variation of stimulus" were tabulated to reveal the effects of content. PRRP collected data on "all the indicative incidental situations in which radio had been admittedly effective in the lives of various people" and then "careful catalogued" variation in response across demographic groups.[98] Again calling upon Vienna Circle research as well as Rudolf Arnheim, Lazarsfeld developed a system of "hunches" to predicate how a demographic group might interpret broadcasting content based upon previous responses.

Between 1937 and 1939 the PRRP delineated four types of "effects," which they defined as: 1) effects upon listeners at the time that they listened in terms of preference or mood, i.e., impressions, 2) effects of a longer-lasting nature upon opinion, behavior, decisions, or actions, i.e., influences, 3) effects upon political attitudes and habits, i.e., changes, and 4) institutional effects upon a "web of social institutions or general mores going beyond effects upon individuals or specific groups of people subject directly to the radio."[99] These effects were identified in relation to program features, single or series studies, types of broadcasts, policies, and the "existence of radio."[100] Once the concept of the phenomenon of listening had been expanded, the PRRP called upon the broader RF consortium to evaluate their results.

English anthropologist Geoffrey Gorer was credited with helping to clarify several tenets of their work. Gorer contributed that radio listening could be thought about as the interplay of "social groups defined by the high number of their common characteristics," and "reactions, especially the common reactions, of individuals to known situations."[101] Effects research measured the direct correlation between what a program provided and different demographics, whereas audience research was a broader category that might consider "conditions of listening." Reception to adjustments in content connected to gratification, whereas patterns of what listeners derived from listening were measured across "stratification studies"[102] with applications beyond radio into cultural affiliations.

By 1939, the PRRP's new "effects" paradigm was already capable of informing public policy research, insofar as it could triangulate results across geographic regions based upon demographic affiliation. The PRRP provided a method to predicate possible responses based upon survey research into the relationship between social context and listening behavior. The PRRP team noted in their publication "Propositions Regarding the Problems and Findings of the Princeton Radio Research Project" that their first two years delineated a new field of radio research through the development of a method to understand educational audiences, which they concluded was a "fishing expedition." But the project's focus on the "principles of outstanding differences" regarding the importance of "tools of communication" in general pointed toward a new, and not yet defined, capacity to study media and public policy.[103] General effects of information, which they had defined as immediate, group, long-term, and tacit outcomes, turned out to not only be applicable to research and development, but useful for measuring general comprehension to the introduction of new information. The panel technique had accidentally revealed "solicitation, selection, and psychological inclination" as core methodological problems in civic life. Questionnaires showed that the influence of radio upon civil society was tied not just to a medium or program, but larger social influences and conditions in which listening was a part.

"Effects" research, according to Hadley Cantril, investigated the "three dimensional" problem of classification according to an area in which an effect was to be studied. According to Cantril this included geographical, class, and personal context, but also the physical conditions and interpersonal proximity in which radio communication took place. Any proposition of "effect" was tied to the material it conveyed on the listener and social institutions, as a combination of technical artifice, personal gratifications, and the differences between other media. Further, "effects" demonstrated the relation between "conditioning factors" of a program and the characteristics of the listener in a situational context.

The second two years of the project endeavored to account for how listener preferences were tied to and changed social conditions, which the team believed could be understood by how listeners described effects, changes to larger institutional patterns, and most abstractly, Lazarsfeld's hunch that attention to "background information" would predict how audiences would respond to content.[104] Between 1937 and 1939 they learned that a broadcast was not just a broadcast—it was a participatory phenomenon, which psychological research could mine for "intrinsic" perspectives about the present, conduct "directive" research that might prescribe future content adjustments, and benefit "inductive" work to inform speculative analysis.[105] "Therefore, there will always be a need for research which discloses the potentialities of radio, knowledge which then can be used for many purposes."[106]

In 1940 FREC was reassigned to the Office of Education, losing its multisector veneer, and PRRP's fidelity to the question of the improvement of educational broadcasting faded. Cantril reported that the question of educational broadcasting led to "the directors of the project repeatedly regretting the necessity for such a procedure."[107] The educational starting point served as inspiration for the "measurement and analysis of its effects" in different areas from program content, to "spheres of human activities," and combinations thereof.[108] But as a disciplinary foundation, Lazarsfeld wrote that their contribution better resided with "principles of outstanding differences" of the "auditory character" of radio to disseminate content. He imagined the concept of "effect" to be a way to analyze the "material it conveys on the listener and on social institutions."[109] An effect could be technical, such as a change in a dramatic play, or indicative of immediate and long-term audience reactions that might lead to lasting changes in habits and attitudes. A media effect indicated more than how a group understood what they heard; it revealed the conditioning factors of the program, listener, and situational in which content was heard. And problems in each area could be researched for "levels of effect" on radio's "own material," decisive features of programs, preferences of different groups, conditions that might imperil the success of broadcasts, effects upon habits and interests, and changes in institutions and other social patterns.[110] Progress in educational broadcasting, Lazarsfeld wrote, should analyze the "amount and kinds of listening with other activities such as reading, interest in art, and hobbies," not just radio instruction alone.

War of the Worlds and the First Cross-Geographic Triangulation of Demographic Response

At the very moment that the PRRP standardized methods for cross-geographic audience measurement, *War of the Worlds* aired. PRRP had completed close to fifty different demographic experiments, but in a closed, survey-research environment the timing of *War of the Worlds* could not have been better. WOTW impacted listeners well beyond a conventional broadcast and became somewhat of a public policy problem due to its framing as a national and military emergency. Over the previous two years, Stanton and Lazarsfeld continuously refined their approaches to sampling characteristics of listeners, the effect of advertisements upon psyche, and the stimulus of political campaigns upon the minds of voters in rural areas. They broke research into two categories, *service research* was created to understand general psychological response beyond enjoyment of programming, and *general research*, which looked to radio's role in the study of a newly nationalizing public. *War of the Worlds* well fit their investigation into the general research model.[111]

The day after the "War of the Worlds" broadcast, a request came from Frank Stanton's employer CBS for an opportunity to test their new "technique." Cantril wrote in one personal letter: "when the broadcast of October 30 occurred, with its responses in mass hysteria over a wide area, the Princeton researchers recognized that here was a perfect opportunity for their inquiry."[112] On the Wednesday following the broadcast two field workers began the first mass communications research canvass—in Orange, New Jersey. They visited the homes of thirty persons who were known to have listened to the broadcast, while other researchers began to tabulate statistics from other sites.

Interviewees reported that they had not been listening very closely, but disruptions to the familiarity of the broadcast in the form of news flashes made them so terrified that they forgot what they had heard just a few minutes before. The play purported to present an invasion by armed beings from Mars, but only four of thirty listeners had understood this storyline. Four thought the invasion was by animal monsters, another four thought it was a natural catastrophe, eight thought that it was an attack by the Germans, and one Jewish woman had interpreted the broadcast as an uprising against the Jews. The only overlapping perception was incitement to panic.[113]

When asked what made it so realistic, the overwhelming response was that the program's introduction of well-known government officials and prominent scientists was persuasive at influencing their response. And more so the technical features of the broadcast, its appearance as an interruption of a dance program, the shifting of the news flashes from place to place, the gasping voice of the announcer, his muffled scream when he was about to break down, all contributed powerfully to the illusion. One woman reported that she saw people literally running down the street screaming. Another reported that her town was immediately deserted. However, these instances were often exaggerated. As Jefferson Pooley and Michael Socolow have written,[114] Cantril found that there were only a small percentage (1–3%) of "panic" responses to the program, significantly lower than popular folklore has led us to believe.

However, the important outcome, as far as Cantril, Stanton, and Lazarsfeld were concerned, was that for the first time a statistically notable sampling of responses to an unplanned media event had been measured. The PRRP was able to paint a realistic and thorough picture of the types of responses that occurred, including sub-divided categories of which demographic groups responded in what way. This satisfied supervisors at FREC, and perhaps more importantly their research impressed the commercial networks.[115] Responses to the broadcast were quite varied. One letter, submitted to the FCC with consternation, spoke of just how upset children were to hear that New Jersey was being attacked signed by, "all of Toledo, Ohio."[116] Other letters were written with awe and deference that Orson Welles had revealed new creative opportunities to the emerging practice of radio flows.[117] The broadcast incited the first mass moment of self-reflexive listener engagement.[118] Everyone had an opinion about the broadcast, and these opinions could be correlated and broken down by demographic affiliations.

As Socolow and Pooley have written,[119] in the aftermath of the study, Cantril rushed to publish the book in his name alone, and neglected several recent methodological breakthroughs in the project, notably Herta Herzog's new attention to the "checking up" phenomenon, the precursor to social context in Lazarsfeld's media effects research. By 1940 the PRRP needed an additional perspective to engage with their study, as well as someone to articulate their increasingly complex findings in policy terms. They were able to triangulate their results across geography, but they still had not figured out how to translate their research into something that could explain to regulators what they had accomplished.

Critical Theory: The Failed Voice of Public Broadcasting Policy

Theodor Adorno came to the attention of Lazarsfeld through Max Horkheimer, the Institute for Social Research, and Lazarsfeld's commitment to engaging with intellectual movements in Germany and Austria. Horkheimer affiliated with Columbia University in 1934. As David Morrison and David Jenemann persuasively write,[120] Lazarsfeld already suspected a methodological continuity between emerging empirical research and critical research. A philosophical research dimension of the PRRP added credibility to an otherwise new method, and with many major Jewish intellectuals seeking to flee Germany at that moment, Lazarsfeld was in the unusual position of being able to offer Adorno with a visa. Once it became clear that Adorno might agree to join the project, they had to find him a title in accordance with his area of specialty. He was offered the position of "Music Director."[121] But the funding and mandate for the project was to understand, measure, and report on the effects of educational programming.

Theodor Adorno made for a potentially significant addition for several reasons: First Adorno might be able to address Lazarsfeld's concern that demographic research might overly demarcate findings, in the process divorcing results from a broader civic context. As Tobias and Levin and von der Linn[122] have noted, Adorno's official capacity was to contribute to the influence of music upon social psychology. But the second and implicit institutional reason for Adorno's entry into the PRRP was to help the Rockefeller-funded project to describe to the FCC how their empirical findings were similar effective to the standardized testing model of the Eight Year Study. Adorno's appointment was meant to fit into a broader federal mandate—to provide evidence for why universities and noncommercial broadcasters deserved radio frequencies, and to interpret and explain how evidence produced by the PRRP aided media reform advocacy to increase educational frequency allocations.[123] Adorno was there to write that the PRRP had produced empirical evidence that educational broadcasting was in fact educational, while helping Lazarsfeld think through how data might serve a broader public service impulse.

The broader methodological issue that Lazarsfeld hoped to work on with Adorno was his concern that the "problems of radio research could not be determined with any degree of accuracy if results were divorced from the special field in which radio broadcasting is going on."[124] The technical elements of programs, especially in the field of music, Lazarsfeld determined, could not be reduced to questions of preference. "Many isolated findings in the field of radio research get their full weight only when they are understood in the light of the total environment in which people live."[125] Cantril agreed, and followed Lazarsfeld's document with a report on the "Inadequacy of Information as Furnished by the Newspaper, the Radio, and the Movies" in which he argued that once responses were interpreted out of context of a directed question, basic "motives and mechanisms" could not be accounted for by quantification of group psychology.[126]

PRRP researchers had been concerned at the inception of the project whether "the techniques, developed and used in Project 15, differ from the research already accomplished by the industry?"[127] In a letter to the Committee of Six asking for funds to bring Adorno onto the project, Lazarsfeld argued that it was not enough to collect large amounts of data and "present them in a disconnected form," a theoretical framework had to be developed to guide empirical research and in interpretation of the findings. A project to derive general ideas about the possibilities and limitations of educational radio by the systematic study of "actual effects made currently with educational programs" required a researcher to "weave back and forth" between field work and conceptual generalizations. And the addition of a humanistic researcher would help to "develop techniques to test and, if possible, to prove the educability of the listener."[128] And it must be noted that Herta Herzog's insight that a listener's community influenced their willingness to receive information encouraged Lazarsfeld to pursue this line of research.

As PRRP research continued to reveal "unexpected facets" not initially anticipated by the project's mandate, Lazarsfeld sought a way to convey his findings "on the present radio audience" to educators and policymakers. Lazarsfeld wrote that if one stopped to consider the real meaning of a "media effect," one would find that it could be answered without "rather careful clarification of the various possible interpretations of the words 'effects' and 'radio.' *Effects upon what?*"[129] Lazarsfeld was concerned that this new turn in positivist research was "not sufficiently profound, and that empirical research was not sufficiently extensive, and thus, perhaps not adequate" to persuade policymakers that the correlation between data and effect was sufficient evidence of student comprehension. If the PRRP hoped to change "administrative policies" and encourage cooperation between civic agencies such as the FCC and Office of Education, technical language had to be clarified for government agencies.

FREC documents show that underlying Adorno's invitation was Lazarsfeld's realization that media content was far more influential on social deliberation than previously understood.[130] If survey research overly demarcated findings, he worried, the project would have the opposite effect as intended—regulators would get a strong sense of which groups responded in what way, but this information would become separated from the larger social context in which listening became relevant. Adorno's appointment was meant to complement the PRRP's broader federal mandate—to interpret and explain how evidence produced by the PRRP aided media reform advocacy to increase educational frequency allocations.

In a December 1939 letter to John Marshall, Lazarsfeld sent two of Adorno's articles, highlighting the "more particular music aspects of the programs" as well as the "interpretation of its social implications."[131] Lazarsfeld believed that Adorno's model of "social critique" would be of "great interest to radio educators,"[132] and provide a "good bridge between mere theory and empirical listener research." In the letter Lazarsfeld contended that Adorno's social critique would help to expound the context of broader conditions of listening and contribute to "program policy in the field of radio music." In one of the more striking lines of their engagement, Lazarsfeld described Adorno's philosophy as "parallel" analysis to administrative research, and Lazarsfeld planned to incorporate Adorno's policy framing of data into final results.

The PRRP team knew in advance that Adorno might not agree with their new methods, and Adorno immediately took a different tack upon joining the project. In specific his paper "On a Social Critique of Radio Music," which he presented during a project colloquium, took a particularly critical stand against the project. Any method that approached "the problem of radio by studying its effects upon the population while regarding the structure of the tool, the structure of society, and the function of the tool," without thinking about broader social ramifications of the specific study, would fail at a civic contribution. Adorno warned against the assumption that radio was something that "performs in it as something given," as a matter of fact, an ethical device that distributed and elicited reactions, and nothing more. This assumption, an "if—so relation: if we do this and this, we have to expect that and that result," could never do more than measure reactions and suggest "treatments" to elicit different reactions. Inevitably, the mere assessment of reactions would result in the development of fragmented data and procedures that produced effects desired by the experiment. At some point, any desired reaction, regardless of the consequences, could be designed by treating audiences as extensions of measurement tools.

Administrative research was fundamentally faulty, according to Adorno, because the subjection of "some groups" to different treatments to measure reactions selected and recommended procedures that produced effects desired by the experiment. Results appeared as "something given" but only pertained to the interrelationship between aim, technique, and particular question asked. Such an approach might improve broadcasting content through incremental steps but could also fall into the hands of modifying behavior "according to the aims of the central agency."[133] The result of the project was just as likely to be implemented to "mold according to the idea of a skilled manipulation of the masses" than improve civic participation.

Much of the essay anticipated his scholarship on Walter Damrosch and famous "Culture Industries" chapter and reflected WOTW findings that audiences were overly deferential to mediated presentations of authority.[134] But often not cited in this foundational piece are Adorno's analyses of the application of empirical research to educational broadcasting practice, which occupy nearly half of the twenty-page document. After examining fan mail received by land-grant Midwestern educational broadcasters, Adorno was "struck" by the apparent enthusiasm of listeners, especially the vast belief in the "highly progressive social function that this program was fulfilling."[135] Reaction to radio was less a response to a social institution than reinforcing appreciation of an ephemeral experience. Echoing Siepmann, Adorno believed that programs were amateurish. For Siepmann the answer was to produce better content, but for Adorno, audience complacency with mediocre content reflected a broader dialectical problem, in which listeners received content with "standardized enthusiasm," and exhibited "refuge" in the announcer's speeches "on behalf" of dominant culture.[136] The listener had the choice to enjoy or not enjoy a program but was not offered an opportunity to consider the ramifications of the content.

Adorno wrote that if Lazarsfeld's "administrative research" was serious about "the question of control and safeguard against biased imagination,"[137] the PRRP would have to devise a system to resist the ideological reproduction of inequities reinforced by representational strategies. How could problems like "pseudo individualization of standardized products" be of use to social ameliorative projects, when embodiment became instrumentalized as a trace within a numeric category? For Adorno, development of policy language in support of the project would have to wait until its researchers confronted the "inadequacy" of typology in accounting for larger social structures. Little discussed in the history of communication research, Adorno's criticisms paralleled the concerns that led to his invitation. One could read his paper as a validation for why PRRP invited him to join the project. All three researchers were worried about what happened to data when presented out of context. Solving or at least addressing the issue was one of Adorno's assignments.

However, the response to Adorno's interpretation of the PRRP initiative was famously hostile. Adorno was brought to the project to translate PRRP findings into applied language, to convince FCC regulators that educational broadcasting had sufficient methods to meet stipulations of the Pursuant of the Communications Act. Members had deliberately homed a methodology for trial-and-error analysis of audiences that could be applied to educational broadcasting production—and in the process they had innovated new and accurate techniques for encapsulating and framing opinion.

Geoffrey Gorer wrote to Marshall that the content of Adorno's paper was the "reaction of an extremely sensitive person to the sound of transmitted music." He was intrigued by Adorno's conclusion, but could "see no evidence to presume" that Adorno's statements were applicable to understanding listeners, calling Adorno's paper an "unproven hypothesis."[138] Gorer worried that for an audience unfamiliar with the German philosophical canon, that the Critical Theory model seemed to be a hypothesis that needed correlation to actual "stimulus and responses."[139] Marshall wrote that he was intrigued by Adorno's approach, but that the real issue was "the utility of the study, and that utility must be measured by the effect which can be anticipated for it in remedying the present deficiencies of broadcasting music." Marshall was inclined to kick Adorno off the project unless his work could be translated into a statement of how to adjust the framing of findings, which would necessarily have to include a "positive statement" of what Adorno believed could be done for music through broadcasting. Adorno was "being paid by the PRRP to produce results which are presumably of value within themselves." It's not clear how Adorno responded to Marshall's request, but shortly after Marshall concluded that Adorno's work would benefit from "a period of rest and consolidation."[140] In June 1941 Marshall "tried to explain as tactfully as possible to Adorno the administrative reasons which prevented a consideration" of further grant money. Marshall consulted with Charles Siepmann about his decision. Siepmann was similarly taken by Adorno's thought but could not figure out how to apply his conclusions. "He is, I fear, essentially an intellectual and not like Lazarsfeld either capable of or concerned to communicate at a popular level of interpretation."[141]

Yet, as Adorno's relationship with other members of the research group deteriorated, there's evidence that Lazarsfeld listened to Adorno's concerns.

While in conversation with Adorno, Lazarsfeld increased his focus to the "situation where public opinion is being formed."[142] Lazarsfeld noted how programs produced short durations of effects on social issues because they simultaneously presented information authoritatively and with neutrality. From those conditions Lazarsfeld concluded that listeners selected elements of communications that confirmed previously held viewpoints. While it was safe to assume that some changes in public opinion would always come about, it was paramount to consider "who the people are who provide for social change the entrance wedge into existing social groups."[143] This signaled a resounding support for the original intent of the FREC project, while expanding empirical purview with at least some heed to a critical social model. Calling his new model a "social philosophy of radio," Lazarsfeld wrote to Marshall in 1940 that until Adorno joined the PRRP the investigators had neglected "a discussion of the more general social effects of radio and its position in the total context of our culture."[144]

A report written under Lazarsfeld's direction in 1940 contended that it was unlikely that listeners would be able to use results of their research directly, but "certain civic and administrative groups" might find several important uses for research data, in specific the FCC, FREC, the Federal Trade Commission, and the Office of Education.[145] Research on educational broadcasting could be classified into two groups: 1) the preference of listeners and potential listeners, and 2) the effects or influences of radio on listeners. There were multiple ways to gauge such preferences including quantitative, relative, general, production, analytical, influence, stimulation, and the shifting of opinions and thinking. Broadcasters could use the PRRP's development of data on relative preferences to "estimate the desirability of changing educational programs to more nearly resemble preferred types"; such data would provide plenty of hints for improvement of existing educational series.[146]

Of greater concern to Lazarsfeld was the question of the influence of educational broadcasts on the "thinking" of those who listen, which he argued was the most important of all educational aims. First-rate educational programs had significant effects on those who listened closely, and listener research would be useful for broadcast production. But research was "urgently needed" to determine what types of opinions were most easily changed. Most research had been dedicated to dramatized programs, and the persuasive nature of forms of delivery needed much closer exploration. Notably missing from the letter was any recommendation for amending educational content to meet regulatory preferences. The study of the effects of media upon public opinion had taken over the original initiative, amplified by concerns about an impending war in Europe, and so, by the early 1940s, it was the relationship between media and public policy in general[147] that began to occupy PRRP researchers.

Charles Siepmann's Influence upon the Institutional Synthesis of Political Economic and Social Science Methods at the Princeton Radio Research Project

Nonetheless, the PRRP had dramatically helped the cause of the media reform movement by showing that educational radio research was not only not a niche area, but in conversation with and generative of broader socio-political discourses. The PRRP team successfully innovated a method for trial-and-error analysis of audiences—and achieved the remarkable goal of making their method reproducible in different control experiments, eliciting similar demographic responses across geographic space. Adorno was brought to the project to consider the context of their findings and help Lazarsfeld posit a broader social purview for the technique, both to the specific question of music education, and in language that would help reformers convince FCC regulators that educational broadcasting was able to meet Syke's Pursuant. Though Adorno left the project, the Rockefeller Foundation, OOE, and FCC still hoped to add a policy expert to the mix.

In contrast to Adorno, Siepmann conducted a series of well-received analyses of educational stations for John Marshall. And he worked well with the research staff, co-writing several seminal ledgers passed among Rockefeller Foundation insiders such as "Research in Mass Communication" with Gorer, Lasswell, Lazarsfeld, Lynd, Marshall, Waples, Bryson, and Slesinger. Compared to Adorno's resistance to the reproductive dimensions of administrative research, Siepmann's contribution to the "Mass Communication" document included strategies for utilizing PRRP research for tangible civic purposes.[148] Though he was quite progressive in his political views, Siepmann was already on board with the tenor of FREC's empirical, evidentiary requirements. According to Robert Lynd, government procedure rested upon knowledge of how to best secure consent, and since policies were assigned in interpretation of public predisposition and of public need, effective models of communicating information about phenomena scientifically were necessary.[149] Wishing to "give what follows a frame of reference not vaguely theoretical," Siepmann argued with his coauthors that public policy had left too much private control over channels of communication. Communication research at its inception began as a model to seek "flexible balance" between spheres of private and public enterprise.[150] They believed that the PRRP had influenced the researchers to discover ways of "securing public policy" for future public policies. Many of the methods that the PRRP explored were originally developed for "private" purposes such as market research, and then transferred to support "public" policies. But the techniques proved to be reliable and had matured to the point where the complexity of method could be gauged to the length of observation through time. The study of mass communication was not only of interest to educational broadcasters, but governmental agencies and industrial and civic groups.[151]

Siepmann further wrote a persuasive set of recommendations to Marshall regarding the future of educational broadcasting administration. Siepmann encouraged Marshall to explore "the pathology of influence" and disclose methods by which needs failed to be met. As a longtime practitioner, Siepmann understood that adjusting radio content required a decisively empirical language with intended cause and effect. Broadcasting content and public policy were fundamentally practical endeavors, and radio's influence upon opinion could be tied directly to adjustments in the aesthetics of content.[152] His goal to improve the appeal of public service programming, and his willingness to apply empirical data became the chosen method of political advocacy on behalf of educational broadcasting and made him a strong replacement for Adorno among the FREC consortium. He was subsequently hired by the FCC to write the "Blue Book."[153]

The Legacy of the Princeton Radio Research Project in the University of Illinois Institute of Communications Research: Media Effects, Political Economy, and Educational Broadcasting Production

A final 1941 PRRP report on educational broadcasting suggested that if educators were to apply FREC research that they would have to organize efficiently to: 1) identify when a problem had occurred at some point in broadcasting conceptualization, production, or reception, and 2) prove with verifiable data that educational broadcasting was in fact educational. The report argued that educators should focus on audience categories, applied to "relative" content and production. By "relative" they referred to situational and contextual application of the research paradigm. Educational broadcasters should examine the "analytical" attributes of audiences in reception of information, as it related to influence, preference, and the changing of opinions, attitudes, and "thinking."[154]

PRRP's synthesis of educational broadcasting practice, philanthropic work, listener research, and policy study, influenced the Institute for Communications Research (ICR) at the University of Illinois. Early communication researchers were focused on the civic paradigm of creating communication content, and with testing the ramifications of the program upon the public. Due to the applied, cross-sector nature that early communications researchers faced, the discipline was uniquely founded as a composite of multiple methodologies, with a close correlation between the questions that were asked about tangible practices and the contours of the methodologies developed to answer those questions.[155] In this way media effects did not carry a direct lineage to humanistic discourses of the Enlightenment. The goal of communication research was to provide clarification regarding perception about a situation, in line with an administrative question posed by an agency or institution.

When Wilbur Schramm was appointed to organize the ICR, he explicitly and repeatedly pointed to the Princeton project and its participants as a founding model for communication research.[156] He appointed its legacy representatives from political economic, media effects, and educational broadcasting sectors. And the ICR was formed to streamline civic approaches to the production of communication, and evaluation of communication methodologies. By the time the ICR was formed, John Marshall's legacy loomed large. Faculty member Robert Hudson worked on the Rocky Mountain Radio Council,[157] Dallas Smythe had worked with the FCC and Charles Siepmann conducting sociological testing on broadcasting institutions,[158] and Schramm himself worked with the OWI during World War II with Rockefeller Foundation consultant Harold Lasswell.[159] Letters reveal close contact between Schramm and many of the PRRP figures, and the ICR archive still includes the original recommendation from Lazarsfeld to appoint Dallas Smythe to conduct sociological research on behalf of educational broadcasting. Crucially, the department was formed as the result of educational broadcasting reform work, and its members were closely tied to NAEB research.[160]

In his 1947 planning document, Schramm wrote that the objectives of the ICR were to contribute knowledge of the communication process, the controls on communication in modern society, the media, their contents, and their audiences, and the social effects of communications.[161] He believed that communication could help "realize the good of men in democratic society," by providing research for customers, penetrating different groups, and contributing to the exchange of opinions between individuals in the creation of social consensus. Core to the founding of the program, Schramm envisioned communication as a discipline still focused on the success of educational radio, which he described as "the most effective media of communication ever devised until television, and the most effective teaching tool ever put into the hands of man." However, beyond producing educational content, communication research held a responsibility to develop methodologies to understand human motives and drives, including attitude formation, the making of information, and political checks.[162]

The founding documents of the ICR points to Lazarsfeld's Office of Radio Research as "first unit organized for research in communications as a social instrument." Parallel to FREC, Illinois endeavored to synthesize different areas of research and practice into one academic discipline.[163] In a conversation with Lazarsfeld in 1948, Schramm delineated how ICR would pull from its influences. Schramm had read the Payne Fund studies, early leadership studies conducted by Gallup polls, and the work of John Marshall in bringing together the PRRP, particularly the work of Rockefeller fellows Lyman Bryson, Douglas Waples, Harold Lasswell, I. A. Richard, and Charles Siepmann. Lazarsfeld jokingly called the PRRP the "Moses of the situation." In 1948 Schramm worked with NAEB pioneers Josef Wright and Frank Schooley to increase the hours of the Illinois station. With Wright, Schramm formed a radio advisory committee that would permit the Institute to work with the school of journalism to develop an "intelligent use of radio," with the station as the testing ground.[164]

Schramm set about organizing two PRRP influenced projects between 1947 and 1952. First, he edited the first anthology of mass communications research in 1949,[165] consolidating the early canon of the discipline. In "Information Theory and Mass Communications"[166] Schramm built on early mass communication work to define a theory of the "information chain," which he characterized as the "passing of communication through one or more states, in which one or more events can occur." Pulling from information technology practice, Schramm applied metaphors such as "input and output" to two categories of information reception systems. He defined the first, structural systems, states independent of past operation. The second, functional systems, depended on past operations capable of learning and discriminating. He argued that communication networks were source data of interpersonal activity and institutional communication units, contributing a sense of correlation between source and destination frequencies. The consequence of the early period of intellectual foment with FREC could be seen in the unusual synthesis of ICR curriculum and the NAEB. Programs were connected to and provided a reason for universities to fund educational stations.

Conclusion

In a 1937 document titled "Amplified Description of Above Project," Cantril wrote that coordinating an inventory of available resources toward the creation of a national network of educational broadcasting research required adequate broadcasting facilities and satisfactory assurance of stable time allotments so that educational series could be monitored. A radio series funded by the FREC's "Project II" could be produced by "capable script writers" to design and prepare broadcasts, with talent perhaps from the networks.[167] Such an endeavor should be widespread and rely upon advance agreement by school superintendents, teachers and classrooms, and weekly attention by students to an entire run of a series, supplemented by a set of instructions and protocols followed by classrooms. This would assure sufficient listening pupils to make "demonstration effective and convincing," and control groups could pursue the same course of study as experimental groups for effective follow-up work by researchers. Cooperating agencies based in state, city, or university stations would broadcast twelve weekly thirty-minute broadcasts on seventh grade geography. The production of one program distributed over many stations kept production costs lower, and such a series would begin with a reliably empirical subject with assuredly repeatable and testable data. Cantril's conviction was that a thorough analysis of techniques and later applications to broad population groups would "be of incalculable value to the educational and commercial broadcasters, and the general welfare of radio in this country."[168] This value was best implemented through continuing interplay between broadcasts, research, audiences, and production. But, of course, the PRRP moved on from educational radio research to make a much bigger contribution to social psychology, advertising research, and mass communications and sociological methodologies.

Media reform strategy played an unexpectedly central role in the constitution of media research and development practices. The concept of equal access to education through technology not only engendered new approaches to technical standards and content production discussed in previous chapters, but an intellectual regime that framed and measured institutional interpretation of policy. Communication research in part emerged to solve a specific, government-mandated problem: how to understand if educational broadcasts were effective at reaching every demographic of student listener?

The project was convened due to the Sykes Pursuant, and was closely monitored by the FCC and OOE, to gauge if educational and commercial radio researchers could collaboratively find a way to meet stipulations of the Communications Act.

The scholars assembled for the project signified a remarkable serendipity of diverging yet complementary talents. Cantril realized that the PRRP could synthesize the methodologies of two emerging disciplines. Stanton arrived already set to streamline extant forms of audience measurement. Lazarsfeld understood the correlation between movements in empirical philosophy and audience measurement. And Herzog contributed a persuasive understanding of the context in which information was received. The innovations of early media effects research were immediately apparent, and PRRP researchers realized that their work applied beyond the question asked of the project.

Revisiting the original dynamic between Adorno and Lazarsfeld reveals that its founders had worried that empirical research would lose sight of its original socio-ethical thrust – defined against the backdrop of equal access to education through technology—illustrated for example in one of Lazarsfeld's letters in which he argued that researchers should ask purposive questions about the "effects upon what?" when quantifying data. The invitation of Adorno was significant for communication research precisely because he was rejected. He resisted standardized models of audience analysis that resembled the technocratic mandates of the FRC as applied to facilities and testing. The consequence was that the Adorno's ejection from the project consolidated communication research's status as an empirically oriented methodology that gauged public response to agency decisions, which tied "administrative research" even closer to grant writing, advertising, metrics, and public relations discourses.

The investments of the PRRP culminated into the first communication program, which consciously grouped together previous decades of research. The PRRP represented a key symbiosis between communication studies and public media history. Early communications research was the most successful advocacy strategy of media reform, and the communication discipline remained dedicated to the materialization of a "4th Network" until the Public Broadcasting Act of 1967 was passed.

CHAPTER 5

Policy

Public Media Policy, 1934–1967:
Lessons from Reform History

The Public Broadcasting Act as a Pastiche
of Communication and Education Policies

By 1952, media reformers had consolidated public broadcasting's early institutional structure: as a decentralized production culture; funded by philanthropic and university underwriters; based in communication departments; where research, development, and audience testing could be conducted; so that quality civic and cultural programming reached students and adult learners. Public media in the United States emerged as the product of a complex set of influences, in which reformers, advocates, practitioners, and regulators pursued strategies to realize an abstract aspiration—equal access to education through technology—as a material practice. That fundamental aspiration often got lost within the logistics of organizing. At the same time the impulse served as a guiding principle that kept the reform movement together. Because reform activities were so connected to the educational sector, the history of noncommercial media regulation closely dialogued with educational regulation.

While the principles of educational access held different sectors together, it was ultimately the technical language that media advocates learned over two decades that won protected frequencies for educational television. The most persuasive argument made by educators, policymakers, and associated government agencies rested not in the significance of content produced by universities, but if educational broadcasting airwaves were reaching every educational audience. Put differently, funding for what became public media was hedged upon the technocratic language of evaluation, facilities, and maintenance stipulated by the public interest mandate. After the Sixth Report and Order of 1952, advocates framed lack of "universal service" to noncommercial media as a violation of the public interest stipulation that facilities be made available for educational audiences. This strategy inevitably compelled communications regulators to allocate funds for educational broadcasting.[1] Many of the concerns and struggles around allocations in 1927, 1928, and 1934 were directly associated with scarcity of available channels. This scarcity problem repeated itself in 1952 with television channels.[2] But after the first protected FM channels were awarded in 1939 and 1945, educational media experienced less and less resistance from policymakers. Once more channels were made available, more educational stations made it onto the airwaves, and less pressure was placed on commercial stations to produce sustaining programs. Reform strategies changed when more frequencies were made available, and educational advocates carved out an infrastructure piece by piece, bill by bill. Before the 1945 FM allocations, the major issue faced by the NAEB was over how to locate channels. After 1945, the question became how to produce and distribute quality broadcasts.

Before and After Frequency Scarcity in the 1930s and 1940s: NAEB Advocacy Strategies from AM to FM

As Victor Pickard has written,[3] the FCC was significantly more progressive under the Roosevelt administration than in the early 1930s and can be argued as having played a supportive role in passing progressive communications legislation. In a letter to Frank Schooley in March of 1946, Franklin Dunham, formerly of NBC, now Chief of Radio at the Office of Education, notified the NAEB that the FCC asked "all noncommercial educational FM broadcast licensees, permittees, applications, and others to submit comments and suggestions in writing to the office of the secretary with 60 days."[4] Progressive FCC Commissioner Clifford Durr[5] announced that if applications were on time that educators could apply for new frequencies. In March 1945 Durr and his staff issued a report titled the "Promulgation of the Rules and Regulations for Non-Commercial Education FM Broadcast Service," that permitted new applications by educators.[6]

In the Durr-conceived document, educators were required to prove that their services were being employed in schools as "illustrative of effective teaching procedures or instructional devices."[7] Proof had to be demonstrable through evidence of testing, administrative reports, and reliable program content. If a station acquired a new frequency, it was responsible to provide samples of student achievement by radio that exhibited sound administration, coordination, and evaluation of projects by committees at universities or community organizations in an assumed service area. Further, educational stations were required to employ functional "PR" departments to explain the work and purpose of schools to the public and provide instruction to accredited institutions. Adult education was defined as providing listeners with useful information of social questions, including news, updates, and weather.

In a pursuant version of the document, titled "Definition II," the FCC stipulated that educational FM stations may now hold licenses as nonprofit, accredited, legal entities. Stations applying for noncommercial frequencies had to have obtained "official recognition or certification" as a "program of public education" that broadcast nonpolitical, nonsectarian education that fulfilled minimum requirements of public educational standards by state and federal governments.[8]

On June 27, 1945, twenty protected FM channels were released primarily to NAEB members in the FM range of 88.1 to 91.9.[9] FM frequencies were slated to expand over the next three years but were probationary, contingent on quality of operation and service, maintenance of channel, power and service area, and meeting guidelines for "standards of good engineering practice."[10] Should stations not meet public interest criteria, the experimental frequencies would be subject to "forfeiture of construction permits."[11] The report further mandated rigid expectations regarding frequency controls, transmitter maintenance, technical operation, station inspection, modulation, operator logs, program logs, voltage, station identification, and other categories. To manage license applications, Allen Miller from the University Broadcasting Council was retained. Miller spent a short time at the Rocky Mountain Radio Council in 1946 after Robert Hudson left to work in the educational broadcasting division at CBS.[12] NAEB President Richard Hull broke membership into regional divisions to monitor rules and regulations. By 1947, the NAEB consolidated its services into three major categories to maintain such oversight: 1) "Getting on the Air," or helping new stations with comparative data on all types of broadcast equipment and spelling out necessary steps for administration including the utilization of transcription services, 2) "Staying on the Air," or maintaining daily programming that met the criteria for effective broadcasts, and 3) "Fight for a Continuing Place for Education on the Air," which included the slow progress toward setting up a Washington office.[13]

In 1947 the FCC was split into three divisions: 1) broadcast, 2) common carrier, and 3) safety and special services. The National Association of Broadcasters lobbied to keep Durr out of the Broadcast Division.[14] The networks were no fan of Durr, and a March 12, 1947 issue of *Variety* reported that Durr was viewed by commercial interests as "corroding the foundations" of "truly free and unmonopolized radio," since he had "struck out sharply against" sale practices for commercial facilities that had been built on public property.[15] While Durr had been a supporter of educational broadcasting, NAEB-affiliated educators still had not developed an official polity approach to support him, though before Durr's tenure concluded[16] the NAEB sent representatives to Washington to lobby for his reappointment. When Durr was replaced, commercial lobbyists painted new educational FM reservations as violating the public interest mandate of the Communications Act, not to mention free speech and rules about editorialization in radio. In a letter to Maurice Novik, labor rights activist and NYC director of educational broadcasting, Richard Hull worried in February 1948 that the FCC's flash of educational sympathy might be overturned, with the "FCC giving every evidence of not knowing what the score is at all. Words like incompetent, confused, etc." were used in a recent conversation with another Washington based affiliate.[17] A new set of hearings was called in late February 1948 regarding "editorialization by broadcast licensees." A public notice was posted on February 6, 1948, that all "special temporary authorizations," or STA's, might be retracted because they were having a detrimental effect on "regular nighttime broadcast service in many areas."[18] Since educators implicitly took "editorial positions" they might not qualify for special frequency assignments, signaling a possible revisitation of the "propaganda station" category of the 1928 General Order 40.

The NAEB did not come to an immediate consensus for how to defend educational broadcasting, and with some chagrin they recused themselves from participation in an upcoming FCC conference on editorialization for fear of an offhand statement being used against them. But the NAEB supplied the following statement to T. J. Slowie, FCC Secretary:

"Speaking for the National Association of Educational Broadcasters, and for those everywhere whose concern is for free men in a free world, for free exchange of information, and for dissemination of truth and understanding, we do wish to underscore and reiterate our concern that while in theory—and perhaps in fact—the broadcaster should have equal rights with the press to free speech that with his power goes responsibility. That the structure of radio is such that a very few thousands of men necessarily exercise great power on the minds and the emotions of millions of citizens. Radio, using its major tool the human voice, nearly always conveys to its listeners a sense of authenticity which may or may not be justified in fact. That radio stations are licensed in the public interest, convenience, and necessity, and by the laws of the United States, the facilities they use are the properties of the citizens of the country. Each licensee holds a temporary franchise on a portion of the public domain—that portion of the radio spectrum which he uses. That true freedom of speech is a vital American heritage which must above all be preserved in these days of fear and suspicion, and prejudice."[19]

In contrast to 1934, the NAEB positioned themselves as technical carriers of the public interest in ways that commercial networks had failed. Rules and regulations were meant to be applied for common welfare, the primary mission of the NAEB, but only a tertiary goal of commercial networks. The commercial lobby, the letter stated, had previously argued on their own behalf that they had the right to editorialize with some context. Yet they had now contended that the FCC threatened their licenses by permitting noncommercial stations the right for editorialization. Much to the pleasant surprise of the NAEB, the document was persuasive, and the hearing was closed.

In March 1948, the NAEB concluded that if the FCC was forced to suspend the new experimental assignments, a new tactic would be necessary—lobbying the senators commissioned with oversight of the FCC. In March 1948 Richard Hull contacted ranking Senators Charles Tobey and Edwin Johnson of the Interstate and Foreign Commerce Committee regarding support for educational broadcasting. In his letter to Tobey, Hull described the NAEB as having rebounded from 1935 to 70 members over 25 states operating 22 AM and 30 FM stations, of which four operated at a 24-hour schedule. Stations were described as equipped to serve specialized local and regional audiences with farm and market reports, music, classroom lectures, and matters of public interest.[20]

Hull wrote that if educational stations lost their frequencies, listeners would lose access to content "located in their immediate vicinity for news, markets, weather, and other items of information. A clear channel station located hundreds of miles away cannot serve this function." Much to their surprise, Chair Edwin Johnson agreed. Not only did he agree, but he introduced a bill (S-2231) to limit clear channel proposals and increase educational localism.[21] It turned out that when Johnson was governor of Colorado the Rocky Mountain Radio Council had persuaded him that an educational network was a constructive service for regional education, and he sought a way to revisit set-aside channels.

His response heartened educational advocates, who held a conference on March 15, 1948, regarding the next strategies that educators might pursue for set-aside frequencies. At the conference members affirmed their dedication to six initiatives that had been progressing for some time: 1) definition of educational radio goals and objectives, 2) better planning and organization toward these ends, 3) working systems for mutual aid, now also to include legal aid, 4) "recognition among ourselves of our very real strength," 5) ways and means to let administrators, the radio industry, and the public know what educational broadcasting offers, and 6) better understanding by station operators for how to appeal to radio audiences. Educators aimed to establish production centers, research agencies, and continued political advocacy, avoiding the urge to be perceived as merely "critics" of regulation.[22] It was time, they determined, to leave the conference with a "clear understanding that the tide has turned," and that educational radio was no longer the "step child of American broadcasting."[23] Colleges, universities, and allied institutions had, through new interconnectivity, begun to "compare favorably with many corporations," Hull believed, and more importantly, educational stations had become new "fountainheads" of radio research.[24]

Charles Siepmann predicted that such an opportunity was set to materialize: radio's "second chance" had arrived with allocation of experimental frequencies, and he believed that it was crucial to protect and build upon this political precedent.[25] The consequent document from the conference, titled "The State of Non-Commercial Broadcasting in the U.S." noted that after years of development and research, there were still only thirty-six US stations licensed specifically for educational purposes, with only ten operating on an equal facility and administrative footing as commercial stations.[26] Educational stations suffered from lack of financial support and public interest. Members neither had the money to stand up to commercial interests in court over facility disputes, nor did more than a few states argue on behalf of noncommercial extension services. But the FCC had set a positive path dependency with the reservations on the new FM band.

The present system, the report stated, was based upon the 1927 Radio Act and continued to "knit [sic] any plan for changing," implicitly disregarding any progress made since 1927 in technological or organizational progress by noncommercial stations.[27] Further, radio technology now permitted split frequencies so that different parts of the same city might receive different signals. A university could presumably broadcast directly to its intended students, neighborhoods, and schools without interrupting other signals.

> "Since metropolitan areas form the basis for allocations on a national scale...the FCC decreed that 40 kc was sufficient, and last year successful tests were conducted between a station in Silver Spring temporarily operating on 1420 kc and WDC Washington on 1450 kc providing that a 30kc split between regional and local station in the same area was feasible. Nothing is said about a complete revision of the allocation structure from one end of the band to the other, allowing a 40kc separation between high powered operations and a 30kc split between regional and local outlets."[28]

It was possible that two stations could occupy the same frequency to broadcast to different audiences in different areas of the same region. The upper end of the AM band was expanded from 1510kHz to 1600kHz in 1940 (the band area originally offered to the Association of College and University Broadcasting Stations before the Communications Act). Since this expansion had taken place, it seemed expedient to inquire about a further wave of expansions from 1610 to 1800. "In effect it could be considered as asking for three times as much as one would expect to get, realizing at the same time thru effective public relations planning that the best defense is offence."[29]

The NAEB believed that it was possible that Edwin Johnson would seriously consider their plan. A proposal argued for "Class III" channels to be shared with commercial interests, and "Class IV" channels for educational use only. By requesting frequency set-asides on the already congested AM band, channels could be assigned for educational purposes, since more coveted FM channels might end up in the hands of commercial stations.[30] A subcommittee was formed to present information about progress of schools and "exchange ideas" with regulatory interests.

Due to foundational audience research and grant writing standards set in the 1930s advocates learned to hedge advocacy not in moral language but the technocratic logic of facilities maintenance. Once precedent for educational access by technology was written into law, facilities became synonymous with student rights under compulsory education laws. Successful media advocacy work between 1952 and 1967 subsequently centered on technical access language to obtain funding and increase channel representation. An additional precedent had been set in 1941 when school districts were unable to provide facilities for primary and secondary education. The Lanham Act set aside wartime funds for construction, maintenance, and operations[31] as contributions to national defense. The Act provided funds for construction, maintenance, and operation, through applications to the federal works agency. Once the precedent was set that a compulsory educational access[32] through technical facilities must be supported by federal aid, the two major informational agencies, the Office of Education and FCC repeatedly appealed to these two laws to make subsequent reform suggestions.[33]

Evidentiary Advocacy Practices and Dallas Smythe's work Building Public Support for Public Media through Educational Policy

By the time educators met at the Allerton House seminars in 1949 and 1950 (discussed in chapter 3), reformers were familiar with the language, practice, and framing of empirical evidence in support of noncommercial media. As the last educational media group standing the NAEB took on multiple roles defined by previous associations: clearinghouse work that John Studebaker had pioneered in the 1930s, facilities consultation suggested by the Communications Act, and the lobby strategies of both the NACRE and NCER.

In October 1949 the NAEB decided to dedicate its full energy to obtaining TV channels. The NAEB lobbied the FCC for additional review time for each application, noting that there were differences in treatment between commercial and educational stations. These letters were noticed by commission member Frieda Hennock, a New York attorney and Democrat. New Chairman Wayne Coy supported the idea of educational television channels and promised to consider the matter at the opening of September 1948 hearings.[34]

Represented by their Washington lawyer Marcus Cohn, the NAEB filed notice with the Association of Land Grant Colleges and Universities (now headed by NAEB member Griffith from Iowa State) for the reservation of channels for noncommercial educational television broadcasts.[35] The Office of Education further spoke on the NAEB's behalf. "A common point of view will be expressed by all the individuals and groups representing education. It is the insistence upon reservations for the future of educational TV channels. The particular means for accomplishing this goal vary somewhat from group to group, but a specific plan is, after all, the final responsibility of the commission."[36] While the NAEB lobbied the FCC, they pressed the agency's overseeing institution through Senator Edwin Johnson. In Johnson's eyes the networks had made a tactical blunder. Commercial broadcasters claimed that reserved frequencies for governmental and educational content infringed upon free speech, but Johnson viewed this as a highly disingenuous position, especially with the connotation that university broadcasts might be synonymous to totalitarian media.

In a 1947 hearing Johnson replied with indignity to commercial broadcasters, cited in a speech by Dallas Smythe in 1950:

"We have heard a great deal about freedom of speech. But the freedom of speech that you are talking about is your right to sell in the market place such speech; and that is exactly what you do when you sell advertising. It is not freedom of speech. There is no freedom about it. It is money on the barrelhead. You sell it, just like you do onions down in the grocery store. You sell it to the advertiser and you collect for it."[37]

Johnson corresponded with several educational broadcasters—Richard Hull, Dallas Smythe, and Keith Tyler. A September 1949 letter from Hull to Johnson reported a phone conversation in which they spoke about NAEB as "the only minority radio voice, and the only radio voice devoted exclusively to educational purposes left in the United States."[38] Another exchange with Keith Tyler at Ohio State in April 1950 discussed an NAEB invitation for Johnson to keynote the second Allerton conference. Johnson replied: "I know of the fine work that is done by your institute and I particularly congratulate you on the general subject of this year's conference. It is my opinion that such a question should be frequently reexamined and reappraised in order that the policies being followed in American radio are kept abreast of today's and tomorrow's needs."[39]

Between 1949 and 1951 several of the NAEB's strategies were inspired by Senator Johnson himself. In one letter to Edwin Johnson, Dallas Smythe appealed that educational broadcasting was not only a benefit to US broadcasting culture, but in line with Johnson's own regulatory philosophy. Broadcasting, Smythe argued, was a uniquely American problem because it balanced the interests of the public with standards upheld by private interests. The FCC, Smythe argued, understood the limits of past legislation and attempted to reserve frequency assignments for broadcasters concerned with community amelioration. But university and educational stations still lacked the central focus of commercial broadcasters to build and maintain frequencies for profit purposes. Universities had to go through several stages of administrative approval before an application would even be possible.

Citing an article by Benjamin Row in the journal *Social Studies* from March 1950, Smythe wrote that in 1949 "it became clear that video was a baby industry, determined to fulfill its destiny as a colossus. It is worth noting that the ingenuity devoted to television may well reap promising rewards for the educator."[40] Educators believed that if they were given a brief amount of time to experiment that educational television would provide immediate benefits for classroom instruction as a visual aid. Smythe appealed to Johnson that a lack of noncommercial options would preclude the development of public interest in education. "At this point let me anticipate a question which inevitably arises: if the public gets the radio programs that market researchers determine to be the public favorites, who are you to tell the public what it should have? Is this a democracy or isn't it?"[41] The early and basic precedent for public interest meant that open frequencies were used correctly. "Public interest," Smythe argued, was originally introduced as an anti-monopoly policy. But due to commercial broadcasting's head start in infrastructural development, public interest ironically came to mean public utilities run by a monopoly of private interests.

Smythe appealed to Johnson that Pursuant (307) recommended progress in the production and reliability of educational programs. The "Blue Book" (of which Smythe was a contributor) pointed to the possible disappearance of such programs without an infrastructure to produce such programming, and the NAEB was the one institution able to develop a stable production culture for community, public service, and educational content.[42] Johnson agreed, though he also stood by Syke's concerns in the Pursuant that educators be able to use assignments constructively before channels were provided, with proof of the educational effectiveness of broadcasts. Several considerations informed by Pursuant (307) comprised final deliberations: 1) should nonprofit educational stations be subject to the same regulatory procedures as commercial stations? 2) were educators going to make sufficient use of frequency assignments if special reservations were offered?, and 3) did "equal access" to broadcasting indicate civic imperatives that commercial broadcasting could and would not provide?

Additional time was provided for the NAEB in October 1948, when the FCC decided that television frequency assignments were much too complex to determine in line with previous regulation and halted the process of granting new television licenses. Originally planned to last only six months, "the freeze" continued until 1952 as the FCC deliberated upon a variety of factors ranging from color television, to VHF and UHF assignments and military utilization of frequencies.[43] The networks' lobbying for clear channel stations waned, and FCC Commissioner Wayne Coy sent special representative Benjamin Cottone, General Counsel for the FCC, to the NAEB's October 1948 annual conference to discuss how the organization might proceed while the FCC considered possible steps.

Cottone pointed out to educators that it was not just the networks that had contested set-aside frequencies but taxicabs, power companies, newspapers, police departments, railroads, and utilities; "even grave diggers" had expressed interest in utilizing FM. Since the FCC could not fully satisfy the demand of all groups, they had been left at a loss for how to proceed, and had in fact favored educators over others, considering the breadth of lobby.[44] Most of the other interests were "articulate, resourceful, and well organized" and had made compelling appeals on their behalf. The FCC still agreed with Sykes, that "radio's channels were too valuable to be left in idleness…if educators fail to utilize them, they will have lost their second and perhaps last chance to own and operate radio stations."[45] But the FCC valued educational broadcasting above other considerations should educators be able to utilize frequencies effectively.

One offer the FCC was prepared to make was for educational stations to take ultra-low power frequencies of 10 watts or less. It would be just enough to cover territory near campuses but would not interfere with commercial networks. This proposal apparently had gained the support of the networks because universities could consequently also be used to develop training centers for commercial broadcasting personnel, and there were possibilities for underwriting of transmitter care, and facilities on behalf of this proposal.[46] Cottone contended that FM would remain a difficult domain for assignments due to frequency scarcity, but that educators should pay close attention to impending television regulation and mount a campaign for set-aside frequencies in that new medium. Cottone encouraged Hull and the NAEB to further increase "Congressional avenues" to pursue protected frequencies. The NAEB filed for ten Experimental Television Allocations on August 22, 1949.

The Committee for Interstate and Foreign Commerce Sides with Educators: Protected Frequency Allocations for NAEB-Affiliated Educational TV Stations and the Sixth Report and Order of 1952

Between 1934 and 1945 the FCC supported educational progress in obtaining frequencies, thanks to an incremental cocktail of technical, lobby, and relationship-building strategies. The NAEB persistently notified the FCC and the Committee for Interstate and Foreign Commerce of their policy positions. Most interested parties agreed that education still could not compete with the networks when it came to speed, efficiency, and economic support. But thanks to the previous decade educators had gotten better at translating their civic ideals into political and technical practices. Internal debates at the FCC wavered back and forth between the typical (and accurate) assessment of educational broadcasting—there were few professional quality stations, it was not clear that educational broadcasting was effective, and professional quality facilities were rare. However, in 1951 discussions about how to interpret the Communications Act had shifted from frequency scarcity to the purpose of postwar broadcasting legislation.

FCC Commissioner Frieda Hennock dominated these discussions. As Susan Brinson has discussed,[47] Hennock was such a strong proponent that she took to publicly arguing for the original Wagner-Hatfield proposal for 25 percent reserved frequencies for television. "Television is the teacher's medium, but to fully harness TV's power educators must have their own independent television stations. Education is too intricate and delicate a process to be handled by any but the most qualified experts in the field—the educators themselves."[48] In March 1951, the FCC conducted a survey called "Other Governmental Sources of Radio Information" to see just how many other federal institutions believed in reserved educational frequencies. They found predictable support at the Office of Education. But to their surprise, the Federal Security Agency decided that school stations should be used for Cold War propaganda,[49] and issued reports on equipment, courses, script catalogs, and radio recordings between 1947 and 1951. The Department of Labor issued reports on employment security, women in radio, education, and unemployment. The Department of Agriculture released a series of mimeographed reports on the use of radio and films for its work. And a poll found that the Department of State was in favor of reserved frequencies for broadcasts of international educational broadcasting initiatives for UNESCO.[50]

Meanwhile educators further consolidated their advocacy into a lobby group called the Joint Committee for Educational Television (JCET). JCET was initiated March 1951. In one of their first releases, JCET offered testimony that argued that noncommercial television offered the best potential for adult populations to take correspondence courses—a major legacy argument of educational media. Much in line with the FCC's internal discussions, the JCET expressed concern that educational reservations should "proceed much more slowly in applying for broadcast stations… If there is no reservation the available channels will all be assigned to commercial interests long before educational stations are ready to apply for them."[51] A congressional hearing was scheduled for March 21, 1951. Thanks to educational broadcasting's new institutional stability, coupled with recent regulation and an education-friendly FCC, momentum shifted to apply the logic of FM reservations to television frequencies.

At the hearings Wayne Coy expressed concern that educational institutions might not be willing to take on the hefty costs and labor needed to use television as an educational tool. Further, Coy was concerned that if final reservations were made as an amendment to the Communications Act that commercial stations would abdicate any public service responsibilities they had held to that point. "I am of the opinion that if the proposed reservation is made final it is important for the commission to emphasize that the reservation of channels for educational stations in no way relieves the licenses of commercial television stations of any responsibility to render a well-rounded program service, including a reasonable proportion of time devoted to programs that meet the educational needs of the community."[52] As was true with radio, commercial stations were capable of producing high quality educational broadcasts at a faster pace than universities, and Coy believed that reservations would reduce commercial investment in educational television.

However, Frieda Hennock made a persuasive plea on behalf of the concept of educational broadcasting. The proposal under debate had not yet guaranteed reserved frequencies, and a failure to provide a "sufficient share" would adversely affect the course of future education.

"Television the most dynamic and effective means of mass communication that modern science has devised, enables the educator to reach into millions of American schools and homes. By now everyone has come to recognize the revolutionary changes that visual instruction has brought about in teaching methods. Television is uniquely qualified to utilize and spread the benefits of this modern and efficient method of education at a minimum cost. As the educators' tool, television can bring about as great an expansion and revitalization of education as the development of printing in the early days of the renaissance...In the hands of the educator, television can become an unparalleled instrument for developing and spreading knowledge and enlightenment—the foundations of a strong and free America."[53]

Hennock argued that the FCC already recognized the "principle" of reserving channels for educational television when conducting internal discussions, and that a reproduction of the errors of the Communications Act would provide for inadequate treatment of educators. "We ought not, while conceding the principle of educational television, kill it in practice."[54] Hennock contended that affirming the principle of public service without buttressing technology could not produce practical results. Adequate means had to be supplied to properly effectuate adoption of public service principles in media ownership. Hennock recommended extending the reservation of channels so that the mandate of "public interest" also applied to noncommercial access. If there was to be a nationwide noncommercial system—a minimum requirement for "adequate use" of television by educators—a provision to safeguard growth needed to be in place. "Education must not be given the giblets of the television turkey."[55] Without set-aside frequencies in 1934, even FREC was largely unable to achieve its stated objectives for aiding experimentation. FREC had been reliant upon grant money from John Marshall. Both had ceased to fund the Committee, and the result was that no federal institution was left to oversee or support educational technology.

The very next day, March 22, 1951, the FCC released a public notice inviting testimony in front of Congress. The FCC planned to issue "some 209 assignments...in many places for noncommercial education use, exclusively," or roughly 10 percent of new television channels under consideration. So as not to interfere with basic public interest requirements for well-run all-day access, a community with fewer than three impending assignments would receive no educational reservations unless there was a "primary educational center" such as a university. In forty-six such cases as university towns the only allocations made were to the universities based upon the testimony of the JCET. The FCC recommended cooperative arrangements in those cases, to be hashed out among educational institutions, and for educational broadcasters to provide at least one television service to all parts of the United States, including one service to each community. Final deliberations for unassigned frequencies were dependent on size of population, geography, and number of TV services available.[56] The *New York Times* reported the end of the freeze on March 23, 1951, with 2000 new stations to 1400 communities.[57] Educational stations would be framed as extensions of "federal" stations, making them subject to different taxes, laws, and considerations than private commercial stations.[58]

To explain the logic of decisions regarding new frequency assignments, Connecticut Senator William Benton, who had overseen the early UBC experiment at the University of Chicago in 1936, joined Edwin Johnson in an interview with *Variety*. The FCC's proposal was beneficial to commercial broadcasters, they argued, because a split between public service and public interest stations would promote the "enduring principles of democracy and free enterprise." A set-aside spectrum for governmental and noncommercial stations limited encroachment of the government upon private activities and encouraged expansion and prosperity of private interests. "Instead of forcing public service broadcasts upon commercial enterprises, which would force them to receive oversight from the government, the commission had revised program structure of licenses in order to determine whether the licensee has rendered a rounded service in the public interest."[59] Part of the offer was that television could introduce its own "code" to avoid governmental regulation, a previously separate debate about government oversight that had now overlapped on the educational question.[60]

William Benton introduced the first version of the bill that became the Sixth Report and Order on May 21, 1951. Benton's resolution (S RES 127) was signed by Ernest McFarland of Arizona and Edwin Johnson. But part of his proposal included a provision for a "subscription method" of educational broadcasting, which would (conveniently) be run by Encyclopedia

Britannica, the company in which he was the Publisher. To maintain federal oversight of educational progress Benton also proposed that a "Blue Book" be published yearly.[61]

Edwin Johnson faced unexpected pressure from his home state of Colorado over educational frequencies. Denver was only designated one channel, and if that single channel were to become educational his city would not receive any network programming. Despite some waffling, Johnson ultimately settled on becoming a great champion of educational television: "I am not opposed to the use of television frequencies for educational purposes per se merely because I proposed the designation of channel 6 as a commercial station. The past few years have strongly demonstrated the superiority of television as a form of communications and its effectiveness in conveying the most elusive of all commodities—thought."[62] As governor of Colorado he was familiar with the difficulty of producing educational broadcasts and did not want access to education through technology to be stifled by one or two private interests. "Television is far too valuable as a national resource and much too intricate and delicate a process to be allowed to waste away through idleness, lack of funds, and experience."[63] Johnson briefly speculated that perhaps the new channel might be subject to a frequency sharing provision.[64] But he was swayed by another internal FCC report in June 1951 titled "Educational Television Survey Report," which found that of the 258 colleges, 123 superintendents, and 46 states surveyed, 74 percent were in support of noncommercial licensing.[65]

In July 1951 the Committee for Interstate and Foreign Commerce (CIFC) faced a decision: compel the FCC to deliberate similarly to the Communications Act, which by default favored commercial networks, or adjust the language of communications policy to protect noncommercial broadcasts. CIFC provided the FCC with the choice to rule in favor of frequency sharing or to extend the precedent set by the 1945 FM allocations. As reported by FCC Secretary Slowie on July 13, 1951, Section 303 of the Communications Act permitted the FCC to classify radio stations based on prescriptions of the nature of services rendered. If the FCC were to organize a classified "assignment table" for possible noncommercial educational stations and then apply the table with uniformity, this would amount to a "direct implementation of the substantive and procedural provisions of Section 303."[66] Further they determined that Section 307(b) commanded equitable distribution of radio service among every state and community if applications for licenses were made. So if a classification was made for a noncommercial frequency band and enough stations applied within that classification, the FCC was impelled to grant equitable access to that classification of service for each community.[67]

When Section (307) was combined with Section 303, Slowie reported, a standard for an educational frequency band could be "applied in all cases, or as a discretionary grant of authority to act by rule if the public interest so requires."[68] The two sections could be read together as one standard to be applied in all cases, whether the commission chose to exercise the rule. Further, an amendment to the Act was possible because Section (c) of the Act provided a congressional mandate in the absence of a "statutory direction to allocate in a manner prescribed by the statute itself." In other words, if an amendment to the Act stipulated that a classification of stations was mandated to hold equal access for their designated purpose, as long as such classified stations were represented in each state, then set-aside frequencies would be available to meet that spectrum of "public interest" requirements.

But this did not let commercial broadcasters off the hook for public service requirements. On July 23, 1951, the FCC reported that it would "require that commercial broadcast stations devote a specified percentage of broadcast time to educational programs."[69] Commercial stations would not be recused from "well rounded" service simply because new classifications might be defined. Section 303 indicated that the commission had authority to prescribe the nature of the service to be rendered by a class of stations, and the stations within that class, by directing that those stations devote a fixed percentage of their broadcasting time to a particular type of service. Commercial stations claimed to offer services that educators had never attempted to offer, and they would be expected to continue doing so.[70] An amendment to the Act included a mandate that new classifications would be set aside for specific purposes, such as aeronautical, industrial, or educational FM, with prescriptions of percentages of time dedicated to meeting allocated classifications. However, in a concession to commercial broadcasters, Johnson offered that the FCC would not actively enforce this provision if networks agreed to follow regulation.

"With respect to non-specialized broadcast services in which stations are licensed to render a rounded service in the public interest to the general public, the commission has consistently interpreted the Communications Act as requiring, as a matter of basic congressional policy, that licensees retain responsibility to make the initial determination as to the specific character of service which would fulfill the statuary mandate. While it has been the commission's position that a well-rounded program structure should include among those programs designed to meet the needs and interests of the people to be served a reasonable amount of educational programs, the commission, in recognition of the basic principle of licensee responsibility and the prohibition against censorship contained in Section 326 of the act has taken the entirely consistent position that it will not prescribe any fixed quantitative program standards for non-specialized broadcast stations."[71]

Educational stations were designated under a wider classification of "non-profit radio programs" with clear institutional licensing as an educational, nonprofit, or community station to qualify for the new classification.

The Sixth Report and Order of 1952 ultimately defined newly reserved channels for "certain communities for use by noncommercial educational television stations."[72] In line with the FM reservations of 1945, the amendment required a clearly detailed description of the purpose of the television applicant's institutional purpose. The new noncommercial classification was applied to public and private educational, state, county, municipality, or other political subdivisions such as boards of educations. The Order permitted educators to apply, if applications supplied accompanying details concerning the educational background of an applicant's practices.[73]

In another round of serendipity, during this process the JCET was granted $90000 by educational broadcasting's newest underwriters, the Ford Foundation.[74] J. Webb Young of Ford had been convinced that the building and maintenance of educational stations was an appropriate application of the foundation's intent to impact "the emotional maturity and unconscious behavior patterns" of the country. This offer buttressed the passing of the Sixth Report, supported strongly by Edwin Johnson.

> "The rendering of the combination of these services will help the cause of education. I am not suggesting nor should any of my comments be interpreted as precluding any educational group from applying for a channel as long as they satisfactorily demonstrate they are financially qualified and otherwise able to operate a station."[75]

Educational broadcasting had survived despite its failings and regulatory hurdles, and the Ford Foundation, now under the supervision of Robert Hutchins (coincidentally one of the University Broadcasting Council supervisors) and C. Scott Fletcher pledged to invest millions of dollars into the standardization of a production culture of educational broadcasting after 1952. The next phase of public media would move to television and focus on streamlining aesthetic practices under Ford Foundation support.[76]

The Sixth Report and Order and the Institutionalization of Public Media: The National Defense of Education Act of 1958 and The Educational Television Facilities Act of 1962

The final version of the Report was filed on April 13, 1952, and upheld the tentative FM assignments from 1945, and even increased them from 209 to 242, split between VHF and UHF. Twenty years of reform research and experimentation into aesthetics, technical practice, curriculum, and methods of distribution had built momentum for an educational infrastructure that persuaded legislators that public service capacities of technology were deserving of some protection from free markets.[77] By the end of the freeze, educators were finally provided with a stable range of television and radio frequencies for which to produce educational content.

Once a set-aside frequency precedent was in place, attention turned to the problem of financing. Looking back at the period between 1952 and 1967, one advocate reminisced that advocacy "had been built around several phases: getting interest and understanding, developing a plan tailored to community needs, activating the plan, and building stations and staff." But the final phase of building a uniformly excellent noncommercial broadcasting constituency seemed permanently cost prohibitive without federal funds. In the early 1960s, one member noted, NET was producing only five hours of programming per week, and the Eastern Educational Network (later WGBH) produced about seven hours. Other noncommercial programs received no consistent support at all.

Advocates looked again to policy to strategize how to fund production, and over subsequent decades after 1952 the public interest mandate transformed from the cause of noncommercial decimation to grounds for obtaining government funding for public media. The National Defense of Education Act of 1958 issued provisions in its Title 3 for educational instructional content research, which included technology but not equipment. Title 7 of the Act put money aside for "experimental and published materials."[78] That a policy not related to broadcasting included funds for educational technology, with grants utilizing the empirical language that had been innovated by public media researchers, helped reformers to further contend that educational broadcasting was a logical extension of educational policy.

As the problem of frequency scarcity declined, the prospects of a legislative "prize" of increasing American public service piqued the interest of several liberal senators. Conceived by Senators Warren Magnuson of Washington and John Pastore of Rhode Island, a new 5-year renewable bill for educational media facilities funding was proposed in line with the National Defense of Education Act, to serve citizens who were not being provided with "equal" access to National Educational Television broadcasts.[79] Magnuson corresponded with NAEB members, who pointed him to their streamlined administrative, content development, and measurement standards.[80]

The bill was written to address several expediencies connected to educational funding. Educational media funding was substantiated by rules set in the Sixth Report and Order, in line with mandates for equal access to educational facilities in the National Defense of Education Act of 1958. It set aside funds for the purpose of equipment, "agency facilitators," and discretionary funds for appointed station managers.[81] It identified four types of recipients: universities, schools, state agencies, and community corporations, stipulating matching grants of up to one million dollars per state, in total of 32 million dollars, distributed as 50 percent toward acquisition and installation of equipment, 25 percent to agency facilitators, and 25 percent as discretionary funds. Funds would be renewed on a yearly basis for five years, through 1967. Senator Warren Magnuson gained widespread support from fellow Democrats, including from station-owner Lyndon Johnson, and the bill was passed as the Educational Television Facilities Act (#87–447) in 1962.[82]

Within the first 3 years of implementation television facilities grew from 84 to 114 stations, and the FCC projected the number would grow as high as 170 by the end of its period. In this time the FCC received 59 applications for new transmitters, conducted 600 closed-circuit instructional television installations, and most astonishingly, educational television viewership grew from four million to thirty-six million, while curricular offerings grew from fifteen shows to over one hundred.[83] By 1966 educational facilities expanded to 20 AM stations, 325 FM stations, and 130 television stations.

During that time other major educational bills were passed that further buttressed support for educational technology.[84] The Elementary and Secondary Education Act of 1965 provided remuneration to schools to buy "equipment," especially for "educationally deprived children," which included provisions for audio-visual materials.[85] And the Higher Education Act of 1965 covered acquisition of closed-circuit direct instruction costs.[86]

The Educational Television Facilities Act revealed the difficulty of relying upon localism to fund a standardized model of educational broadcasting. The FCC found that distributing money did not guarantee appropriate state investment in educational technology. Few of those 59 applications actually became functional stations. One report called the Act a "crazy quilt pattern of assistance available for Educational Television (ETV) equipment installations."[87] The report anticipated criteria for "maximum possible uniformity with the acquisition of ETV equipment, provisions for operation, maintenance staffing, etc." Another report pointed to concern over non-standardization of types of facilities. Some were "very large regional or national," while others were "major city stations with multiple studio capabilities," all the way down to "middle sized cities with 2-studio and mobile production capabilities" and "small city stations with 1 studio production capacity."[88]

Facilities and the Public Interest: The Department of Health, Education, and Welfare's Drafting of the first "Public Television" Bill, and the Carnegie Commission Report

By the time the Educational Television Facilities Act was set to expire, the FCC and Congress were persuaded that even broader legislation was necessary to contain the unprecedented expansion in construction of educational television facilities due to the act between 1963 and 1966, and to address the unexpected increase in qualified inequality to educational content under new legislation.[89] The Department of Health, Education, and Welfare concluded that "the expiring Facilities Act accomplished its limited objective by encouraging the establishment of stations and expanding the coverage of a number of existing stations."[90] However it had only provided "limited matching for the purchase of equipment," and some states lacked interest in receiving federal funds. The Act did not assist in day-to-day operating expenses, and no support was provided for research or "manpower development." Approaching 1967 policymakers were faced with several choices regarding the policy: take no action and permit the program to expire, extend for additional time with the same provisions, extend with amendments, or propose a replacement Act.[91] By that point so much money had been invested, with such astonishing growth in such a short time, that a more pervasive bill seemed necessary.

Around the same time the Carnegie Commission released a well-cited and widely distributed report.[92] Among strategic recommendations found in the Report, Dean Coston, undersecretary at the Department of Health, Education, and Welfare, proposed to fund educational television with a tax on commercial broadcasters.[93] At first policymakers took this idea seriously. Early drafts of a Public Television Act proposed a tax of 0.6 percent to 1.4 percent, with later iterations recommending 1 percent to 3 percent taxes on network income to fund public television. The predictable result was that educators soon had networks lobbying on their side to fund a public corporation, federally financed but separate from governmental control.

Institutional memory ran long in this area, and the Office of Education testified that educational television would improve "learning bodies of subject matter, intellectual skills, problem solving, social relationships, and good attitudes toward learning."[94] To cap, Rosel Hyde, Chairman of the FCC, argued that a central institution would "promote the development of noncommercial educational broadcasting by extending and improving its provisions for grants for the construction of educational broadcasting facilities."[95] Such a change would additionally authorize a needed official research wing, to evaluate curricular implementation of technology contracted by the Department of Health, Education, and Welfare. The Ford Foundation sweetened the deal, by promising an additional thirty-five million dollars of underwriting per year through 1970.[96]

The first proposal for a Public Television Act was amended at the very last second to include radio, becoming the Public Broadcasting Act of 1967. It began as the five-year renewal of the Educational Television Facilities Act, and after much political wrangling, it was written with three Titles: 1) expansion and improvement of facilities, including Corporation for Public Broadcasting (CPB) oversight of construction, regional systems, and money for bureaucratic connectivity between institutions; 2) the creation of a nonprofit public corporation that would provide grants for content, authorize and receive philanthropic gifts, describe standards and functions, assist in operations, and avoid exercising control over content; and 3) to create a division for television and radio professional development, including grants to researchers, traineeships and internships, and distribution of compensation for training.[97] The Public Broadcasting Act was the culmination of close to forty-five years of advocacy and experimentation, beginning with the Communications Act. By 1967 educators had built a national infrastructure, coordinated across multiple sectors, to institutionalize a mission statement as a federal broadcasting agency. The Act carried with it the idiosyncrasies of the institutional scaffolding of the 1930s, and the tenor of the trial-and-error machinations of media reform.

Conclusion

After 1934 educational media defined itself in terms of its mission statement, and slowly designed a media industry in line with its founding principles instead of a profit model. Consequent advocacy strategies reflected a patchwork of university, government, state, and philanthropic attempts to complete the task of providing an educational space through technology. Public media can be studied as a political history in which grassroots, government, and philanthropy groups collaborated to realize the aspiration that "democratic media" might exist among a free market of special interests. Noncommercial media started at a disadvantage. Its early broadcasts lacked performance and aesthetic standards, while practitioners were forced to compete with commercial radio performers for scarce radio frequencies. Because educators began so strong in concept yet so weak in practice, they initially failed to secure a spot on the dial. But their fidelity to nonprofit use of technology kept their lobby going and, over decades, eventually became a commonly agreed-upon goal for American broadcasting. Even commercial broadcasters were on board, as the networks decided by the 1950s that they weren't keen to be the stewards of a public service model that was neither profitable nor predictable for audience metrics. Between the 1940s and 1960s the NAEB and progressive policymakers called upon the rhetoric of compulsory education, technical research, and public interest standards to not only make the case but make it impossible for the government to *not* set aside frequencies for educational radio and television.

Conclusion

Media History and the Public of
Political Economic Research

This book details how the media reform movement helped to build the foundations of public media following the Communications Act. It follows several historical threads, from the origin of philanthropic funding, the influence of the federal educational sector, the complicated relationship between educators and commercial broadcasters, and the logistics of early media network experiments, with reference to the emergence of political economic research, and changes in reform strategy before and after the Act. A study of this history reveals the tenacity and techniques of successful media strategies that changed media policy over time. There's not a clean, clear line between activism and policy changes after 1934, so this book tries to show how momentum grew and shifted along technical, regulatory, organizational, and intellectual tracks until they culminated in public policy. Educational policy impacted multiple lines of discourse around media policy, and the final structure for proto-public media was a hybrid of expectations from each sector.

It's worth making a few observations about how this book interprets the arc of reform work. As Robert McChesney notes, reformers began as an *activist* movement that initially appealed to legislators to set aside protected frequencies for educators. But after 1934, I argue, the movement became something more like an *advocacy*. Here I'll make a few analytical distinctions, less to authoritatively define these terms than clarify the trajectory that each reform method engendered. Media activism tended to do good work identifying a social contradiction, problem, or transgression in order to make an issue conspicuous for the broader public. Activism, for example pre-1934 NCER, successfully raised awareness about the issue of educational access yet tended to occur after a political process was already in motion, or a transgression such as decimation of broadcast licenses had already concluded. In a general sense, activism as we usually think about it is fundamentally important for clarifying, hailing, or interrupting political, institutional, and organizational processes.[1] But event capacity of activism alone—without other strategies—is limited to correcting a field of visibility. The benefits of reform advocacy relied upon activism to clarify specific issues at hand but took a methodologically different turn. Reform advocacy after 1934 examined and then articulated future-oriented infrastructural strategies and was structured to change and interrupt political decisions through calculated steps, tactics, and anticipated benchmarks.

From a historiographical standpoint, media advocacy calls upon past events, and tends to be present and future oriented, with the goal of changing relations endemic to a geographic or relational context. The goal of an advocacy is less to make a contradiction conspicuous, though that certainly might be one goal, than to carve out space for its position, and possibly take a dominant regulatory role. Put differently, the marker for advocacy success is different from activist success. A successful activism focuses attention, while a successful advocacy plans to organize policy and behavior. An activism has succeeded when social agents better understand and are more invested in a social issue,[2] when an impending crisis has been averted, a social vision accepted, a policy passed, or relations are practiced in mundanity. The time frame for an advocacy is much longer, and a proponent of a reform issue might not live to see the culmination of their work.

I make these distinctions as a thought experiment after years of archival work that continuously presented two historiographical problems about reform strategy. The first problem was that advocates and practitioners implemented notably different approaches to organization before and after the Communications Act. I try to account for that shift by making a distinction between present/past-focused activist work, and present-/future-based advocacy to build reform institutions, as imagined by the post-Act reform coalition. What strategies did the NCER take before and after 1934 and why? Second, as mentioned above, the history of media reform between 1934 and 1952 resists association with one centralized institution, figure, or coordinated effort. This history instead unfolds along parallel tracks, across sectors, over close to two decades, culminating in the Allerton House Seminars and Sixth Report and Order. It is clear that post-Act advocates were unified by fidelity to a vision of justice met through educational research. And under this auspice, Dallas Smythe and Richard Hull at the NAEB developed disciplinary strategies associated with political economy of media research.

The history of political economy of media research is a fascinating case study for the very reason that its investments and methodologies exemplify this period's idealisms, concessions, emerging methodologies, and external influences. American political economy of media work turns out to have started as a policy strategy of educational media reform, designed to solve contradictions instituted by the Radio Act and Communications Act. The crisis over frequency allocations inspired a series of targeted reports that became a core mechanism of communication research itself. It's a solution-based methodology that was designed to solve a problem. By the time Dallas Smythe helped to build the Illinois School, he was deeply invested in research to prove why noncommercial media was our best opportunity for democratic media. Smythe conducted empirical research to solve a policy problem that emanated from government and private sector discourses. One of the key virtues of political economic research is that it examines institutional decision-making processes with an inverted eye in the American market: equity *first*, and the logics of industry accumulation second.

System-Building in Media Research History

The institution of public media materialized as an ultimate culmination of over forty years of idealism brought back to earth by adjustments, economic pressures, political concessions, and the limits set by universities themselves. Similar to political economic research, communication research is shaped by how its innovators began their project as an attempt to solve contradictions in government policy by developing evidentiary methodologies. Unique to the Princeton Radio Research Project, the positivist impulse to sort the existential dimensions of mental life into preformularized categories inspired breakthroughs in demographic and survey research. Communication studies convened as a twentieth century intellectual phenomenon that addressed technocratic questions. Communication represents a fundamentally different set of investments than the humanities, and continues to provide an efficient, practical, and useful methodology for public decision-making. Communications research in part began as a strategy of media reform and served as the logic for the development of an alternative noncommercial media infrastructure. Put differently, the historical symbiosis between public broadcasting and communication research reveals something striking about the relationship between institutional mission statements and consequent methodological and technical decisions. PRRP researchers were asked to make a case for special frequency allocations for noncommercial media when the approach was not only not profitable, but not well supported, nor was it even clear that radio was an effective use of classroom time. The project was in part successful at persuading government agencies because its researchers formularized listener subjectivity into reportable patterns capable of predicating response to stimuli and the introduction of new phenomena.

Adorno and Lazarsfeld disagreed about how to interpret, meet, and report upon these findings. But their infamous encounter also ran deeper than that. Adorno departed with a fundamental disagreement over how to characterize human embodiment.[3] Their argument signified an epistemic break over who counts as having been "recognized" within social science research. Can an individual be interpreted as a category? Or does research require that nuanced and thorough description be applied to account for the integrity of every person? If it's the latter, how does one report upon and interpret mass public sentiment about fast-moving social phenomena, not to mention make significant decisions about important events? The irony of Adorno's PRRP engagement is that Adorno abandoned media reform work altogether after he lost his funding. Communication researchers not only stuck with educational broadcasting for decades but were instrumental in designing public broadcasting itself. On that point, one outcome of the post-Act landscape was that the aspiration for equal access to education mobilized the creation of an entire academic discipline that was inflected by language, institutional pressures, and limits framed within the Communications Act.

This strikes at a deeper point that has kept me in archives for years. Media and Communication Studies was founded as a system building approach to increase democratic participation. At one point "Media Studies" was synonymous with scholars who, for at least part of their service agenda, aspired to construct an alternate media system. One intended purpose of this book is to re-pose the New Deal-era question: when an activist group is faced with failure, how do they implement strategic changes? What strategies have historically, tangibly changed path dependencies in policy and institutional decision-making? Any such response must be qualified with a warning about the positionality of the historical figures: largely white men at universities with significant privilege, who, for the primary period that this book covers, did not work with the diverse groups identified by educational broadcasting's mission statement. Yet this history nonetheless reveals something for contemporary scholarship about how media reform has interpreted and addressed policy, without assuming that reform is synonymous with rights advocacy.

The same activists in Robert McChesney's foundational book not only did not disappear after the Act, but continued with their work, and developed new strategies. This history points to key moments when institutional and political changes became sustainable. The durability of belief in educational access was central to these connected changes. Reform became a movement that took on a life of its own outside of individual actors. It's a historical case example of how institutions imagine and implement strategies for effective reform work. Noncommercial media history is unique in that it's one of the few media histories in the twentieth century that aspired to change major legislation and actually succeeded. Without assuming that new public projects should reproduce this specific movement, there's a spirit that can and must be recaptured if we intended to protect democratic institutions.

Podcasts, Diversity, and Facilities-Based Lobby: The Historical Relationship between Public Media and the Educational Sector

As a history of a particular strain of media activism that anticipated a federal service, there are three takeaways that this book offers for public media scholarship. The first point has been well chronicled by my colleagues but is worth punctuating: media activism can be traced through historical and logistical practices. Activist movements often feature arresting and inspiring speeches. By focusing research on media activism on mundane trial-and-error processes situated around a mission statement, this project contextualizes the day-to-day labors of multiple activist and institutional groups. As educational media reform work chalked up regulatory and funding victories over decades, advocates eventually no longer had to advocate, and noncommercial media took on a different veneer.

After forty years noncommercial media in the United States was institutionalized as a federally funded corporation with television and radio wings.[4] Public media's founding policy and mission statement carries the imprint of the previous decades of programming and research.[5] Politically, public media exists thanks to a strange cocktail of educational policy,[6] communication mandates, and successful lobby. The service provides everything from children's programming to science and personal interest stories that complement public media's journalistic focus.[7] PBS and NPR are continuously assailed by free market politics. Nixon, Bush, and Trump have repeatedly suggested in their yearly budgets that public media be completely defunded and its infrastructure replaced with commercial media industries. Noncommercial media industries have thrived, but continuously face new struggles and challenges.

Public media's capacity to field attacks while maintaining its mission has become a point of persistent concern. One thing that public media history shows us is that the service only makes sense as a non-advertising institution. It's quite possible that NPR, PBS, and affiliates will continue to exist for some time, but it's not clear if "public media" will survive as a public service institution built upon a mission statement, or if the nomenclature will refer to a style or genre. This book has not made claims about what public media "should" be. But there's one clear solution that would almost certainly protect the service. Public media should reconnect with public education. It's possible for the service to work with primary and secondary schools and revisit its original classroom extension and literacy mission.

Protecting public media includes (re)connecting digital and podcasting services to the educational sector.[8] Education provides the broadest renewable, diverse audience, helps to fulfill mandates to reach both large and small experiences with content,[9] and perhaps most importantly at this juncture, might attract more public sector funding. The future of public media might well be its past. The service long succeeded by evolving from radio instruction to provide sound content on par with network and cable programming.[10] But what keeps public radio unique and crucial for US democracy, is its service mission, famously penned for NPR by University of Wisconsin alumni and founding program director Bill Siemering. The mission statement was conceived after decades of activism, research, and collaboration, without a profit motive, and without the influence of special interests. There are some indications that the service is already moving in this direction. New delivery models from podcasting[11] to digital interfaces have expanded the audience and reach of public media. From opportunities for non-appointment engagement to niche audio programming, in many ways public media is offering a service closer to its early vision than in previous decades.[12]

Notes

Introduction

1. John Marshall minutes from lunch with Hilda Mathieson, September 10, 1936. Box 53, Folder 696, Rockefeller Archive Center, Sleepy Hollow, NY.

2. See Darrel Newton, *Paving the Empire Road: BBC Television and Black Britons* (Manchester University Press, 2011).

3. Charles Siepmann Iowa State Notes, April 1-June 9, 1937, Box 53, Folder 701, Rockefeller Archive Center, Sleepy Hollow, NY.

4. Charles Siepmann University of Illinois Notes, April 1-June 9, 1937, Box 53, Folder 701, Rockefeller Archive Center, Sleepy Hollow, NY.

5. Charles Siepmann Network Radio Notes, April 1-June 9, 1937, Box 53, Folder 701, Rockefeller Archive Center, Sleepy Hollow, NY. Also see David Weinstein, *The Eddie Cantor Story: A Jewish Life in Performance and Politics* (Boston: University Press of New England/Brandeis University Press, 2017).

6. Kathy Fuller-Seeley, *Jack Benny and the Golden Age of American Radio Comedy* (Berkeley: University of California Press, 2017).

7. Charles Siepmann University of Iowa at Iowa City Notes, April 1-June 9, 1937, Box 53, Folder 701, Rockefeller Archive Center, Sleepy Hollow, NY.

8. Charles Siepmann "Radio at Universities in the United States of America: A Report to the Trustees of the Rockefeller Foundation," 60-page collection of multiple documents: evaluations, recommendations based upon his tour, and declarations of approach to educational radio, 1937. Box 53, Folder 701, Rockefeller Archive Center, Sleepy Hollow, NY.

9. See Dyfrig Jones, *Paul Lazarsfeld and Media Reform at the Ford Foundation* (Sleepy Hollow, Rockefeller Archive Center, 2019) and Anna McCarthy, *Citizen Machine: Governing by Television in 1950s America* (NYC: The New Press, 2010).

10. Deborah Wilson David, "The American Origins of BBC Local Radio," *Journal of Radio & Audio Media* 25, no. 2 (July 3, 2018): 298–310.

11. Carl Menzer to Harold McCarty, December 3, 1936, Box 2, Folder 1, National Association of Educational Broadcasters Papers, Wisconsin Historical Society, Madison, WI.

12. National Association of Educational Broadcasters Constitution of 1934, Box 1, Folder 1934, National Association of Educational Broadcasters Papers, Wisconsin Historical Society, Madison, WI.

13. Laurie Ouellette, *Viewers like You? How Public TV Failed the People* (NYC: Columbia University Press, 2002).

14. Victor Pickard, "Communication's Forgotten Narratives: The Lost History of Charles Siepmann and Critical Policy Research." *Critical Studies in Media Communication* 33, no. 4 (September 27, 2016): 337–51.

15. For expert analysis on the development of tropes in early commercial radio broadcasting, see Elana Levine, *Her Stories: Daytime Soap Opera and U.S. Television History* (Durham, NC: Duke University Press, 2020).

16. See Inger L. Stole, *Advertising at War: Business, Consumers, and Government in the 1940s* (Champaign-Urbana, University of Illinois Press, 2012).

17. Robert McChesney, *Telecommunications, Mass Media, and Democracy: The Battle for the Control of US Broadcasting, 1928–1935* (New York: Oxford University Press, 1993).

18. Dempsey, John Mark, and Eric Gruver. "The American System: Herbert Hoover, the Associative State, and Broadcast Commercialism." *Presidential Studies Quarterly* 39, no. 2 (April 6, 2009): 226–44. https://doi.org/10.1111/j.1741–5705.2009.03673.

19. Patricia Aufderheide. *Communications Policy and the Public Interest: Telecommunications Act of 1996* (New York: Guilford Press, 1997).

20. Transcript of Codel Interview with Anning Prall, March 30, 1935. Box 332, Folder 3950, Rockefeller Archive Center, Sleepy Hollow, NY.

21. Harold Hill, *History of the National Association of Educational Broadcasters,* (Wisconsin Historical Society, 1954).

22. Christine Ehrick, *Radio and the Gendered Soundscape: Women and Broadcasting in Argentina and Uruguay, 1930–1950* (Cambridge University Press, 2015).

23. Christina Dunbar-Hester. "What's Local? Localism as a Discursive Boundary Object in Low-Power Radio Policymaking," *Communication, Culture & Critique* 6, no. 4 (December 14, 2013): 502–24.

24. Alexander Russo, *Points on the Dial: Golden Age Radio Beyond the Networks* (Durham: Duke University Press, 2010).

25. Gwenyth L. Jackaway, *Media at War: Radio's Challenge to the Newspapers, 1924–1939* (Westport, CT: Praeger, 1995).

26. Allison Perlman, *Public Interests: Media Advocacy and Struggles over U.S. Television* (New Brunswick: Rutgers University Press, 2016).

27. Victor Pickard, *America's Battle for Media Democracy: The Triumph of Corporate Libertarianism and the Future of Media Reform* (Cambridge: Cambridge University Press, 2014).

28. Jefferson Cowie, and Nick Salvatore. "The Long Exception: Rethinking the

Place of the New Deal in American History," *International Labor and Working-Class History* 74, no. 1 (November 7, 2008): 3–32.

29. Josef Wright's description of the *Pursuant*, Internal Memo, 1934, Box 1, National Association of Educational Broadcasters Papers, Madison, WI.

30. Hugh Slotten. *Radio's Hidden Voice: The Origins of Public Broadcasting in the United States* (Urbana: University of Illinois Press, 2009).

31. Robert K. Avery, "The Public Broadcasting Act of 1967: Looking Ahead by Looking Back," *Critical Studies in Media Communication* 24, no. 4 (October 2007): 358–64; "The Public Broadcasting Act of 1967: Radio's Real Second Chance," *Journal of Radio & Audio Media* 24, no. 2 (July 3, 2017): 189–99.

32. Sonja Williams, *Word Warrior: Richard Durham, Radio, and Freedom* (Urbana: University of Illinois Press, 2015).

33. For more on media "form" see: Anna Kornbluh, *The Order of Forms: Realism, Formalism, and Social Space* (Chicago: University of Chicago Press, 2019).

34. David Barsamian. *The Decline and Fall of Public Broadcasting* (Cambridge, Mass: South End Press, 2001).

35. See David Goodman and Joy Hayes, *New Deal Radio: The Educational Radio Project* (New Brunswick: Rutgers University Press, 2022).

36. David Goodman, *Radio's Civic Ambition: American Broadcasting and Democracy in the 1930s* (Oxford University Press, 2011).

37. Cynthia Meyers, *A Word from Our Sponsor: Admen, Advertising, and the Golden Age of Radio* (New York: Fordham University Press, 2013).

38. Jennifer Stoever, *Sonic Color Line: Race and the Cultural Politics of Listening* (New York: NYU Press, 2016).

39. James F Hamilton, "Historical Forms of User Production," *Media, Culture & Society* 36, no. 4 (May 7, 2014): 491–507.

40. Michele Hilmes, *Network Nations: A Transnational History of British and American Broadcasting* (New York: Routledge, 2011).

41. Susan Douglas, *Inventing American Broadcasting* (Baltimore: Johns Hopkins University Press, 1989).

42. Heather Hendershot, *What's Fair on the Air?: Cold War Right-Wing Broadcasting and the Public Interest* (Chicago: University of Chicago Press, 2011).

43. Laura Garbes, "Sound Archive Access: Revealing Emergent Cultures," *Journal of Radio and Audio Media* 26(1) (2019): 79–83.

44. See Andrea Stanton, *This Is Jerusalem Calling: State Radio in Mandate Palestine* (Austin: University of Texas Press, 2013); and Alejandra Bronfman, *Isles of Noise: Sonic Media in the Caribbean* (Chapel Hill: University of North Carolina Press, 2016).

45. Glenda R. Balas, "From Underserved to Broadly Served: The Class Interests of Public Broadcasting," *Critical Studies in Media Communication,* 24, no. 4 (December 7, 2007): 365–69.

46. Laura Garbes, "How a CPB task force advanced a prescient vision for diversity in public radio," *Current*, Retrieved from https://current.org/2017/11/how-a-cpb-task -forceadvanced-a-prescient-vision-for-diversity-in-public-radio.

47. Christopher Chavez, *The Sound of Exclusion: NPR and the Latinx Public* (Albuquerque: University of Arizona Press, 2021).

48. Jason Loviglio, "Sound Effects: Gender, Voice, and the Cultural Work of NPR," *The Radio Journal: International Studies in Broadcast and Audio Media*, 5(2) (2008): 67–81; also see John Durham Peters, "The Public Voice of Radio," *Communication in History*, Paul Heyer and Peter Urquhart, eds, (New York: Routledge, 2018).

49. Laurie Ouellette, *Viewers like You? How Public TV Failed the People*.

50. See Carol Stabile, *The Broadcast 41: Women and Anti-Communist Blacklist* (Boston: MIT Press, 2020).

51. See Keisha Blain, *Until I am Free: Fannie Lou Hamer's Enduring Message to America* (Boston: Beacon Press, 2021).

52. Bill Kirkpatrick, "A Blessed Boon: Radio, Disability, Governmentality, and the Discourse of the 'Shut-In,' 1920–1930," *Critical Studies in Media Communication, 29*, no. 3 (November 9, 2011): 165–84.

53. Christine Acham. *Revolution Televised: Prime Time and the Struggle for Black Power* (Minneapolis: University of Minnesota Press, 2004); Angela Tate, "Sounding Off: Etta Moten Barnett's Archive, Diaspora, and Radio Activism in the Cold War," *Resonance: The Journal for Sound and Culture*, 2(3), (2021): 395–410.

54. Bambi Haggins and Kristen Warner, "Flashback/Flashblack," *Journal of e-Media Studies*, 4(1), (2015).

55. Nabil Echchaibi, *Voicing Diasporas: Ethnic Radio in Paris and Berlin in between Culture and Renewal* (Lanham, MD: Lexington Books, 2011).

56. Josh Shepperd. "The Political Economic Structure of Early Media Reform Before and After the Communications Act of 1934," *Resonance: The Journal for Sound and Culture*, 1 (3) (2020): 244–66. See Aswin Punathambeker, *Media Industry Studies* (New York: Polity, 2020).

57. Eileen R. Meehan and Ellen Riordan, *Sex and Money: Feminism and Political Economy in the Media* (Minneapolis: University of Minnesota Press, 2002).

58. Ralph Engelman, *Public Radio and Television in America: A Political History* (NY: Sage, 1996).

59. Stuart Cunningham, & David Craig, "Creator Governance in Social Media Entertainment," *Social Media + Society*, Issue 28, November (2019).

60. The earliest "how to" educational radio books appear in the late 1920s and continued to be published until roughly the 1970s.

61. Katherine Rye Jewell, "Buttermore's Dream Come True: WRAS at Georgia State and the Sound Politics of Cultural Radio, 1978–1983," *Resonance: The Journal of Sound and Culture*, 3, no 2, (2022): 145–62.

62. Jack Mitchell, *Wisconsin on the Air* (Madison: Wisconsin Historical Society Press, 2017).

63. Randall Davidson, *9XM Talking: WHA Radio and the Wisconsin Idea* (Madison: University of Wisconsin Press, 2007).

64. George Gibson, *Public Broadcasting: The Role of the Federal Government, 1912–1976* (Santa Barbara: Praeger, 1977).

65. Eric Rauchway, "The New Deal Was on the Ballot in 1932," *Modern American History* 2, no. 02 (July 22, 2019): 201–13.

66. Timothy Havens, Amanda D. Lotz, Serra Tinic, "Critical Media Industry Studies: A Research Approach." *Communication, Culture & Critique* 2(2) (2009): 234–53.

67. John Macy, *To Irrigate the Wasteland* (Berkeley: University of California Press, 1974).

68. Derek Vaillant, *Sounds of Reform: Progressivism and Music in Chicago, 1873–1935* (Chapel Hill: University of North Carolina Press, 2004).

69. Brian Rosenwald. *Talk Radio's America: How an Industry Took Over a Political Party that Took Over the United States* (Cambridge, MA: Harvard University Press, 2019).

70. Kyle Asquith, "Knowing the Child Consumer Through Box Tops: Data Collection, Measurement, and Advertising to Children, 1920–1945," *Critical Studies in Media Communication* 32, no. 2 (March 4, 2015): 112–27.

71. Eric Rothenbuhler, "Commercial Radio as Communication," *Journal of Communication* 46(1), (1996): 125–43.

72. See Julie Beth Napolin, *The Fact of Resonance: Modernist Acoustics and Narrative Form* (New York: Fordham University Press, 2020).

73. Victoria Cain, "From Sesame Street to Prime-Time School Television: Educational Media in the Wake of the Coleman Report," *History of Education Quarterly* 57, no. 4 (November 6, 2017): 590–601; also see Kathryn Ostrofsky, "Taking Sesame to the Streets: Young Children's Interactions with Pop Music's Urban Aesthetic in the 1970s," *Journal of Popular Music Studies*, 24(3), (2012).

74. It's worth reading Christopher Sterling across multiple texts, discussing the central role of logistics and policy in content decisions. Christopher H. Sterling, "The Rise of Radio Studies: Scholarly Books Over Four Decades," *Journal of Radio & Audio Media* 16, no. 2 (November 6, 2009): 229–50.

75. Michael Huntsberger, "Politics and Poster Children: A Historical Assessment of Radio Outcomes in the Public Broadcasting Act of 1967," *Journal of Radio & Audio Media* 24, no. 2 (September 22, 2017): 213–25.

76. NAEB Bulletin, February 20, 1931, Box 101, National Association of Educational Broadcasters Papers, box 101, Wisconsin Historical Society, Madison, WI.

77. Jack Lule. "The Public Broadcasting Act of 1967: Forty Years Later." *Critical Studies in Media Communication* 24, no. 4 (October 2007): 357–57.

78. Juergen Habermas, *The Structural Transformation of the Public Sphere: An Inquiry into a Category of Bourgeois Society*, trans. Thomas Burger. (Cambridge, MA: The MIT Press, 1989).

79. Sue Curry Jansen. "Phantom Conflict: Lippmann, Dewey, and the Fate of the Public in Modern Society," *Communication and Critical/Cultural Studies* 6, no. 3 (August 6, 2009): 221–45.

80. John Dewey. *Experience and Education* (New York: Simon and Schuster, 1938).

81. See Sonia Robles, *Mexican Waves: Radio Broadcasting Along Mexico's Northern Border* (Albuquerque, NM: University of Arizona Press, 2019).

82. Dallas W. Smythe, "On the Political Economy of Communications," *Journalism & Mass Communication Quarterly*, 37 (4), (1960): 563–72.

83. See Willard D. Rowland, Jr., *The Institution of U.S. Public Broadcasting: In Public Television in America*, eds. Eli M. Noam, Jens Waltermann (Gutersloh: Bertelsmann Foundation Publishers, 1998). Willard D. Rowland, Jr., "The Illusion of Fulfillment: The Broadcast Reform Movement," *Journalism Monographs*, Issue 79 (1982).

84. David Park, Jefferson Pooley. *The History of Media and Communication Research: Contested Memories* (Peter Lang: 2008).

85. For more on transnational exchanges with the BBC, see Ian Whittington, *Writing the Radio War: Literature, Politics, and the BBC, 1939–1945* (Edinburgh University Press, 2018).

86. Hynek Jerabek, *Paul Lazarsfeld's Research Methodology* (Prague: Karolinum Press, 2006).

87. A. Brad Schwartz, *Broadcast Hysteria: Orson Welles's War of the Worlds and the Art of Fake News* (New York: Hill and Wang, 2016).

88. Hadley Cantril, *The Invasion from Mars* (London: Routledge, 1940).

89. Charles Siepmann, Dallas Smythe, *Public Service Responsibility of Broadcast Licensees* ["The Blue Book"], (Washington, DC: FCC, 1946).

Chapter 1. Advocacy

1. See Lori Emerson, Darren Wershler, and Jussi Parikka, *The Lab Book: Situated Practices in Media Studies* (Minneapolis: University of Minnesota Press, 2022); Lisa Gitelman, *Always Already New: Media, History, and the Data of Culture* (Boston: MIT Press, 2008); Carolyn Marvin, *When Old Technologies Were New: Thinking about Electric Communication in the Late 19th Century* (Oxford University Press, 1990).

2. Vincent Mosco, *The Political Economy of Communication*, Second Revised Edition (London: SAGE, 2009).

3. See Christopher Ali, *Media Localism: The Politics of Place* (Urbana: University of Illinois Press, 2017).

4. For more on media infrastructures, see Nicole Starosielski, "Warning: Do Not Dig: Negotiating the Visibility of Critical Infrastructures," *Journal of Visual Culture*, 11(1), (2012): 38–57.

5. Michael Apple, *Ideology and Curriculum* (London: Routledge, 2018).

6. Lizabeth Cohen, *Making a New Deal: Industrial Workers in Chicago, 1919–1939* (Cambridge: Cambridge University Press, 1992).

7. Mary Beltran, *Latino TV: A History* (New York: NYU Press, 2022).

8. Aniko Bodroghkozy, *Equal Time: Television and the Civil Rights Movement* (Urbana: University of Illinois Press, 2012).

9. Alain Badoiu, *Being and Event* (London: Bloomsbury, 2013).

10. Antonio Gramsci, *Selections from the Prison Notebooks* (New York: Columbia University Press, 2011).

11. Robert Hudson, "Allerton House 1949, 1950." *Hollywood Quarterly*, Volume V, Number 3 (1951).

12. Janice Peck, "Itinerary of a Thought: Stuart Hall, Cultural Studies, and the Unresolved Problem of the Relation of Culture to "Not Culture," *Cultural Critique*, 48(1), 200–249.

13. Robert Blakely, *To Serve the Public Interest* (Syracuse: Syracuse University Press, 1979).

14. Michael J. Socolow, "Radio's Waves of History: Media Activism and National Radio Network Historiography in the United States," *Journal of Radio and Audio Media* 27, no. 2 (July 2, 2020): 208–33.

15. Report of the Secretary of the Interior, February 15, 1930, Box 358, National Archives I, Washington, DC.

16. John Dewey, *Democracy and Education* (Carbondale: Southern Illinois University Press, 1980).

17. https://wcftr.commarts.wisc.edu/exhibits/radio-pioneers-madison.

18. Tom McCourt, *Conflicting Communication Interests in America: The Case of National Public Radio.* (Westport, CT: Praeger Publishers, 1999); Robert Pepper, *The Formation of the Public Broadcasting Service* (New York: Arno Pres, 1979); Tom Streeter, *Selling the Air: A Critique of the Policy of Commercial Broadcasting in the United States* (Chicago: University of Chicago Press, 1996).

19. Paul Saettler, "Historical Overview of Audio-Visual Communication," *Audio Communication Review*, Vol. 2, No. 2, (1954): 109–17.

20. Caroll Atkinson, *Radio in State and Territorial Education* (Boston: Meador Publishing Company, 1942).

21. Larry Cuban, *Teachers and Machines: The Classroom Use of Technology Since 1920* (Palo Alto: Stanford, 1986).

22. Michael S. Katz, *A History of Compulsory Education Laws* (Bloomington, IN: Phil Delta Kappa, 1976).

23. Emily Raucher, "Educational Expansion and Occupational Change: US Compulsory Schooling Laws and the Occupational Structure 1850–1930," *Social Forces*, Vol. 93, No 4. (2015): 1397–1422.

24. Adriana Lleras-Muney, "Were Compulsory Attendance and Child Labor Laws Effective?" *Journal of Law and Economics*, Vol 45, No 2: 401–35.

25. William Reese, *Power and Promise of School Reform* (New York: Teacher College Press, 1980).

26. See Philip M. Napoli, *Audience Economics: Media Institutions and the Audience Marketplace* (New York: Columbia University Press, 2003)

27. Edward J. Banas, W. Frances Emory, "History and Issues of Distance Learning," *Public Administration Quarterly* Vol. 22, No. 3, (1998): 365–83.

28. See Media History Digital Library (https://mediahistoryproject.org/), and Eric Hoyt, *Ink-Stained Hollywood: The Triumph of American Cinema's Trade Press* (Berkeley: University of California Press, 2022).

29. Herbert Kliebard, *The Struggle for the American Curriculum, 1893–1958,* 2nd edition (New York: Routledge, 1995).

30. First Constitution of ACUBS, 1926. WHS, Box 110.

31. H. Hill, A History of the NAEB. Wisconsin Historical Society.

32. William Reese, *Power and Promise of School Reform* (New York: Teacher College Press, 1980).

33. Once public extensions were created, they also tended to act as sites for democratic exchange in the form of town hall meetings, which Reese describes as "social centers."

34. Internal Correspondence from B. B. Brackett to T. M. Beaird, March 1, 1932, Box 1, National Association of Educational Broadcasters Papers, Wisconsin Historical Society, Madison, WI.

35. Tracy Tyler on the National Committee on Education by Radio, to the National Association of Educational Broadcasters (as Association of College and University Broadcasting Stations). May 24, 1929. Box 1, National Association of Educational Broadcasters Papers, Wisconsin Historical Society, Madison, WI.

36. Ibid.

37. "What Educational Stations are Doing," Box 1, National Association of Educational Broadcasters Papers, Wisconsin Historical Society, Madison, WI.

38. Susan Douglas, Inventing American Broadcasting, 1899–1922. Josh Shepperd, "Radio Pioneers in Madison," Wisconsin Center for Film and Theater Research, 2008.

39. Ibid.

40. NAEB Ledgers, 1925–1930, Box 1, National Association of Educational Broadcasters Papers, Wisconsin Historical Society, Madison, WI.

41. See Edgar Dale Papers, Unprocessed, Box 141–151–6. Ohio State University Archives, Columbus, OH.

42. Alan Stavitsky, "From Pedagogic to Public: The Development of U.S. Public Radio's Audience-Centered Strategies, WOSU, WHA, and WNYC, 1930–1987," dissertation (Columbus: Ohio State University, 1990).

43. R. Higgy on history of Ohio Emergency Radio Junior College, Letter on Sept. 9, 1935. Box 101, National Association of Educational Broadcasters Papers, Wisconsin Historical Society, Madison, WI.

44. Higgy in NAEB Bulletin, March 31, 1931, Box 19, Folder 1931, National Association of Educational Broadcasters Papers, Wisconsin Historical Society, Madison, WI.

45. Higgy to NAEB, Dec. 17, 1931, Box 19, Folder 1931, National Association of Educational Broadcasters Papers, Wisconsin Historical Society, Madison, WI.

46. B. B. Brackett to Ted Beaird, 1931. Box 1, National Association of Educational Broadcasters Papers, Wisconsin Historical Society, Madison, WI.

47. B. B. Brackett internal note to NAEB, Feb 6, 1932. Box 110, National Association of Educational Broadcasters Papers, Wisconsin Historical Society, Madison, WI.

48. F. H. Lumley to NAEB, "The Needs of Educational Broadcasting, 1932, Box

19, National Association of Educational Broadcasters Papers, Wisconsin Historical Society, Madison, WI.

49. NAEB Special Bulletin, Oct 9, 1931, Box 19, National Association of Educational Broadcasters Papers, Wisconsin Historical Society, Madison, WI.

50. Armstrong Perry to NAEB, 1931, Box 101, National Association of Educational Broadcasters Papers, Wisconsin Historical Society, Madison, WI.

51. Ibid.

52. Morse Salisbury, Chief of Radio Service at U.S. Department of Agriculture. "Educational Broadcasting, 1928–1933," Box 19, National Association of Educational Broadcasters Papers, Wisconsin Historical Society, Madison, WI.

53. Ibid.

54. For more on media and liveness, see: Mark Williams, "History in a flash: Notes on the Myth of TV 'Liveness,'" *Collecting Visible Evidence*, Jane Gaines and Michael Renov, eds, Visible Evidence Series, 6, (1999): 292–312.

55. Letter from Bess Goodykoontz, Dec. 17. 1931, Box 19, National Association of Educational Broadcasters Papers, Wisconsin Historical Society, Madison, WI.

56. B. B. Brackett, Letter to Clarence Dill nominating J. C. Jensen to upcoming Federal Commutations Commission, 1931, Box 1, Folder 1931, National Association of Educational Broadcasters Papers, Wisconsin Historical Society, Madison, WI.

57. Josef Wright, internal memo 1931, Box 19, National Association of Educational Broadcasters Papers, Wisconsin Historical Society, Madison, WI.

58. Letter from Tyler to Herman James, 1932, Box 19, National Association of Educational Broadcasters Papers, Wisconsin Historical Society, Madison, WI.

59. Letter from Tyler to Wright, Jan. 9, 1933, Box 19, National Association of Educational Broadcasters Papers, Wisconsin Historical Society, Madison, WI.

60. David Moss and Jonathan Lackow, "Capturing History: The Case of the Federal Radio Commission in 1927," Ch. 8 in *Preventing Regulatory Capture: Special Interest Influence and How to Limit It*, ed. Daniel Carpenter and David Moss (Cambridge: Cambridge University Press, 2019).

61. Payne Fund, record of the committee meeting, December 30, 1930, Box 38, Folder 743, Payne Fund Papers, Western Reserve Historical Society, Cleveland, OH.

62. Levering Tyson to Neville Miller of the NAB, December 10, 1938, Box 104, Folder 4, National Association of Broadcasters Papers, Wisconsin Historical Society, Madison, WI.

63. Joy Elmer Morgan, Memorandum, October 1, 1932, Box 42, Folder 813, Payne Fund Papers, Western Reserve Historical Society, Cleveland, OH.

64. Benjamin Darrow, *Radio the Assistant Teacher* (Columbus: R. G. Adams and Company, 1932).

65. Edgar Dale, report, December 5, 1938, Keith Tyler Papers, Accession 141–151–6. 55, Ohio State University Archives, Columbus, OH.

66. Francis Payne Bolton, letter to Franklin Dunham of RCA, October 29, 1930, Box 69, Folder 1352, Western Reserve Historical Society, Payne Fund Papers.

67. Armstrong Perry, "Organization Set Up," memorandum, November 5, 1930, Box 69, Folder 1352, Payne Fund Papers, Western Reserve Historical Society, Cleveland, OH.

68. National Committee on Education by Radio, "Memorandum Regarding Conference on Radio in Education," November 8, 1930, Box 69, Folder 1352. Western Reserve Historical Society, Payne Fund Papers, Cleveland, OH.

69. Hugh Slotten, *Radio and Television Regulation, 1920–1960* (Baltimore: Johns Hopkins Press, 2000).

70. Levering Tyson to Neville Miller, December 10, 1938, Box 104, Folder 4, National Association of Educational Broadcasters Papers, Wisconsin Historical Society, Madison, WI.

71. Katie Day Good, *Bring the World to the Child: Technologies of Global Citizens in American Education* (Boston: MIT Press, 2020).

72. See Rodney Benson, "Rethinking the Sociology of Media Ownership," in L. Grindstaff, Ming-Cheng M. Lo, and John R. Hall, eds, *Routledge Handbook of Cultural Sociology* (London: Routledge): 387–96.

73. David Goodman, *Radio's Civic Ambition: American Broadcasting and Democracy in the 1930's* (New York: Oxford Press, 2011).

74. Robert Kunzman, David Tyack, "Educational Forums of the 1930s: An experiment in Adult Civic Education," *American Journal of Education*, Vol. 111, No. 3 (May 2005): 320–40.

75. Ibid.

76. John W. Studebaker, *Plain Talk* (Washington, DC: National Home Library Foundation, undated).

77. William Reese, *Power and Promise of School Reform.* (New York: Teacher College, 1980); John W. Powell, *Channels of Learning: The Story of Educational Television* (New York: Public Affairs Press, 1962).

78. John W. Studebaker, "On Managing Meetings for Freedom Forums," (Pamphlet, 1942).

79. Ibid.

80. Josh Shepperd, "Infrastructure in the Air: The Office of Education and the Development of Public Broadcasting in the United States, 1934–1944," *Critical Studies in Media Communication*, Volume 31, Number 3 (2014): 230–43.

81. John W. Studebaker, "Liberalism and Adult Civic Education," *The Annals of the American Academy of Political and Social Science November* (182), (1935): 63–72.

82. John W. Studebaker, *Twentieth Century Educational Approaches in the Use of Communication* (Washington, DC, Office of Education, 1940).

83. Studebaker, "Liberalism and Adult Civic Education."

84. John W. Studebaker, *Classification of Educational Radio Research* (Washington, DC: Report of the Federal Radio Education Committee, 1940).

85. Paul Clifford Pickett, "The Contributions of John Ward Studebaker," doctoral dissertation (Iowa City, 1967).

86. Ibid.

87. John W. Studebaker, *Classification of Educational Radio Research* (Washington, DC: Report of the Federal Radio Education Committee, 1941).

88. See Murendehle M. Juwayeyi, "Congressional Concerns Over Partisanship and a Lack of Professional Independence: Critical Junctures and the Evolution of U.S. Government Information Agencies," *Journalism and Communication Monographs*, 23(3), (2021): 164–233.

89. Armstrong Perry, "Memorandum of Intention," October 24, 1930, Box 69, Folder 1352, Payne Fund Papers, Western Reserve Historical Society, Cleveland, OH.

90. See Michael Keith, *Selling Radio Direct* (Waltham, MA: Focal Press, 1992).

91. Susan Smulyan, *Selling Radio: The Commercialization of American Broadcasting, 1920–1934* (Washington, DC: Smithsonian Institution Press, 1994).

92. Carl Menzer to Harold Ingham, August 1934. Box 1, Folder 1934, National Association of Educational Broadcasters Papers, Wisconsin Historical Society, Madison WI.

93. Willis Phillips to Harold Ingham, September 4, 1934, Box 1, Folder 1934, National Association of Educational Broadcasters Papers, Wisconsin Historical Society, Madison WI.

94. Ibid.

95. Letter from Josef Wright to James H. Hanley at the Federal Radio Commission, August or September 1934, Box 1, Folder 1934, National Association of Educational Broadcasters Papers, Wisconsin Historical Society, Madison WI.

96. Josef Wright, letter to all members, August 15, 1934, Box 1, National Association of Educational Broadcasters Papers, Wisconsin Historical Society, Madison WI.

97. Ibid.

98. B. B. Brackett to J. W. Stafford, August or September 1934, Box 1, Folder 1934, National Association of Educational Broadcasters Papers, Wisconsin Historical Society, Madison WI.

99. Carl Menzer to Harold Ingham, August 1934, Box 1, Folder 1934, National Association of Educational Broadcasters Papers, Wisconsin Historical Society, Madison WI.

100. Ibid.

101. Agenda for Conference on January 8, 1937, Regarding the Future of the FREC, E. O. Sykes, Presiding. Box 359, Folder 3706, Rockefeller Archive Center, Sleepy Hollow, NY.

102. Chris Robé, Todd Wolfson, and Peter N. Funke, "Rewiring the Apparatus: Screen Theory, Media Activism, and Working-Class Subjectivities," *Rethinking Marxism* 28, no. 1 (January 2, 2016): 57–72.

103. See David Haus, *Expertise at War: The National Committee on Education by Radio, the National Association of Broadcasters, the Federal Radio Commission, and the Battle for American Radio*, dissertation (Bowling Green, 2006).

104. Amanda Keeler, "Defining a Medium: The Educational Aspirations for Early Radio," *Journal of Radio and Audio Media* 23, no. 2 (July 2, 2016): 278–87.

105. John Marshall, "The Webster-Case Memorandum on Broadcasting and other related aids to Education," November 9, 1936, Box 360, Folder 3709, Rockefeller Archive Center, Sleepy Hollow.

106. Levering Tyson, "Memorandum of Points Brought Out in First Annual Assembly," NACRE, Meeting May 21, 1931," Box 360, Folder 3709, Rockefeller Archive Center, Sleepy Hollow.

107. Levering Tyson, "A Proposal of the Establishment of a National Council on Radio in Education," Box 360, Folder 3709, Rockefeller Archive Center, Sleepy Hollow.

108. H. W. Chase to Trevor Arnett of Rockefeller Foundation General Education Board, April 2, 1935, Box 358, Folder 3693, Rockefeller Archive Center, Sleepy Hollow.

109. Confidential Internal Report, "Radio in RF and GEB Program: Retrospect and Prospect," June 1937, Box 358, Folder 3693, Rockefeller Archive Center, Sleepy Hollow.

110. Levering Tyson to NAEB, 1933. Untitled and Undated, Box 101, National Association for Educational Broadcasters Papers, Wisconsin Historical Society, Madison, WI.

111. Levering Tyson, "Educational News Bulletin from Western State Teacher's College," October, Volume 6, #1, 1936, Box 101, National Association for Educational Broadcasters Papers, Wisconsin Historical Society, Madison, WI.

112. Levering Tyson, "What is Educational Broadcasting? An Urgent Need," 1936, Box 101, National Association for Educational Broadcasters Papers, Wisconsin Historical Society, Madison, WI.

113. Ibid.

114. See Hilmes, *Network Nations*, 2011

115. Grant Application by David H. Stevens, November 15, 1935, Box 52, Folder 694, Rockefeller Archive Center, Sleepy Hollow.

116. "Americans Aping British Speech Are Chided by London Linguist" Untitled News Clipping form James' Tour, Box 52, Folder 694, Rockefeller Archive Center, Sleepy Hollow.

117. Ibid.

118. Ibid.

119. John Marshall Diaries, Internal Memo on Lloyd James, February 5, 1936, Box 52, Folder 695, Rockefeller Archive Center, Sleepy Hollow.

120. Lloyd James to John Marshall, April 16, 1936, Box 52, Folder 695, Rockefeller Archive Center, Sleepy Hollow.

121. Ibid.

122. John Marshall, personal notes from UK visit, September 3–7, 1936, Box 53, Folder 696, Rockefeller Archive Center, Sleepy Hollow.

123. John Marshall Diaries, Internal Memo, August 31, 1938, Box 5, Folder 50, Rockefeller Archive Center, Sleepy Hollow.

124. Ralph Engelman, *Public Radio and Television in America: A Political History.* (Thousand Oaks: SAGE, 1996.)

125. Tracy Tyler to NAEB, February 18th, 1935, Box 1, Folder 1935, National Association of Educational Broadcasters Papers, Wisconsin Historical Society, Madison, WI.

126. Edgar Dale, untitled history of the Payne Fund, filed December 5, 1938, Keith Tyler Papers, accession 141–151–6, Ohio State University Archives, Columbus, OH.

127. Howard Evans to Gertrude Warren, February 19, 1935, Box 38, Folder 722, Payne Fund Papers, Western Reserve Historical Society, Cleveland, OH.

128. Bob Lochte. "Christian Radio in a New Millennium," *Journal of Radio and Audio Media* 15, no. 1 (May 14, 2008): 59–75; Thomas A Wikle and Jonathan C. Comer, "Translator Networks and the New Geography of Religious Radio," *Journal of Radio and Audio Media* 17, no. 1 (May 6, 2010): 48–62.

129. A. G. Crane, proposal for "Supplemental Broadcasting System," September 9, 1935, Box 101, National Association for Educational Broadcasters Papers, Wisconsin Historical Society, Madison, WI.

130. A. G. Crane to NAEB, "An American Public Broadcasting Service," March 11, 1939, Box 2, National Association for Educational Broadcasters Papers, Wisconsin Historical Society, Madison, WI.

131. Tracy Tyler, letter to NAEB, Feb 18, 1935, Box 1, National Association for Educational Broadcasters Papers, Wisconsin Historical Society, Madison, WI.

132. Proposal for "Supplemental Broadcasting System," September 9, 1935, Box 101, National Association for Educational Broadcasters Papers, Wisconsin Historical Society, Madison, WI.

133. Ibid.

134. A. G. Crane, "Selling Radio to College Authorities," note to NAEB, 1936, Box 101, National Association for Educational Broadcasters Papers, Wisconsin Historical Society, Madison, WI.

135. Crane, "Selling Radio to College Authorities."

136. Burton Wheeler, NCER Notes on Testimony, Box 42, Folder 815, Payne Fund Papers, Western Reserve Historical Society, Cleveland, OH.

137. Howard Evans, "Toward a More Democratic Radio," 1939, Box 2, Folder 4, National Association for Educational Broadcasters Papers, Wisconsin Historical Society, Madison, WI.

138. Preamble to the Constitution of 1934, Box 1, Folder 1934, National Association for Educational Broadcasters Papers, Wisconsin Historical Society, Madison, WI.

139. Editorial from "Radio Guide," September 15, 1934, Box 1, Folder 1934, National Association for Educational Broadcasters Papers, Wisconsin Historical Society, Madison, WI.

140. Ibid.

141. Update from the University of Kentucky, Box 110, National Association for Educational Broadcasters Papers, Wisconsin Historical Society, Madison, WI.

142. University of Washington to NAEB, Box 1, National Association for Educational Broadcasters Papers, Wisconsin Historical Society, Madison, WI.

143. Ibid.

144. Ted Beaird, internal memo to NAEB, Box 1, National Association for Educational Broadcasters Papers, Wisconsin Historical Society, Madison, WI.

145. Harold McCarty to NAEB members, Box 101, National Association for Educational Broadcasters Papers, Wisconsin Historical Society, Madison, WI.

146. Ibid.

147. Minutes from NCER meeting in Washington, Jan. 20–21, 1936, Box 2, National Association for Educational Broadcasters Papers, Wisconsin Historical Society, Madison, WI.

148. Ibid.

149. NCER Pamphlet, "Radio Education through Public and Institutionally Owned Stations," Box 110, National Association for Educational Broadcasters Papers, Wisconsin Historical Society, Madison, WI.

150. W. I. Griffith, internal memo, "Some Radi Nubbins from the State where the Tall Corn Grows," 1936, Box 101, National Association for Educational Broadcasters Papers, Wisconsin Historical Society, Madison, WI.

151. For broader context about documentary production, see Daniel Marcus, "Primary Methods: Non-Fiction," in Michael Kackman and Mary Celeste Kearney, eds., *The Craft of Criticism: Critical Media Studies in Practice* (New York: Routledge: 2018).

152. Ibid.

153. Ibid.

154. Ibid.

155. Ibid., section on "Recommendations."

156. Siepmann, Charles, *Radio's Second Chance* (Boston: Little, Brown, and Company, 1946).

157. Victor Pickard, "The Battle Over the FCC Blue Book: Determining the Role of Broadcast Media in a Democratic Society, 1945–48," *Media, Culture and Society* 33, no. 2 (March 23, 2011): 171–91.

158. Richard Hull to Harold Engel, December 9, 1946, Box 4, Folder, National Association for Educational Broadcasters Papers, Wisconsin Historical Society, Madison, WI.

159. Ibid.

160. Richard Hull to H. P. Constane, August 22, 1946, Box 4, Folder 2, National Association for Educational Broadcasters Papers, Wisconsin Historical Society, Madison, WI.

161. Ibid.

162. Richard Hull to E. W. Ziebarth, January 7, 1948, NAEB Papers, Box 4, Folder 5, National Association for Educational Broadcasters Papers, Wisconsin Historical Society, Madison, WI.

Chapter 2. Funding and Collaboration

1. See Michele Hilmes, *Network Nations.*

2. Eugene Coltrane, Brief Statement of Support of Representative Fulmer's Resolu-

tion for a Stud of Radio Broadcasting, 1933, Box 38, Folder 782, Payne Fund Papers, Western Reserve Historical Society, Cleveland, OH.

3. George Zook, Report on the Conference with the American Council of Education, February 16, 1936, Box 38, Folder 788, Payne Fund Papers, Western Reserve Historical Society, Cleveland, OH.

4. Edgar Dale, untitled history of the Payne Fund, filed December 5, 1938, Accession 141–151–6, Keith Tyler Papers, Ohio State University Archives, Columbus, OH.

5. Joy Elmer Morgan, Memorandum, October 1, 1932, Box 42, Folder 813, Payne Fund Papers, Western Reserve Historical Society, Cleveland, OH.

6. Edgar Dale, untitled history of the Payne Fund, filed December 5, 1938, Accession 141–151–6, Keith Tyler Papers, Ohio State University Archives, Columbus, OH.

7. Brent Malin, "Mediating Emotion: Technology, Social Science, and Emotion in the Payne Fund Motion-Picture Studies," *Technology and Culture*, 50, no. 2 (2009): 366–90.

8. See Lisa Rabin, "A Social History of U.S. Educational Documentary: The Travels of Three Shorts, 1945–1958," *Film History: An International Journal*, 29(3), (2017): 1–24.

9. David Stevens, "Program in the Humanities," 1933, Report, Box 29, General Educational Board, Rockefeller Archive Center, Sleepy Hollow, NY.

10. "New Program in the Humanities," April 10, 1935: D.R. 491, Folder 156, Box 29, Rockefeller Archive Center, Sleepy Hollow, NY.

11. Ibid.

12. "Program in the Humanities," (undated), 1933: D.R. 491, Folder 159, Box 29, Rockefeller Archive Center, Sleepy Hollow, NY.

13. Rachel C. Donaldson, "Teaching Democracy: Folkways Records and Cold War Education," *History of Education Quarterly* 55, no. 1 (January 20, 2015): 58–81; David King Dunaway, "The Conglomeration of Public Radio: A Tale of Three Cities," *Journal of Radio and Audio Media* 21, no. 1 (January 2, 2014): 177–82.

14. Jerome Bourdon and Cecile Meadela, "Ratings as Politics. Television Audience Measurement and the State: An International Comparison." *International Journal of Communication*, June 2015.

15. Craig Kridel and R. V. Bullough, *Stories of the Eight-year Study* (Albany, NY: SUNY Press, 2007).

16. W. W. Charters, Proposal for an Evaluation of Radio Broadcasts for Schools, 1937, Box 5, Werrett Wallace Charters Papers. Ohio State University Archives, Columbus, OH.

17. Ralph Tyler, *Service Studies in Higher Education*, Bureau of Educational Research (Columbus: Ohio State University, 1932).

18. Keith Tyler and Norma Woelfel, *Radio and the School: A Guidebook for Teachers and Administrators* (New York: World Book Company, 1945).

19. Brian C. Gregory, "Educational Radio, Listening Instruction, and the NBC Music Appreciation Hour," *Journal of Radio and Audio Media* 23, no. 2 (July 2, 2016): 288–305.

20. John Marshall, Notes on Meeting with Franklin Dunham of NBC, January 24, 1935, Marshall Diaries, Rockefeller Archive Center, Sleepy Hollow, NY.

21. Letter to David Sarnoff, August 17. 1934, Box 26, Folder 27, NBC Papers.

22. Harry Adams Bellows, Commercial Broadcasting and Education. Box 4, Folder 1, National Broadcasting Company Papers, Wisconsin Historical Society, Madison, WI.

23. See Christopher Terry, "Minority Ownership: An Undeniable Failure of FCC Media Ownership Policy," *Widener Journal of Law, Economics, and Race*, 5, 2013: 18–36.

24. Lee McGuigan, "Procter & Gamble, Mass Media, and the Making of American Life," *Media, Culture and Society* 37, no. 6 (April 29, 2015): 887–903.

25. Internal NBC Brief on the FCC Pursuant to the Communications Act, Box 26, Folder 27, National Broadcasting Company Papers, Wisconsin Historical Society, Madison, WI.

26. Franklin Russell, Internal Memo, July 31, 1934, Box 26, Folder 27, National Broadcasting Company Papers, Wisconsin Historical Society, Madison, WI.

27. Joy Elmer Morgan of the NCER, Letter, October 26, 1934, Box 26, Folder 27, National Broadcasting Company Papers, Wisconsin Historical Society, Madison, WI.

28. Internal NBC Report on FCC Hearings, November 9, 1934, Box 26, Folder 27, National Broadcasting Company Papers, Wisconsin Historical Society, Madison, WI.

29. H. K. Norton, internal memo to NBC reporting on Wagner-Hatfield Amendment proposal, 1933, Box 26, Folder 27, National Broadcasting Company Papers, Wisconsin Historical Society, Madison, WI.

30. Louis G. Caldwell, "Regulation of Broadcasting by the Federal Government," *Variety Radio Directory* (Media History Digital Library, 1937).

31. For more on radio advertising strategy, see Richard K. Popp, "Information, Industrialization, and the Business of Press Clippings, 1880–1925," *Journal of American History*, 101(2), (2014): 427–53.

32. Testimony by Dr. James Francis Cook at Hearing of NBC before Interstate Commerce Commission, October 18, 1934, Box 26, Folder 27, National Broadcasting Company Papers, Wisconsin Historical Society, Madison, WI.

33. Statement by Merlin Aylesworth to FCC, October 5, 1934, Box 19, Folder 64, National Broadcasting Company Papers, Wisconsin Historical Society, Madison, WI.

34. Will Mari, *The American Newsroom: A History, 1920–1960* (Columbia: University of Missouri Press, 2021).

35. For more on early radio and newspapers, see Michael Stamm, *Sound Business: Newspapers, Radio, and the Politics of New Media* (Philadelphia: University of Pennsylvania Press, 2016).

36. Harry Adams Bellows, Commercial Broadcasting and Education. Box 4, Folder 1, National Broadcasting Company Papers, Wisconsin Historical Society, Madison, WI.

37. Internal NBC Brief on the FCC Pursuant to the Communications Act, Box 26, Folder 27, National Broadcasting Company Papers, Wisconsin Historical Society, Madison, WI.

38. Ibid.

39. Ibid.

40. Report of the Federal Communications Commission to Congress *Pursuant* to Section *307* (c) of the Communications Act of 1934, Box 360, Folder 3710, Rockefeller Archive Center, Sleepy Hollow, NY.

41. Ibid.

42. Ibid.

43. David Hamilton, "Patents: a Neglected Source in the History of Education," *History of Education* 38, no. 2 (2009): 303–10.

44. Letter from Allen Miller to David Stevens, March 12, 1935, Box 284, Folder 3394, Rockefeller Archive Center, Sleepy Hollow, NY.

45. Report of the Federal Communications Commission to Congress *Pursuant* to Section *307* (c) of the Communications Act of 1934, Box 360, Folder 3710, Rockefeller Archive Center, Sleepy Hollow, NY.

46. Ibid.

47. Ibid.

48. Letter from E. O. Sykes, FCC Chairman of Broadcast Division, to Raymond D. Fosdick, President of Rockefeller Foundation, December 3, 1936. Box 332, Folder 3950, Rockefeller Archive Center, Sleepy Hollow, NY.

49. Report of the Federal Communications Commission to Congress *Pursuant* to Section *307* (c) of the Communications Act of 1934, Box 360, Folder 3710, Rockefeller Archive Center, Sleepy Hollow, NY.

50. Sykes, undated quote on Educational Broadcasting, Rockefeller Archive Center, Box 358, Folder 3693, Rockefeller Archive Center, Sleepy Hollow, NY.

51. E. O. Sykes, undated quote on Educational Broadcasting, Rockefeller Archive Center, Box 358, Folder 3693 Rockefeller Archive Center, Sleepy Hollow, NY.

52. Report of the Federal Communications Commission to Congress *Pursuant* to Section *307* (c) of the Communications Act of 1934, Box 360, Folder 3710, Rockefeller Archive Center, Sleepy Hollow, NY.

53. Report of the Federal Communications Commission to Congress *Pursuant* to Section *307* (c) of the Communications Act of 1934, Box 360, Folder 3710, Rockefeller Archive Center, Sleepy Hollow, NY.

54. Transcript of Codel Interview with Anning Prall, March 30, 1935, Box 332, Folder 3950, Rockefeller Archive Center, Sleepy Hollow, NY.

55. John Marshall, Diary Entry, December 18, 1936, Box 254, Folder 3035, Rockefeller Archive Center, Sleepy Hollow, NY.

56. George Zook to the Rockefeller Foundation, March 10, 1937, Box 254, Folder 3034, Rockefeller Archive Center, Sleepy Hollow, NY.

57. David Sarnoff, "Broadcasting in the American Democracy," December 12, 1936, Box 254, Folder 3035, Rockefeller Archive Center, Sleepy Hollow, NY.

58. Ibid.

59. A. F. MacLennan, "Transcending borders: reaffirming radio's cultural value in Canada and beyond," *Journal of Radio and Audio Media*, 23(2), (2016): 197–99.

60. Harold Ickes, Department of the Interior, "Readin, Ritin, and Radio," Document filed December 29, 1936, Box 254, Folder 3035, Rockefeller Archive Center, Sleepy Hollow, NY.

61. John Studebaker, "Radio in the Service of Education," Filed December 29. 1936, Box 254, Folder 3035, Rockefeller Archive Center, Sleepy Hollow, NY.

62. William Boutwell, "Increased Radio Activity in Schools Is Seen by Educational Radio Script Exchange," June 16, 1937, Box 332, Folder 3951, Rockefeller Archive Center, Sleepy Hollow, NY.

63. E. O. Sykes and John Studebaker to Raymond Fosdick, December 3, 1936, Box 332, Folder 3950, Rockefeller Archive Center, Sleepy Hollow, NY.

64. Ibid.

65. John Studebaker to Stacy May, October 3, 1936, Box 332, Folder 3950, Rockefeller Archive Center, Sleepy Hollow, NY.

66. Ibid.

67. Grant-in-Aid, Rockefeller Foundation to Federal Radio Education Committee, October 22, 1936, Box 332, Folder 3950, Rockefeller Archive Center, Sleepy Hollow, NY.

68. John Marshall, Diary Notes, Filed December 18. 1936, Box 254, Folder 3034, Rockefeller Archive Center, Sleepy Hollow, NY.

69. Neil Verma, *Theater of the Mind: Imagination, Aesthetics, and American Radio Drama* (Chicago: University of Chicago Press, 2012).

70. Bret Gary, *Nervous Liberals* (New York: Columbia University, 1999).

71. Hilmes, 2011.

72. Rockefeller Archive Center, http://www.rockarch.org/publications/resrep/buxton.pdf.

73. Rockefeller Archive Center, http://www.rockarch.org/publications/resrep/tobias.pdf.

74. John Marshall, Notes on Second Conference, June 10, 1937, Box 254, Folder 3035, Rockefeller Archive Center, Sleepy Hollow, NY.

75. John Marshall, internal memo, filed March 24, 1937, Box 332, Folder 3951, Rockefeller Archive Center, Sleepy Hollow, NY.

76. David Stevens, "The Humanities in Theory and in Practice," March 31, 1937, D.R. 491, Folder 158, Box 29, Rockefeller Archive Center, Sleepy Hollow, NY.

77. Ibid.

78. Program in the Humanities.

79. For more on recorded sound equipment and policy, see Alex Sayf Cummings, *Democracy of Sound: Music Piracy and the Remaking of American Copyright in the Twentieth Century* (New York: Oxford University Press, 2013).

80. Geo Wiley, "Radio in Education: Recommendations Relative to Experiments in Radio Education," October 4, 1934, Box 360, Folder 3710, Rockefeller Archive Center, Sleepy Hollow, NY.

81. Geo Wiley, "Report Committee on Radio Education" undated, packaged with 1934 report, Box 360, Folder 3710, Rockefeller Archive Center, Sleepy Hollow, NY.

82. Ibid.

83. Ibid.

84. David Stevens, "Radio in the Schools," Internal Memo, November 30, 1934, Box 358, Folder 3693, Rockefeller Archive Center, Sleepy Hollow, NY.

85. Ibid.

86. For acoustic design see Emily Thompson, *The Soundscape of Modernity: Architectural Acoustics and the Culture of Listening in America, 1900–1933* (Boston: MIT Press, 2004); Jonathan Sterne, *The Audible Past: Cultural Origins of Sound Reproduction* (Durham: Duke University Press, 2003).

87. Rockefeller Foundation Trustees Meeting, "Radio" and "Broadcasting in the Public Interest," April 10, 1935, Box 2, Folder 11, Rockefeller Archive Center, Sleepy Hollow, NY.

88. Ibid; also see Ted Striphas, *The Late Age of Print* (New York: Columbia University Press, 2009).

89. Elena Razlogova, *The Listener's Voice: Early Radio and the American Public*, (Philadelphia: University of Pennsylvania Press, 2011).

90. See Smulyan, *Selling Radio*.

91. Shawn Vancour, *The Sounds of Radio: Aesthetic Formations of 1920s American Broadcasting*, doctorial dissertaion (Madison: University of Wisconsin-Madison, 2008); Alexander Todd Russo, "Roots of Radio's Rebirth: Audiences, Aesthetics, Economics, and Technologies of American Broadcasting, 1926–1951," dissertation (Providence: Brown University, 2004); Michael Socolow, "To Network a Nation: N.B.C., C.B.S., and the Development of National Network Radio in the United States, 1925–1950," dissertation (Washington, DC: Georgetown University, 2001).

92. Mark Ethridge, Our Mutual Responsibilities, Testimony for the FCC, May 16, 1938, Box 1, Folder 1, National Association of Broadcasters Papers, Wisconsin Historical Society, Madison, WI.

93. Mark Ethridge and John Hogan, Report at NAB, Box 1, Folder 1, National Association of Broadcasters Papers, Wisconsin Historical Society, Madison, WI.

94. "The Work of the Federal Radio Education Committee," October 22, 1936, Box 332, Folder 3950, Rockefeller Archive Center, Sleepy Hollow, NY.

95. John Marshall on the Federal Radio Education Committee, January 12, 1937, Box 332, Folder 3951, Rockefeller Archive Center, Sleepy Hollow, NY.

96. "The Work of the Federal Radio Education Committee," October 22, 1936, Box 332, Folder 3950, Rockefeller Archive Center, Sleepy Hollow, NY.

97. Wm. D. Boutwell to John Studebaker, "What the Office of Education Can Do," October 3, 1936, Box 332, Folder 3950, Rockefeller Archive Center, Sleepy Hollow, NY.

98. Ibid.

Chapter 3. Distribution and Facilities

1. See Clifford J. Doerkson, *American Babel: Rogue Radio Broadcasters of the Jazz Age* (Philadelphia: University of Pennsylvania Press, 2005).

2. Joy Elizabeth Hayes, "White Noise: Performing the White, Middle-Class Family on 1930s Radio," *Cinema Journal* 51, no. 3 (2012): 97–118.

3. For an important tool unpacking records connected to sound industries, see Douglas Gomery, *The Coming of Sound* (London: Routledge, 2004).

4. See Wick Rowland, *Challenges to Public Service Broadcasting* (Berlin: Aspen Institute, 1986).

5. See Hayes and Goodman, 2022

6. Amanda Keeler, "A Certain Stigma of Educational Radio: Judith Waller and 'Public Service' Broadcasting," *Critical Studies in Media Communication* 34, no. 5 (October 15, 2017): 495–508; for more on NBC and gendered administrative practices also see Catherine Martin, "In their Own Little Corner: The Gendered Sidelining of NBC's Information Department," *Journal of Radio and Audio Media*, 26(1), 2019: 88–103.

7. Judith Waller, *Radio, the Fifth Estate* (New York: Houghton Mifflin, 1946).

8. Judith Waller and Franklin Dunham, Interdepartmental Correspondence, October 27, 1934, Box 26, Folder 27, National Broadcasting Company Papers, Wisconsin Historical Society, Madison, WI.

9. John Royal with Judith Waller, Internal NBC Education Mission Statement, November 3, 1936, Box 36, Folder 37, National Broadcasting Company Papers, Wisconsin Historical Society, Madison, WI.

10. Ibid.

11. For more on the history of public media hosts, see: Lisa Napoli, Susan, Linda, Nina, and Cokie: The Extraordinary Story of the Founding Mothers of NPR (NYC: Abrams Press, 2021).

12. John Royal and James Angell, Internal Memo, November 12, 1938, Box 93, National Broadcasting Company Papers, Wisconsin Historical Society, Madison, WI.

13. Ibid.

14. Ibid.

15. For more on radio transcriptions, see Claudia Calhoun, "When the Stars Aligned: Radio and Histories of Media Convergence," *Journal of Radio and Audio Media*, 26(1), 2019: 147–52.

16. B. B. Brackett to Harold McCarty, July 3, 1936, Box 2, Folder 1, National Association of Educational Broadcasters Papers, Wisconsin Historical Society, Madison, WI.

17. John Marshall, Notes on Conversation with Keith Tyler on the Bureau of Educational Research at Ohio State University, March 2, 1937, Marshall Diaries, Rockefeller Archive Center, Sleepy Hollow, NY.

18. See Sherman Dorn and C. Ydesen, "Toward a Comparative and International History of School Testing and Accountability," Educational Policy Analysis Archives, 22(115), (2014)

19. John Marshall, Notes on Menzer's 'Discouraging Conditions' at the University of Iowa, June 1, 1937, Marshall Diaries, Rockefeller Archive Center, Sleepy Hollow, NY.

20. Carl Menzer, NAEB Official Correspondence, March 23, 1925, Box 2, National

Association of Educational Broadcasters Papers, Wisconsin Historical Society, Madison, WI.

21. Carl Menzer to Harold McCarty, December 3, 1936, Box 2, Folder 1, National Association of Educational Broadcasters Papers, Wisconsin Historical Society, Madison, WI.

22. Josef Wright to Carl Menzer, Harold McCarty, and W. I. Griffith, October 1937, Box 2, Folder 3, National Association of Educational Broadcasters Papers, Wisconsin Historical Society, Madison, WI.

23. James Ebel to Carl Menzer, September 1937, Box 2, Folder 2, National Association of Educational Broadcasters Papers, Wisconsin Historical Society, Madison, WI.

24. For more on radio regionalism, see Bala James Baptiste, *Race and Radio: Pioneering Black Broadcasters* (Jackson: University of Mississippi Press, 2019).

25. Gilbert Williams to Carl Menzer, April 19, 1938, Box 2, National Association of Educational Broadcasters Papers, Wisconsin Historical Society, Madison, WI.

26. For more on program transcription and MBS, see Alex Russo, *Roots of Radio's Rebirth.*

27. Carl Menzer, internal memo, "Report of Tests Conducted at Station WSUI on Recording Equipment," 1936, Box 2, Folder 1, National Association of Educational Broadcasters Papers, Wisconsin Historical Society, Madison, WI.

28. Ibid.

29. NAEB Release, March 27, 1937, Box 2, National Association of Educational Broadcasters Papers, Wisconsin Historical Society, Madison, WI.

30. Internal notes on 1937 *Variety* article, Box 2, Folder 2, National Association of Educational Broadcasters Papers, Wisconsin Historical Society, Madison, WI.

31. NAEB Newsletter, March 20, 1937, National Association of Educational Broadcasters Papers, Wisconsin Historical Society, Madison, WI.

32. Minutes from March National Conference on Educational Broadcasting, Document filed December 1936, Box 2, Folder 1, National Association of Educational Broadcasters Papers, Wisconsin Historical Society, Madison, WI.

33. Reported in letter with NCER, September 1935, Box 2, Folder 1, National Association of Educational Broadcasters Papers, Wisconsin Historical Society, Madison, WI.

34. For a description about what's at stake with radio archival clearing housework, see David Seubert, "Preserving Radio Broadcasts: Thoughts on Future Directions," *Journal of Archival Organization,* 17(1–2), 2020: 13–18.

35. Studebaker to NAEB, 1936, Box 19, National Association of Educational Broadcasters Papers, Wisconsin Historical Society, Madison, WI.

36. Frank Schooley, List of past duties as Secretary of NAEB, 1938, Box 2, Folder 3, National Association of Educational Broadcasters Papers, Wisconsin Historical Society, Madison, WI.

37. John W. Studebaker, *Report of the Radio Committee to the National Association of State Universities* (Washington, DC: Pamphlet, 1936).

38. John W. Studebaker, *The Federal Radio Education Committee* (Washington, DC: Pamphlet, 1936).

39. Schooley to Kirwin at FREC, undated 1940, Princeton Radio Research Project, Federal Radio Education Committee Papers, Princeton University Libraries, Princeton, New Jersey.

40. Studebaker to FCC Commissioner Fly, undated 1944, Princeton Radio Research Project, Federal Radio Education Committee Papers, Princeton University Libraries, Princeton, New Jersey.

41. John W. Studebaker, FREC pamphlet.

42. Ibid.

43. Ibid.

44. Pickett, 1967 dissertation.

45. See David Goodman and Joy Hayes, *New Deal Radio: The Educational Radio Project* (New Brunswick: Rutgers University Press, 2022).

46. John W. Studebaker, *The Educational Radio Project of the Office of Education* (Washington, DC: Pamphlet, 1937); Barbara Savage, *Broadcasting Freedom: Radio, War and Politics of Race, 1938–1948* (Chapel Hill: University of North Carolina Press, 1999).

47. See Goodman and Hayes, 2022; Pickett, 1967 dissertation.

48. Ibid.

49. John Studebaker, "Report of Progress of Federal Radio Education Committee," Address given at Second National Conference on Educational Broadcasting, November 30, 1937, Box 359, Folder 370, Rockefeller Archive Center, Sleepy Hollow, NY.

50. Ibid.

51. Office of Education Report to Department of the Interior, "Local Government Radio Script Series," Report filed August 4, 1937, Box 254, Folder 3036, Rockefeller Archive Center, Sleepy Hollow, NY.

52. Savage, *Broadcasting Freedom*.

53. Studebaker, Educational radio project.

54. John Marshall to David Stevens, September 15, 1936, Box 53, Folder 696, Rockefeller Archive Center, Sleepy Hollow, NY.

55. John Marshall, minutes from lunch with Hilda Mathieson, September 10, 1936, Box 53, Folder 696, Rockefeller Archive Center, Sleepy Hollow, NY.

56. Ibid.

57. John Marshall, telephone conversation minutes with Felix Greene, March 8, 1937, Box 53, Folder 697, Rockefeller Archive Center, Sleepy Hollow, NY.

58. Marshall to B. E. Nicholls, February 10, 1937, Box 53, Folder 697, Rockefeller Archive Center, Sleepy Hollow, NY.

59. Ibid.

60. "Revised Schedule for Mr. Siepmann's Visits to Regional Broadcasting Stations," Filed April 2, 1937, Box 53, Folder 699, Rockefeller Archive Center, Sleepy Hollow, NY.

61. Charles Siepmann, personal handwritten notes, April 1-June 9, 1937, Box 53, Folder 701, Rockefeller Archive Center, Sleepy Hollow, NY.

62. Siepmann personal notes, Review of Iowa.

63. Siepmann personal notes, Review of Iowa.

64. Siepmann personal notes, Review of Iowa.

65. Charles Siepmann, personal handwritten notes, April 1-June 9, 1937, Review of Wisconsin, Box 53, Folder 701, Rockefeller Archive Center, Sleepy Hollow, NY.

66. Ibid.

67. Charles Siepmann review of Ohio State, Filed June 14, 1937, Box 53, Folder 701, Rockefeller Archive Center, Sleepy Hollow, NY.

68. Ibid.

69. Siepmann personal notes, Review of Illinois.

70. Siepmann personal notes, Review of NBC-California.

71. Ibid.

72. Charles Siepmann, "Radio at Universities in the United States of America: A Report to the Trustees of the Rockefeller Foundation," 60-page collection of multiple documents: evaluations, recommendations based upon his tour, and declarations of approach to educational radio, 1937, Box 53, Folder 701, Rockefeller Archive Center, Sleepy Hollow, NY.

73. Ibid.

74. Ibid.

75. Siepmann, "Radio at Universities."

76. John Marshall, Inter-office Correspondence to General Education Board on Charles Siepmann's Report, December 16, 1937, Accession 2771, Box 397, Rockefeller Archive Center, Sleepy Holly, NY.

77. Ibid.

78. Siepmann, "Radio at Universities."

79. Ibid.

80. Joseph Wright's description of the *Pursuant*, internal memo, 1934, Box 1, National Association of Educational Broadcasters Papers, Wisconsin Historical Society, Madison, WI.

81. Grant-in-Aid Application, University Broadcast Council, June 21, 1935, Folder 3394, Box 284, Rockefeller Archive Center, Sleepy Hollow, NY.

82. Ibid.

83. John Marshall, Internal Memo, June 21, 1935, Box 284, Folder 3394, Rockefeller Archive Center, Sleepy Hollow, NY.

84. Allen Miller, "The Problem of Educational Broadcasting and a Plan for Its Solution," April 8, 1935: Folder 3394, Box 284, Rockefeller Archive Center, Sleepy Hollow, NY.

85. Also see Josh Shepperd, "Rockefeller Underwriting of Local, Regional, and National Broadcasting Experiments, 1934–1940," https://www.issuelab.org/resources/28023/28023.pdf.

86. Ibid.

87. Ibid.

88. Grant-in-Aid Application, University Broadcasting Council, June 21, 1935, Folder 3394, Box 284, Rockefeller Archive Center, Sleepy Hollow, NY.

89. Ibid.

90. First Annual Report of the University Broadcasting Council, "A Year's Experiment in Cooperation," July 1, 1936, Box 284, Folder 3394, Rockefeller Archive Center, Sleepy Hollow, NY.

91. Ibid.

92. "Resume of the Broadcasting Activities of Chicago, DePaul, and Northwestern Universities with Special Consideration of the Achievement of the University Broadcasting Council," February 1938, Box 285, Folder 3398, Rockefeller Archive Center, Sleepy Hollow, NY.

93. Interview with Levering Tyson by John Marshall for RF, April 22, 1935, Box 284, Folder 3395, Rockefeller Archive Center, Sleepy Hollow, NY.

94. Ibid.

95. See Mike Conway, *Contested Ground: 'The Tunnel' and the Struggle over Television News in Cold War America* (Amherst: University of Massachusetts Press, 2019).

96. Letter from Miller to Marshall, July 22, 1937, Folder 3397, Box 285, Rockefeller Archive Center, Sleepy Hollow, NY.

97. Letter from Miller to Marshall, August 21, 1936, Folder 3395, Box 285, Rockefeller Archive Center, Sleepy Hollow, NY.

98. Allen Miller to John Marshall, July 15, 1936, Folder 3395, Box 285, Rockefeller Archive Center, Sleepy Hollow, NY.

99. "Entertainment in Erudition? UBC Proves It," Larry Wolters, *Chicago Tribune*, February 28, 1937, Box 285, Folder 3397, Rockefeller Archive Center, Sleepy Hollow, NY; also see Noah Arceneaux, "The Wireless Press and the Great War: An Intersection of Print and Electronic Media, 1924–1921," *Journal of Radio and Audio Media*, 26(2), 2019: 318–35.

100. Charles Siepmann, "University Broadcasting Council," April 19, 1937 Report, Box 285, Folder 3396, Rockefeller Archive Center, Sleepy Hollow, NY.

101. Miller to Marshall, April 28th, 1937, Folder 3397, Box 285, Rockefeller Archive Center, Sleepy Hollow, NY.

102. Ibid.

103. Miller to Marshall, April 30, 1937, Box 285, Folder 3397, Rockefeller Archive Center, Sleepy Hollow, NY.

104. Miller to Marshall, July 22, 1937, Box 285, Folder 3397, Rockefeller Archive Center, Sleepy Hollow, NY.

105. Ibid.

106. John Marshall Diaries, Interview with William Benton, December 29, 1937, Folder 3397, Box 285, Rockefeller Archive Center, Sleepy Hollow, NY.

107. John Marshal, internal memo about conversation with William Benton, December 29, 1937, Box 285, Folder 3397, Rockefeller Archive Center, Sleepy Hollow, NY.

108. Ibid.

109. Letter from William Benton to John Marshall, February 16, 1938, Folder 3398, Box 285, Rockefeller Archive Center, Sleepy Hollow, NY.

110. John Marshall to Robert Hutchins, February 18, 1938, Box 285, Folder 3398, Rockefeller Archive Center, Sleepy Hollow, NY.

111. John Marshall Assessment of the UBC Project, March 1941, Box 285, Folder 3403, Rockefeller Archive Center, Sleepy Hollow, NY.

112. A. G. Crane, Preliminary Prospectus for a Rocky Mountain Public Radio Service, April 29, 1937, Box 279, Folder Folder 3320, Rockefeller Archive Center, Sleepy Hollow, NY.

113. John Marshall Diaries, interview with A. G. Crane. April 13. 1937, Box 277, Folder 3307, Rockefeller Archive Center, Sleepy Hollow, NY.

114. John Marshall Diaries on A.G. Crane, April 13, 1937, Box 277, Folder 3307, Rockefeller Archive Center, Sleepy Hollow, NY.

115. Rocky Mountain Radio Council, "A Need Discovered," undated, probably 1939 or 1940. Box 278, Rockefeller Archive Center, Sleepy Hollow, NY.

116. Charles Siepmann's review of RMRC, Filed June 14, 1937, Box 53, Folder 701, Rockefeller Archive Center, Sleepy Hollow, NY.

117. John Marshall Diaries, from a conversation with Crane at the Institute on Education by Radio, Columbus, May 3–5, 1937, Box 277, Folder 3307, Rockefeller Archive Center, Sleepy Hollow, NY.

118. Ibid.

119. Ibid.

120. A. G. Crane to John Marshall, February 1, 1938, Box 277, Folder 3307, Rockefeller Archive Center, Sleepy Hollow, NY.

121. A. G. Crane to John Marshall, August 13, 1938. RF, Box 277, Folder 3307, Rockefeller Archive Center, Sleepy Hollow, NY.

122. Crane to Guy Ford at University of Minnesota, March 1938, Box 2, Folder 2, National Association of Educational Broadcasters, Wisconsin Historical Society, Madison WI.

123. Ibid.

124. Crane to Ford.

125. Crane to Marshall, August 20, 1938, Box 277, Folder 3308, Rockefeller Archive Center, Sleepy Hollow, NY.

126. Rocky Mountain Radio Council, "A Preliminary Plan for Broadcasting Service to the Schools of the Colorado-Wyoming Region," September 21, 1938, Box 277, Folder 3308, Rockefeller Archive Center, Sleepy Hollow, NY.

127. Ibid.

128. Rocky Mountain Radio Council, "Rocky Mountain Radio Project: A Plan for Cooperative, Regional, Broadcasting in Public Interest," July 22, 1939, Box 278, Folder 3310, Rockefeller Archive Center, Sleepy Hollow, NY.

129. Rocky Mountain Radio Council, "Program Preparatory to Opening of Rocky Mountain Public Radio Program," May 22, 1939, Box 277, Folder 3308, Rockefeller Archive Center, Sleepy Hollow, NY.

130. Rocky Mountain Radio Council, "Rocky Mountain Radio Project: A Plan for Cooperative, Regional, Broadcasting in Public Interest," July 22, 1939, Box 277, Folder8, Rockefeller Archive Center, Sleepy Hollow, NY.

131. Ibid.

132. A. G. Crane to John Marshall, May 22, 1939, Box 277, Folder 3308, Rockefeller Archive Center, Sleepy Hollow, NY.

133. A. G. Crane to John Marshall, July 22, 1939, Box 278, Folder 3310, Rockefeller Archive Center, Sleepy Hollow, NY.

134. Robert Hudson to John Marshall, July 25, 1939, Box 278, Folder 3310, Rockefeller Archive Center, Sleepy Hollow, NY.

135. John Marshall Diaries, September 15, 1939, Box 278, Folder 3310, Rockefeller Archive Center, Sleepy Hollow, NY.

136. Paul Lazarsfeld to John Marshall, February 26, 1940, Box 277, Folder 3307, Rockefeller Archive Center, Sleepy Hollow, NY.

137. Robert Hudson to John Marshall, March 4, 1940, Box 278, Folder 3311, Rockefeller Archive Center, Sleepy Hollow, NY.

138. Heidi Tworek, "The Savior of the Nation? Regulating Radio in the Interwar Period," *Journal of Policy History*, Vol. 27(3), (2015): 465–91.

139. A. G. Crane to John Marshall, September 25, 1939, Box 278, Folder 3311, Rockefeller Archive Center, Sleepy Hollow, NY.

140. Rocky Mountain Radio Council, "First Four Months of Operations, November 1, 1939-February 29, 1940, Box 278, Folder 3312, Rockefeller Archive Center, Sleepy Hollow, NY.

141. A. G. Crane to John Marshall, July 22, 1939, Box 277, Folder 3308, Rockefeller Archive Center, Sleepy Hollow, NY.

142. John Marshal Diaries, November 20, 1937, Box 360, Folder 3712, Rockefeller Archive Center, Sleepy Hollow, NY.

143. Reported in April 1941 Application for Renewal Funds, Box 278, Folder 3315, Rockefeller Archive Center, Sleepy Hollow, NY.

144. Ibid.

145. Harold Lasswell, "An Architectural Symbol for America," April 23, 1941, Box 1554, NC-148 Record Group 208, Entry 294, U.S. National Archives OWI Papers, College Park, MD.

146. James R. Schiffman, "Undervaluing Mutual: The FCC's Missed Opportunity to Restructure Radio Broadcasting in the New Deal Era," *Journal of Radio and Audio Media* 24, no. 2 (September 22, 2017): 302–19.

147. See James Baughman, *Television's Guardians: The FCC and the Politics of Programming, 1958-1967* (Knoxville: University of Tennessee Press, 1985).

148. Richard Hull, 1949 Update to NAEB, Box 5, Folder 1, National Association of Educational Broadcasters Papers, Wisconsin Historical Society, Madison, WI.

149. John Marshall in personal diaries, Barclay Leathem's Letter, June 21, 1949, Box 5, Folder 51, Rockefeller Archive Center, Sleepy Hollow, NY.

150. Ibid.

151. George Stoddard to John Marshall, March 30, 1949, Box 5, Folder 51, Rockefeller Archive Center, Sleepy Hollow, NY.

152. John Marshall to Wilbur Schramm, March 11, 1949, Box 5, Folder 51, Rockefeller Archive Center, Sleepy Hollow, NY.

153. For more see Janet Wasko, "The Study of the Political Economy of the Media in the Twenty-First Century," *International Journal of Media and Cultural Politics*, 10(3), 2014: 259–71.

154. Wilbur Schramm Bio, Box 8, 1948 (Box 1,2,3), Rockefeller Archive Center, Box 4, Folder 23, Rockefeller Archive Center, Sleepy Hollow, NY.

155. Wilbur Schramm to John Marshall, March 16, 1949, Rockefeller Archive Center, Box 4, Folder 23, Rockefeller Archive Center, Sleepy Hollow, NY.

156. Letter from Wilbur Schramm to John Marshall, March 16, 1949, Box 4, Folder 23, Rockefeller Archive Center, Sleepy Hollow, NY.

157. Ibid.

158. Grant in Aid to the University of Illinois, April 11, 1949, Box 4, Folder 23, Rockefeller Archive Center, Sleepy Hollow, NY.

159. Letter from Wilbur Schramm to John Marshall, March 16, 1949, Box 4, Folder 23, Rockefeller Archive Center, Sleepy Hollow, NY.

160. Seminar Remarks by Paul Lazarsfeld, July 2, 1949, Box 5, Folder 3, National Association of Educational Broadcasters Papers, Wisconsin Historical Society, Madison, WI.

161. Ibid, Remarks by Charles Siepmann; John Marshall, June 28–29 notes.

162. Ibid.

163. Richard Hull to Wilbur Schramm, July 14, 1949, Box 4, Folder 23, Rockefeller Archive Center, Sleepy Hollow, NY.

164. Irving Merrill to Wilbur Schramm, July 23, 1949, Box 5, Folder 1, National Association of Educational Broadcasters Papers, Wisconsin Historical Society, Madison, WI.

165. Probst (roundtable) to Schramm, July 15, 1949, Box 5, Folder 1, National Association of Educational Broadcasters Papers, Wisconsin Historical Society, Madison, WI.

166. Wilbur Schramm to John Marshall, November 4, 1949, Box 4, Folder 23, Rockefeller Archive Center, Sleepy Hollow, NY.

167. John Marshall, Internal Notes, October 24, 1949, Box 5, Folder 51, Rockefeller Archive Center, Sleepy Hollow, NY.

168. Ibid.

169. John Marshall, Internal Diaries, August 24, 1949, Box 5, Folder 51, Rockefeller Archive Center, Sleepy Hollow, NY.

170. John Marshall to Lily Endowment, October 26, 1949, Box 5, Folder 51, Rockefeller Archive Center, Sleepy Hollow, NY.

171. Ibid.

172. Radio Programming in Colleges and Universities, 1950, Box 4, Folder 24, Rockefeller Archive Center, Sleepy Hollow, NY.

173. Ibid.

174. Wilbur Schramm to John Marshall, February 3, 1950, Box 4, Folder 23, Rockefeller Archive Center, Sleepy Hollow, NY.

175. "Proposal for a Second Allerton Seminar for Non-Commercial Broadcasters," March 18, 1950, Box 4, Folder, Rockefeller Archive Center, Sleepy Hollow, NY.

176. Ibid.

177. Ibid.

178. Wilbur Schramm to John Marshall, November 4, 1949, Box 4, Folder 23, Rockefeller Archive Center, Sleepy Hollow, NY.

179. John Marshall, "Possible Program in Radio," January 9, 1950, Box 5, Folder 51, Rockefeller Archive Center, Sleepy Hollow, NY.

180. Richard Hull to Lincoln Foundation, October 10, 1949, Box 5, Folder 5, National Association of Educational Broadcasters Papers, Wisconsin Historical Society, Madison, WI.

181. Ibid.

182. Allerton House, "Public Affairs in Radio," July 15, 1950, Box 5, Folder 3, National Association of Educational Broadcasters Papers, Wisconsin Historical Society, Madison, WI.

183. Lee De Forest, November 4, 1949, Box 5, Folder 5, National Association of Educational Broadcasters Papers, Wisconsin Historical Society, Madison, WI; For more on Lee De Forest, see Mike Adams, *Lee De Forest: King of Radio, Television, and Film*, (Copernicus Press, 2011).

184. Dallas Smythe to NAEB, November 4, 1949, Box 5, Folder 5, National Association of Educational Broadcasters Papers, Wisconsin Historical Society, Madison, WI.

185. NAEB, "Radio Programming in Colleges and Universities: 'Future Basis for Research,'" undated, 1949, Box 5, Folder 5, National Association of Educational Broadcasters Papers, Wisconsin Historical Society, Madison, WI.

186. February 3, 1950: Schramm to Marshall, Box 5, Folder 3, National Association of Educational Broadcasters Papers, Wisconsin Historical Society, Madison, WI.

187. Ibid.

188. Wilbur Schramm, "A Second Allerton Seminar for Non-Commercial Broadcasters," March 17, 1950, Box 5, Folder 3, National Association of Educational Broadcasters Papers, Wisconsin Historical Society, Madison, WI.

189. John Marshall to Wilbur Schramm, February 5, 1950, Box 4, Folder 23, Rockefeller Archive Center, Sleepy Hollow, NY. Also see Balas, Glenda. "Eavesdropping at Allerton: The Recovery of Paul Lazarsfeld's Progressive Critique of Educational Broadcasting." *Democratic Communique* 24, 2011.

190. Wilbur Schramm to John Marshall, March 17, 1950, Box 4, Folder 23, Rockefeller Archive Center, Sleepy Hollow, NY.

191. Allison L. Rowland and Peter Simonson. "The Founding Mothers of Communication Research: Toward a History of a Gendered Assemblage," *Critical Studies in Media Communication* 31, no. 1 (January 11, 2013): 3–26.

192. Robert Hudson to Chester I. Barnard, President of the Rockefeller Foundation, Box 4, Folder 23, Rockefeller Archive Center, Sleepy Hollow, NY.

193. David Hendy, "Radio's Cultural Turns," *Cinema Journal* 48, no. 1 (2008): 130–38.

194. Robert Hudson, "Allerton House 1949, 1950," *Hollywood Quarterly*, Volume V, Number 3 (1951).

195. See Colin Burnett, *The Invention of Robert Bresson: The Auteur and his Market* (Bloomington: Indiana University Press, 2017) for a fascinating account of the relationship between aesthetic production and critical reception.

196. Co-written by 23 NAEB members, "Educational Broadcasting: Its Aims and Responsibilities," Box 4, Folder 23, Rockefeller Archive Center, Sleepy Hollow, NY.

197. Ibid.

198. Ibid.

199. Hudson, "Allerton House 1949, 1950."

200. "Educational Broadcasting: Its Aims and Responsibilities."

201. Ibid.

202. Robert Hudson, August 1, 1950, Box 6, National Association of Educational Broadcasters Papers, Wisconsin Historical Society, Madison, WI.

203. Richard Hull to Judith Waller, August 26, 1950, Box 6, National Association of Educational Broadcasters Papers, Wisconsin Historical Society, Madison, WI.

204. Seymour Siegel letter, July 27, 1950, Box 6, National Association of Educational Broadcasters Papers, Wisconsin Historical Society, Madison, WI.

205. John Cabbe to Richard Hull, July 21, 1950, Box 6, National Association of Educational Broadcasters Papers, Wisconsin Historical Society, Madison, WI.

206. Richard Hull, July 28, 1950, "NAEB network and Allerton House Meeting," NAEB Files, Box 6, National Association of Educational Broadcasters Papers, Wisconsin Historical Society, Madison, WI.

207. Richard Rider to UNESCO, February 15, 1951, Box 6, National Association of Educational Broadcasters Papers, Wisconsin Historical Society, Madison, WI.

208. Richard Rider Internal memo to Arthur Wildhagen, February 28, 1951: "officially known as NAEB Tape Network." NAEB Files, Box 6, National Association of Educational Broadcasters Papers, Wisconsin Historical Society, Madison, WI.

209. Letter from Allen Miller, August 28, 1950, now at KWSC, Pullman Washington. NAEB Files, Box 6, National Association of Educational Broadcasters Papers, Wisconsin Historical Society, Madison, WI.

210. https://current.org/2017/09/under-two-visionary-directors-new-yorks-wnyc-became-an-incubator-of-pubmedia-innovation.

211. Cynthia B Meyers, "From Radio Adman to Radio Reformer: Senator William Benton's Career in Broadcasting, 1930–1960," *Journal of Radio and Audio Media* 16, no. 1 (May 6, 2009): 17–29; also see Ira Wagman, "Locating UNESCO in Histories of Communication Study," in The *International History of Communication Study*, ed. by Peter Simonson and David Park (Routledge, 2015).

212. See Andy Lanset, *WNYC Director Seymour N. Siegel: Public Radio Visionary*, 2012, https://www.wnyc.org/story/184376-wnyc-director-seymour-n-siegel/.

213. Paul Walker to Dallas Smythe, Feb. 19, 1952, NAEB Papers, Box 6, National Association of Educational Broadcasters Papers, Wisconsin Historical Society, Madison, WI.

214. Richard Hull, "The University and Radio Education," August 22, 1949, Box 5, Folder 4, National Association of Educational Broadcasters Papers, Wisconsin Historical Society, Madison, WI.

215. Kate Moylan, *The Cultural Work of Community Radio* (London: Rowman and Littlefield, 2019).

216. Paddy Scannell and David Cardiff, *A Social History of British Broadcasting* (Oxford: Oxford University Press, 1991); Jamie Medhurst, *Early Years of Television and the BBC* (Edinburgh: Edinburgh University Press, 2022); David Hendy, *The BBC: A Century on the Air* (London: Public Affairs, 2022).

Chapter 4. The Emergence of Communication Studies

1. John Marshall, Note about meeting at Ohio State, May 3–5, 1937, Marshall Diaries, Sleepy Hollow, NY.

2. John Marshall, February 20, 1936, January 2nd to August 21, 1936, Marshall Diaries, Rockefeller Archive Center, Sleepy Hollow, NY.

3. John Marshall, April 24, 1936, January 2nd to August 21, 1936, Marshall Diaries, Rockefeller Archive Center, Sleepy Hollow, NY.

4. John Marshall Interview with Hadley Cantril, May 15, 1936, January 2nd to August 21, 1936, Marshall Diaries, Rockefeller Archive Center, Sleepy Hollow, NY.

5. W. Towers, "Lazarsfeld and Adorno in the States: A case study in Theoretical Orientations," *Annals of the International Communication Association*, 1(1), (1977): 133–45.

6. John Marshall Interview with Edward R. Murrow, September 10, 1936, January 2nd to August 21, 1936, Marshall Diaries, Rockefeller Archive Center, Sleepy Hollow, NY.

7. See Dorothy Ross, *The Origins of American Social Science* (Cambridge: Cambridge University Press, 1990).

8. John Marshall Interview with Philip Cohen at NYU Radio Workshop, August 20th and 21st, 1936. Marshall Diaries, Rockefeller Archive Center, Sleepy Hollow, NY.

9. John Marshall, Minutes for Annual Institute for Education by Radio at Ohio State University, May 4–6, 1936, January 2nd to August 21, 1936, Marshall Diaries, Rockefeller Archive Center, Sleepy Hollow, NY.

10. John Studebaker, Radio in the Service of Education, December 10, 1936, speech, Box 254, Folder 3034, Rockefeller Archive Center, Sleepy Hollow, NY.

11. Ibid.

12. "Evaluation of School Broadcasts: Proposal for an Extension of the Evaluation

of School Broadcasts Project," 1939, Box 361, Folder 3719, Rockefeller Archive Center, Sleepy Hollow, NY.

13. Ibid.

14. John Marshall Diaries, "Reporting on the University Bureau of Radio Research," Document filed March 10, 1938, Box 226, Folder 2163, Rockefeller Archive Center, Sleepy Hollow, NY. See also Day Good, Katie. "Radio's Forgotten Visuals," *Journal of Radio and Audio Media* 23, no. 2 (July 2, 2016): 364–68.

15. Allison Perlman, "Television Up in the Air: The Midwest Program on Airborne Television Instruction, 1959–1971," *Critical Studies in Media Communication* 27, no. 5 (2010): 477–97.

16. John Marshall Diaries, internal note, March 15, 1937, Box 361, Folder 3719, Rockefeller Archive Center, Sleepy Hollow, NY.

17. Keith Tyler, "Proposal for an Evaluation of Radio Broadcasts for Schools," Filed March 25, 1937, Box 360, Folder 3716, Rockefeller Archive Center, Sleepy Hollow, NY.

18. Ibid.

19. Ibid.

20. Keith Tyler, "Illustrations of Kinds of Evidence Which Seem to be Appropriate in Connection with a Sampling of the More Important Objectives of Some School Broadcasts," undated, 1937, Box 360, Folder 3716, Rockefeller Archive Center, Sleepy Hollow, NY.

21. John Marshall, Notes from January 19, 1935, Meeting, Marshall Diaries, January 2nd to August 21, 1936, Rockefeller Archive Center, Sleepy Hollow, NY.

22. Keith Tyler, "Evaluation of School Broadcasts, Ohio State University," Box 360, Folder 3716, Rockefeller Archive Center, Sleepy Hollow, NY.

23. Ibid.

24. "Report of the Reviewing Committee: Ohio State University Radio Evaluation," undated, 1937 or 1938, Box 360, Folder 3718, Rockefeller Archive Center, Sleepy Hollow, NY.

25. "Brief Progress Report: Evaluation of School Broadcasts, a Study Sponsored by the Federal Radio Education Committee of the Federal Communications Committee," November 29, 1938, Box 360, Folder 3718, Rockefeller Archive Center, Sleepy Hollow, NY.

26. "Confidential Dictionary of Objectives for Selected Broadcasts," March 21, 1939, Box 360, Folder 3718, Rockefeller Archive Center, Sleepy Hollow, NY.

27. Ibid.

28. "Some Possible Findings of Present Research Studies," April 18, 1939, internal document, Box 361, Folder 3719, Rockefeller Archive Center, Sleepy Hollow, NY.

29. Ibid.

30. Jack Mitchell, *Wisconsin on the Air* (Madison: Wisconsin Historical Society Press, 2017).

31. Hugh Slotten, *Radio's Hidden Voice: The Origins of Public Broadcasting in the United States* (Urbana: University of Illinois Press, 2009).

32. See Timothy Shaffer, "Democracy in the Air: Radio as a Complement to Face-to-Face Discussion in the New Deal," *Journal of Radio and Audio Media*, 26(1): 21–34.

33. John Marshall Diaries, Conversation with Harold McCarty and Harold Engel, April 24, 1936, Box 362, Folder 3736, Rockefeller Archive Center, Sleepy Hollow, NY.

34. Ibid.

35. Ibid.

36. The Radio Committee of the University of Wisconsin, "Outline for a Research Project in School Broadcasting," Box 362, Folder 3735, Rockefeller Archive Center, Sleepy Hollow, NY.

37. Jennifer Hyland Wang, "Did They Say What They Thought? Gender, Sound, and Oral History in a Wisconsin Women's Radio Program," *Journal of Radio and Audio Media*, 26:1 (2019): 63–74.

38. For more on how commercial broadcasters perfected this approach, see Ross Melnick, *American Showman: Samuel "Roxy" Rothafel and the birth of the Entertainment Industry, 1908–1935* (New York: Columbia University Press, 2014).

39. Ibid.

40. University of Wisconsin Radio Committee, "Preliminary Survey of Fields of Inquiry in Establishing a University Program of Instruction by Radio," March 16, 1938, Box 363, Rockefeller Archive Center, Sleepy Hollow, NY.

41. The Radio Committee of the University of Wisconsin, "Outline for a Research Project..."

42. John Marshall interview with Harold McCarty, October 9, 1936, Box 362, Folder 3736, Rockefeller Archive Center, Sleepy Hollow, NY.

43. "Experimental Procedure in Educational Evaluation," undated, Box 362, Folder 3736, Rockefeller Archive Center, Sleepy Hollow, NY.

44. State Radio Council of Wisconsin, "Statement of Policy Relative to the Use of the Radio Broadcasting Channels Licensed to Agencies of the State," December 6, 1938, Box 363, Rockefeller Archive Center, Sleepy Hollow, NY.

45. Ibid.

46. Ibid.

47. Wisconsin State Radio Council, "Report of the Committee on School Broadcasting," September 13, 1940, Box 363, Rockefeller Archive Center, Sleepy Hollow, NY.

48. John Marshall, "History and Educational Results of the Wisconsin Research Project in School Broadcasting," May 25, 1942, Accession 751, Box 362, Rockefeller Archive Center, Sleepy Hollow, NY.

49. Report of the Committee of Six, March 12, 1937, Box 332, Folder 3951, Rockefeller Archive Center, Sleepy Hollow, NY.

50. Inter-Office Report of Federal Radio Education Committee, January 12, 1937, Box 332, Folder 3952, Rockefeller Archive Center, Sleepy Hollow, NY.

51. Ibid.

52. John Studebaker, "Report of Progress of Federal Radio Education Committee," November 30, 1937, Box 359, Folder 3705, Rockefeller Archive Center, Sleepy Hollow, NY.

53. Hadley Cantril on Project 15, October 15, 1936, Box 359, Folder 3706, Rockefeller Archive Center, Sleepy Hollow, NY.

54. "Project I (Old Project No. 15)," Internal RF Report, March 12, 1937, Box 332, Folder 3951, Rockefeller Archive Center, Sleepy Hollow, NY.

55. "The Work of the Federal Radio Education Committee," undated 1936, Box 332, Folder 3952, Rockefeller Archive Center, Sleepy Hollow, NY.

56. Hadley Cantril, Invitation to Frank Stanton, Undated. Frank Stanton Papers, Box 20, Folder 11, Stanton-Lazarsfeld Program Analyzer, 1937–1945. Washington, DC: Library of Congress.

57. Inter-Office Correspondence, Studebaker Office, FREC, Jan. 12, 1937, Box 332, Folder 3952, Rockefeller Archive Center, Sleepy Hollow, NY.

58. John Marshall, letter to Rockefeller Foundation Trustees, May 24, 1937, Box 271, Folder 3234, Rockefeller Archive Center, Sleepy Hollow, NY.

59. See Brian Kane, "Phenomenology, Physiognomy, and the 'Radio Voice,'" *New German Critique*, 129 (43.3) (November 2016): 91–112.

60. Ibid.

61. Ibid.

62. Hadley Cantril and Gordon Allport, *The Psychology of Radio* (New York: Harper and Brothers, 1936).

63. John Marshall, "First impressions from reading projects," Feb. 8, 1937, Box 271, Folder 3234, Rockefeller Archive Center, Sleepy Hollow, NY.

64. Ibid.

65. Hadley Cantril, "A Preliminary Study to Devise a Method for Ascertaining the Effectiveness and the Effects of Radio Programs of a Broad Cultural Nature," Undated, 1936, Box 271, Folder 3233, Rockefeller Archive Center, Sleepy Hollow, NY.

66. Ibid.

67. Unsigned, but likely Frank Stanton, Hadley Cantril, or Paul Lazarsfeld, "What the Industry Knows," Internal Document, April 26, 1937, Box 271, Folder 3234, Rockefeller Archive Center, Sleepy Hollow, NY.

68. Ibid.

69. Hadley Cantril, "A Preliminary Study to Devise a Method for Ascertaining the Effectiveness and the Effects of Radio Programs of a Broad Cultural Nature."

70. Hadley Cantril, Internal note, May 1937, Box 271, Folder 3234, Rockefeller Archive Center, Sleepy Hollow, NY.

71. Hadley Cantril, "Revised Prospectus of Original Project II in the Report of the Sub-Committee on Conflicts and Cooperation," Box 359, Folder 3706, Rockefeller Archive Center, Sleepy Hollow, NY.

72. Hadley Cantril, "Work Accomplished," March 7, 1939, Box 271, Folder 3240, Rockefeller Archive Center, Sleepy Hollow, NY.

73. Unsigned, "What the Industry Knows."

74. Hadley Cantril, "Radio in the Elementary School, A Psychological Analysis and Interpretation," May 15, 1936, Box 271, Folder 3233, Rockefeller Archive Center, Sleepy Hollow, NY.

75. Ibid.

76. Jefferson Pooley and Michael Socolow, "Checking up on *The Invasion from Mars*: Hadley Cantril, Paul F. Lazarsfeld, and the making of a misremembered classic," *International Journal of Communication,* 7, (2013).

77. Hadley Cantril, "Radio," May 1937, Box 271, Folder 3233, Rockefeller Archive Center, Sleepy Hollow, NY.

78. Princeton Radio Project document prepared by Lazarsfeld, November 7, 1938, Box 271, Folder 3236, Rockefeller Archive Center, Sleepy Hollow, NY.

79. Hadley Cantril (1936). Invitation to Frank Stanton.

80. See Michael Socolow, "The Behaviorist in the Boardroom: The Research of Frank Stanton, Ph.D," *Journal of Broadcasting and Electronic Media,* 52(4), (2008): 526–43.

81. Frank Stanton, "Listener Research Techniques (Confidential)," November 1938, Revised July 1939, Box 271, Folder 3241, Rockefeller Archive Center, Sleepy Hollow, NY.

82. Cantril, May 11, 1937 letter.

83. Stanton report.

84. Ibid.

85. Application for renewal of PRRP, September 1941, Box 273, Folder 3253, Rockefeller Archive Center, Sleepy Hollow, NY.

86. Paul Lazarsfeld to Cantril and Stanton, copied to Marshall, Memorandum, "From Technical to Social Knowledge," January 15, 1938, Box 222, Folder 2660, Rockefeller Archive Center, Sleepy Hollow, NY.

87. Application for more funds (7th issued grant application, 1941), in project description history, Box 222, Folder 2664, Rockefeller Archive Center, Sleepy Hollow, NY.

88. Ibid.

89. Paul Lazarsfeld, "Princeton Radio Research Project, Outline of Presentation," found in a series of 1939 letters to John Marshall on project development, Box 271, Folder 3237, Rockefeller Archive Center, Sleepy Hollow, NY.

90. "Project I (Old Project No. 15)," undated, 1937, Box 271, Folder 3234, Rockefeller Archive Center, Sleepy Hollow, NY.

91. Hynek Jerabek, "Paul Lazarsfeld-The Founder of Modern Empirical Sociology: A Research Biography," *International Journal of Public Opinion Research*, 13(3), (2001); David E. Morrison, "Kultur and Culture: The Case of Theodor W. Adorno and Paul F. Lazarsfeld," *Social Research*, 45(2), (1978): 331–55.

92. Paul Lazarsfeld, "On the Use of Elaborate Personal Interviews for the Princeton Radio Research Project," August 1936, Box 271, Folder 3234, Rockefeller Archive Center, Sleepy Hollow, NY.

93. Ibid.

94. Paul Lazarsfeld, "Propositions Regarding the Problems and Findings of the Princeton Radio Research Project," March 10, 1939, Box 271, Folder 3240, Rockefeller Archive Center, Sleepy Hollow, NY.

95. Document by PRRP members, "Research in Mass Communication for Private Circulation Only," July 1940, Box 271, Folder 3243, Rockefeller Archive Center, Sleepy Hollow, NY.

96. Peter Simonson, Junya Morooka, Bingjuan Xiong, and Nathan Bedsole, "The Beginnings of Mass Communication: A Transnational History," *Journal of Communication*, 69, (2019): 513–38; Herman S. Hettinger, "Forward to Radio: The Fifth Estate," *Annals of the American Academy of Political and Social Science* (1935): 177.

97. PRRP Staff, "What Research Can do For Educational Broadcasting," September 17, 1940, Box 222, Folder 2662, Rockefeller Archive Center, Sleepy Hollow, NY.

98. Ibid.

99. Ibid.

100. "Summary of Discussion of Communications Seminar," March 15, 1940, Box 224, Folder 2679, Rockefeller Archive Center, Sleepy Hollow, NY.

101. Geoffrey Gorer, "Confidential First Volume of the Report of the Work done by the Princeton Radio Project," June 7, 1939, Box 224, Folder 2678, Rockefeller Archive Center, Sleepy Hollow, NY.

102. Paul Lazarsfeld, "Notes on Audience Research," 1940, Box 224, Folder 2678, Rockefeller Archive Center, Sleepy Hollow, NY.

103. Paul Lazarsfeld to John Marshall, September 18, 1939, Box 224, Folder 2674, Rockefeller Archive Center, Sleepy Hollow, NY.

104. Cantril, "Propositions Regarding the Problems and Findings of the Princeton Radio Research Project," Internal memo, March 10, 1939, Box 271, Folder 3240, Rockefeller Archive Center, Sleepy Hollow, NY.

105. Ibid.

106. Ibid.

107. Cantril, "Propositions Regarding the Problems and Findings of the Princeton Radio Research Project," Internal memo, March 10, 1939, Box 271, Folder 3240, Rockefeller Archive Center, Sleepy Hollow, NY.

108. Ibid.

109. Ibid., section titled "Propositions on the conception of 'EFFECT.'"

110. Ibid.

111. Hadley Cantril, "Report on *War of the Worlds*," Box, 252, Folder 3236, Rockefeller Archive Center, Sleepy Hollow, NY.

112. Ibid.

113. Ibid.

114. Jefferson Pooley and Michael Socolow, "Checking up on The Invasion from Mars."

115. See James N. Gilmore and Sidney Gottlieb, eds, *Orson Welles in Focus: Texts and Contexts* (Bloomington: Indiana University Press, 2018).

116. Letter from Toledo, Ohio. RG 173, FCC Office of the Executive Director General Correspondence, 1927–1946, FCC Records, National Archives, Washington, DC.

117. Ibid.

118. For more on audience response, see Jonathan Gray, "Antifandom and the

Moral Text: Television without Pity and Textual Dislike," *American Behavioral Scientist*, 48(7), 2005: 840–58.

119. Pooley and Socolow, "Checking up on The Invasion from Mars."

120. David Morrison, *Paul Lazarsfeld: The Biography of an Institutional Innovator* (Leicester: University of Leicester Press, 1976). David Jenemann, *Adorno in America* (Minneapolis, University of Minnesota Press, 2007).

121. See Jenemann, 2009

122. http://www.rockarch.org/publications/resrep/tobias.pdf.

123. I've written more about context of Adorno's invitation: Josh Shepperd, "Theodor Adorno, Paul Lazarsfeld, and the Public Interest Mandate of Early Communications Research, 1935–1941," *Communication Theory*, 32(1), February 2022: 142–60.

124. Lazarsfeld to Marshall on Adorno, undated, Folder 3241, Box 252, Rockefeller Archive Center, Sleepy Hollow, NY.

125. Ibid.

126. Cantril, "Inadequacy of Information as Furnished by the Newspaper, the Radio, and the Movies," Internal Memo to John Marshall, Box 273, Folder 3245, Rockefeller Archive Center, Sleepy Hollow, NY.

127. Cantril to Marshall, May 11, 1937, Box 271, Folder 3233, Rockefeller Archive Center, Sleepy Hollow, NY.

128. Paul Lazarsfeld, philosophy of the project to "The Committee of Six," November 7, 1938, Box 271, Folder 3236, Rockefeller Archive Center, Sleepy Hollow, NY.

129. Lazarsfeld, internal memo, May 1941, Box 222, Folder 2664, Rockefeller Archive Center, Sleepy Hollow, NY.

130. See David Jenemann, *Adorno in America* (Minneapolis, University of Minnesota Press, 2007).

131. Paul Lazarsfeld to John Marshall, December 27, 1939, Box 222, Folder 2661, Rockefeller Archive Center, Sleepy Hollow, NY.

132. Ibid.

133. Ibid.

134. Also see Shawn VanCour, "Educating Tomorrow's Media Workers: Television Instruction at American Institutions of Higher Learning, 1945–1960," *Critical Studies in Media Communication* 33, no. 2 (March 14, 2016): 195–209.

135. Ibid.

136. See Martin Jay, *Adorno* (Cambridge: Harvard University Press, 1984); Fredric Jameson, *Late Marxism: Adorno, Or, The Persistence of the Dialectic* (New York: Verso, 2007).

137. Ibid.

138. Geoffrey Gorer, Review of Adorno's Paper, January 2, 1940, Box 271, Folder 3243, Rockefeller Archive Center, Sleepy Hollow, NY.

139. Ibid.

140. John Marshall, internal memo, January 5, 1940, Box 222, Folder 2661, Rockefeller Archive Center, Sleepy Hollow, NY.

141. Charles Siepmann to John Marshall, December 12, 1940, Box 222, Folder 2661, Rockefeller Archive Center, Sleepy Hollow, NY.

142. Paul Lazarsfeld to John Marshall, "Suggested Panel Study," January 15, 1940, Box 222, Folder 2661, Rockefeller Archive Center, Sleepy Hollow, NY.

143. Ibid.

144. Paul Lazarsfeld to John Marshall, September 23, 1940. RAC, Box 222, Folder 2661. Rockefeller Archive Center, Sleepy Hollow, NY.

145. PRRP Staff, "What Research Can do For Educational Broadcasting," September 17, 1940, Box 222, Folder 2662, Rockefeller Archive Center, Sleepy Hollow, NY.

146. Ibid.

147. See Brett Gary, *Nervous Liberals: Propaganda Anxieties from WWI to the Cold War* (New York: Columbia University Press, 1999).

148. G. Gorer, Letter to John Marshall on Adorno, January 20, 1940, Box 271, Folder 3243, Rockefeller Archive Center, Sleepy Hollow, NY.

149. Robert Lynd, Application for Renewal of Grant for Office of Radio Research, 1940 or 1941 (undated), Columbia University: The Need for Fundamental Radio Research. Box 222, Folder 2662, Rockefeller Archive Center, Sleepy Hollow, NY.

150. "Research in Mass Communication."

151. Ibid.

152. See Victor Pickard, "Communication's Forgotten Narratives: The Lost History of Charles Siepmann and Critical Policy Research," *Critical Studies in Media Communication*, 33(4), 2016: 337–51.

153. Charles Siepmann to John Marshall, February 1, 1939, Folder 50, Box 2, Accession 246–247, Rockefeller Archive Center, Sleepy Hollow, NY.

154. HM Beville and Cuthbert Daniel, under Lazarsfeld, "Classification of Educational Radio Research," February 27, 1941, Box 222, Folder 2660, Rockefeller Archive Center, Sleepy Hollow, NY.

155. See Jefferson Pooley, "Wilbur Schramm and the 'Four Founders' History of U.S. Communication Research," *Communications. Media. Design.*, 2(4), (2017); Wilbur Schramm, *The Beginnings of Communication Study in America: A Personal Memoir* (Thousand Oaks: Sage, 1997).

156. Wilbur Schramm, "Plan for the Institute of Communications Research," 1947, Box 3, Institute for Communications Research Papers. University of Illinois Libraries, Champaign-Urbana, Illinois

157. Ibid.

158. Ibid.

159. Wilbur Schramm, "Project for a College Press Campaign for Victory," Office for Emergency Management Office Memorandum, February 25, 1942, NC-148, Entry E-93, Box 596, U.S. National Archives OWI Papers, Washington, DC.

160. Wilbur Schramm, *The Impact of Educational Television* (Urbana: University of Illinois Press, 1960).

161. Institute for Communications Research Plan.

162. Ibid.

163. Paul Lazarsfeld, "Problems Facing a New Communications Research," January 19, 1948, Box 3, Institute of Communications Research Papers, University of Illinois Libraries, Urbana, Illinois.

164. John Nerone, "To Rescue Journalism from the Media." *Cultural Studies* 23, no. 2 (March 30, 2009): 243–58.

165. W. Wilbur Schramm, (ed.), *Mass communications* (Urbana: University of Illinois Press, 1949).

166. Wilbur Schramm, "Information Theory and Mass Communication," 1953 document, Box 3, Institute of Communications Research Papers, University of Illinois Libraries, Urbana-Champaign, Illinois.

167. FREC Report, "Revised Prospectus of Original Project II in the Report of the Sub-Committee on Conflicts and Coordination," undated but probably 1936, Box 332, Folder 3951, Rockefeller Archive Center, Sleepy Hollow, NY.

168. Hadley Cantril to John Marshall, December 31, 1936, Box 271, Folder, 3233, Rockefeller Archive Center, Sleepy Hollow, NY.

Chapter 5. Policy

1. Allison Perlman, "Television Up in the Air: The Midwest Program on Airborne Television Instruction, 1959–1971," *Critical Studies in Media Communication* 27, no. 5 (July 28, 2010): 477–97.

2. See Susan Murray's important book for more on television regulation and technical development: Susan Murray, *Bright Signals: A History of Color Television* (Durham: Duke University Press, 2018).

3. Victor Pickard, *America's Battle for Media Democracy: The Triumph of Corporate Libertarianism and the Future of Media Reform* (Cambridge: Cambridge University Press, 2014).

4. Franklin Dunham to Frank Schooley, March 28, 1946, Box 4, Folder 1, National Association of Educational Broadcasters Papers, Wisconsin Historical Society, Madison, WI.

5. Victor Pickard, "Media Activism from Above and Below: Lessons from the 1940s American Reform Movement," *Journal of Information Policy* 5 (2015): 109–28.

6. T. J. Slowie Report before FCC, "Promulgation of Rules and Regulations for the Non-Commercial Educational FM Broadcast Service," May 28, 1946, Correspondence, Box 4, Folder 2, National Association of Educational Broadcasters Papers, Wisconsin Historical Society, Madison, WI.

7. Ibid.

8. Ibid.

9. FCC Order 7424, June 27, 1945, Box 4, Folder 1, National Association of Educational Broadcasters Papers, Wisconsin Historical Society, Madison, WI.

10. Ibid., "Rules Relating to Equipment."

11. Ibid., "Broadcasting Administrative Procedure."

12. Allerton House Conference Schedule, Participant Descriptions, August 1, 1949, Box 265, Folder 4, Rockefeller Archive Center, Sleepy Hollow, NY.

13. Ralph Steetle to Richard Hull regarding internal NAEB policy, September 8, 1947, Box 4, Folder 2, National Association of Educational Broadcasters Papers, Wisconsin Historical Society, Madison, WI.

14. *Variety* Magazine, March 12, 1947, National Association of Educational Broadcasters Papers, Wisconsin Historical Society, Madison, WI.

15. Ibid.

16. See Victor Pickard, "The Air Belongs to the People: The Rise and Fall of a Postwar Radio Reform Movement," *Critical Studies in Media Communication*, 30(4), (2013): 307–26.

17. Richard Hull to Maurice Novik, February 1948, Box 4, Folder 3, National Association of Educational Broadcasters Papers, Wisconsin Historical Society, Madison, WI.

18. Ibid.

19. Richard Hull to T. J. Slowie, February 28, 1948, Box 4, Folder 5, National Association of Educational Broadcasters Papers, Wisconsin Historical Society, Madison, WI.

20. Richard Hull to Charles Tobey. March 13, 1948, Box 4, Folder 5, National Association of Educational Broadcasters Papers, Wisconsin Historical Society, Madison, WI.

21. Richard Hull to NAEB, March 13, 1948, Box 4, Folder 5, National Association of Educational Broadcasters Papers, Wisconsin Historical Society, Madison, WI.

22. Richard Hull to NAEB, March 15, 1948, Box 4, Folder, National Association of Educational Broadcasters Papers, Wisconsin Historical Society, Madison, WI.

23. Ibid.

24. Ibid.

25. Charles Siepmann, *Radio in Wartime* (Kent, England: Hassel Street Press, 2021).

26. National Association of Educational Broadcasters, "The State of Non-Commercial Broadcasting in the U.S.," undated 1948, Box 4, Folder 5, National Association of Educational Broadcasters Papers, Wisconsin Historical Society, Madison, WI.

27. Ibid.

28. Ibid.

29. Ibid.

30. Richard Hull, Internal Memo, May 1, 1948, Box 4, National Association of Educational Broadcasters Papers, Wisconsin Historical Society, Madison, WI.

31. Carl Kaestle and Maris Vinovkis, "The Federal Role in Elementary and Secondary Education, 1940–1980," *Harvard Education Review*, Vol 52, No. 4. (Nov. 1982).

32. See E. A. Krug, *The Shaping of the American High School, Volume 2* (Madison: University of Wisconsin Press, 1972).

33. Chris M. Herbst, "Universal Child Care, Maternal Employment, Children's

Long-Run Outcomes, Evidence from the U.S. Lanham Act of 1940," *IZA Discussion Papers*, No. 7896, Institute for the Study of Labor, Bonn.

34. Richard Hull to Alvin Gaines, Regarding Coy's remarks to Hull, September 7, 1948, Box 4, Folder 8, National Association of Educational Broadcasters Papers, Wisconsin Historical Society, Madison, WI.

35. Report of the Committee on Radio, Association of Land-Grant Colleges and Universities, October 1949. Box 5, Folder 5, National Association of Educational Broadcasters Papers, Wisconsin Historical Society, Madison, WI.

36. Testimony of Office of Education, July 8, 1949, Box 32, Committee for Interstate and Foreign Commerce Papers, National Archives 1, Washington, DC.

37. Dallas Smythe to Edwin Johnson: "A National Policy on Television?," May 5, 1950, Box 36, Committee for Interstate and Foreign Commerce Papers, National Archives 1, Washington, DC.

38. Richard Hull to Edwin Johnson, September 23, 1949, Box 32, Committee for Interstate and Foreign Commerce Papers, National Archives 1, Washington, DC.

39. Edwin Johnson to Keith Tyler, April 1950, Box 34b, Committee for Interstate and Foreign Commerce Papers, National Archives 1, Washington, DC.

40. Dallas Smythe to Edwin Johnson: "A National Policy on Television?," May 5, 1950, Box 36, Committee for Interstate and Foreign Commerce Papers, National Archives 1, Washington, DC.

41. Ibid.

42. Ibid.

43. Report of the Committee on Radio, "Television Hearings are Education's Last Chance," Association of Land-Grant Colleges and Universities, October 1949, box 5, Folder 5, National Association of Educational Broadcasters Papers, Wisconsin Historical Society, Madison, WI. Also See Murray, 2018.

44. Benjamin Cottone, Talk at NAEB Annual Meeting, October 12, 1948, Box 4, Folder 6, National Association of Educational Broadcasters Papers, Wisconsin Historical Society, Madison, WI.

45. Ibid.

46. Ibid.

47. Susan Brinson, *Personal and Public Interests: Frieda B. Hennock and the Federal Communications Commission* (Los Angeles: Praeger, 2001).

48. Freida Hennock, Feb 28, 1951, in *Variety*, Box 43, Committee for Interstate and Foreign Commerce Papers, National Archives 1, Washington, DC.

49. See Jane Leftwich Curry, "Polish Regime Countermeasures against Radio Free Europe," in *Cold War Broadcasting: Impact on the Soviet Union and Eastern Europe*, ed. by A. Ross Johnson and R. Eugene Parta (New York: Central European University Press, 2010).

50. Internal FCC Records on Bill 1378, March 1, 1951. NARA1, CIFC, Box 35b.

51. FCC Proposed Rule Making Hearing, March 21, 1951, NARA1, CIFC, Box 38.

52. Wayne Coy, "Views on Educational Broadcasting" by FCC Members at Hear-

ing, 1951, Box 38, Committee for Interstate and Foreign Commerce Papers, National Archives 1, Washington, DC.

53. Frieda Hennock, "Views on Educational Broadcasting" by FCC Members at Hearing, 1951, Box 38, Committee for Interstate and Foreign Commerce Papers, National Archives 1, Washington, DC.

54. Ibid.

55. See A. J. Bauer, "Propaganda in the Guise of News: Fulton Lewis Jr. and the Origins of the Fairness Doctrine," *Radical History Review*, 141, (2021): 7–29.

56. FCC Public Notice, March 22, 1951: "FCC Proposes Partial Lifting of TV Freeze," Box 38, Committee for Interstate and Foreign Commerce Papers, National Archives 1, Washington, DC.

57. "Freeze to End, 2000 New Stations to 1400 communities," *New York Times,* March 23, 1951, Box 38, Committee for Interstate and Foreign Commerce Papers, National Archives 1, Washington, DC.

58. Letter from Dallas Smythe to Edwin Johnson, 1950, Box 35b, Committee for Interstate and Foreign Commerce Papers, National Archives 1, Washington, DC.

59. Edwin Johnson and William Benton to *Variety* in 1951, "Self Regulation vs Government Interference," Box 36, Committee for Interstate and Foreign Commerce Papers, National Archives 1, Washington, DC.

60. For more on the legacy of commercial regulation, see Jennifer Holt, *Empires of Entertainment: Media Industries and the politics of Deregulation, 1980–1996* (New Brunswick: Rutgers University Press, 2011).

61. William Benton, Resolution (S RES 127), May 21, 1951, Box 35b, Committee for Interstate and Foreign Commerce Papers, National Archives 1, Washington, DC.

62. Johnson on Educational Broadcasting, Internal Memo, Box 35b, Committee for Interstate and Foreign Commerce Papers, National Archives 1, Washington, DC.

63. Ibid.

64. Edwin Johnson, filed Jun 21, 1951, Box 37, Committee for Interstate and Foreign Commerce Papers, National Archives 1, Washington, DC.

65. "Educational Television Survey Report," June 11, 1951, Box 43, Committee for Interstate and Foreign Commerce Papers, National Archives 1, Washington, DC.

66. Ibid.

67. Ibid.

68. Ibid.

69. FCC Release, July 23, 1951, Box 38, Committee for Interstate and Foreign Commerce Papers, National Archives 1, Washington, DC.

70. William Boddy, "'Thrills Sweep Like Electric Currents through Multitudes': Spectacle, Sociality, and Media Competition in Mid-Century America," *Historical Journal of Film, Radio and Television* (February 17, 2021): 1–24.

71. Max Goldman as General Acting Counsel, July 23, 1951, Box 37, Committee for Interstate and Foreign Commerce Papers, National Archives 1, Washington, DC.

72. Sixth Report and Order, Box 37, Committee for Interstate and Foreign Commerce Papers, National Archives 1, Washington, DC.

73. TJ Slowie, June 26, 1952, Box 37, Committee for Interstate and Foreign Commerce Papers, National Archives 1, Washington, DC.

74. July 16, 1951, report in "Broadcasting," Box 45, Committee for Interstate and Foreign Commerce Papers, National Archives 1, Washington, DC.

75. Edwin Johnson, 1952, Box 45, Committee for Interstate and Foreign Commerce Papers, National Archives 1, Washington, DC.

76. Victor Pickard, "The Air Belongs to the People: The Rise and Fall of a Postwar Radio Reform Movement," *Critical Studies in Media Communication* 30, no. 4 (October 15, 2013): 307–26.

77. See Caroline Jack, "Producing Milton Freidman's Free to Choose: How Libertarian Ideology Became Broadcasting Balance," *Journal of Broadcasting and Electronic Media*, 62(3): 514–30.

78. Congressional Record, S7037, May 17, 1967, Box 1. Dean Coston Papers, University of Maryland, College Park, MD.

79. Alanson Willcox, General Council, Department of Health, Education, and Welfare, Memorandum on May 3, 1967. Box 1, Dean Coston Papers, University of Maryland, College Park, MD.

80. Senator Warren Magnuson, Subcommittee on Educational Television, Oct 28, 1966. Box 2, Dean Coston Papers, University of Maryland, College Park, MD.

81. Wayne Urban, *More Than Science and Sputnik: The National Defense of Education Act of 1958* (Tuscaloosa: University of Alabama Press, 2010).

82. Senate Committee Attitude and the Educational Television Facilities Act (P.L. 87–447), June 30, 1967, Box 1, Dean Coston Papers, University of Maryland, College Park, MD.

83. "USOE Programs of Support in Relation to Educational Television Facilities: A Summary Review" prepared by the Educational Televisions Facilities Branch, BAVE, April 14, 1966, Box 2, Dean Coston Papers, University of Maryland, College Park, MD.

84. Staff Report, "Programs Administered by the Department of Health, Education, and Welfare Which Make Available Financial Support for Educational Television," July 1, 1967. Box 2, Dean Coston Papers, University of Maryland, College Park, MD.

85. Raymond J. Stanley, "Radio/TV Communications Systems and Federal Educational Legislation," October 24, 1966. Box 2, Dean Coston Papers, University of Maryland, College Park, MD.

86. USOE Report.

87. Ibid.

88. Chalmers H. Marquis, "Educational Television Broadcasting: A Five-Year Projection," October 13, 1966, Box 2, Dean Coston Papers, University of Maryland, College Park, MD.

89. Carolyn Brooks, "Documentary Programming and the Emergence of the National Educational Television Center as a Network, 1958–1972," dissertation (Madison: University of Wisconsin-Madison, 1994).

90. Subcommittee on Educational Television, Legislative Proposal, October 28, 1966, Box 2, Dean Coston Papers, University of Maryland, College Park, MD.

91. Ibid.

92. James Killian, Letter to Wilbur J. Cohen, April 25, 1966, Box 2, Dean Coston Papers, University of Maryland, College Park, MD.

93. Dean Coston, "Proposal to the Office of Education: A Study of Technology for Education," February 14, 1967, Dean Coston Papers, University of Maryland, College Park, MD.

94. Ibid.

95. Rosel H. Hyde. Statement of FCC Chair before the Subcommittee on Communications of the Senate Committee on Commerce on S. 1160, 90th Congress, 1st Session, the "Public Television Act of 1967," April 11, 1967, Box 1, Dean Coston Papers, University of Maryland, College Park, MD.

96. Charles L. Schultze, "Memorandum for Task force on Financing Public Television Section Four, Recommendations for Financing Public Broadcasting," July 7, 1967, Box 2, Dean Coston Papers, University of Maryland, College Park, MD.

97. April 11 Hearing on S.1160: The Public Television Act of 1967, Three Purposes, Titles I, II, and III. Box 1, Dean Coston Papers, University of Maryland, College Park, MD.

Conclusion

1. Kathleen Battles and Eleanor Patterson, "Special Forum: Radio Preservation as Social Activism," *New Review of Film and Television Studies*, 16(4), (2018): 415–19.

2. Dolores Ines Casillas, *Sounds of Belonging: U.S. Spanish Language Radio and Public Advocacy* (New York: NYU Press, 2014).

3. See Dorothy Ross, *The Origins of American Social Science* (Cambridge: Cambridge University Press, 1991).

4. Alan Stavitsky, "Public Radio Turns 50: Introduction to the Symposium," *Journal of Radio and Audio Media* 24, no. 2 (July 3, 2017): 186–88.

5. Donica Mensing, "Public Radio at a Crossroads: Emerging Trends in U.S. Public Media," *Journal of Radio and Audio Media* 24, no. 2 (July 3, 2017): 238–50.

6. See Deborah L. Jaramillo, *The Television Code: Regulating the Screen to Safeguard the Industry* (Austin: University of Texas Press, 2018).

7. David King Dunaway, "The Conglomeration of Public Radio: A Tale of Three Cities," *Journal of Radio and Audio Media* 21, no. 1 (January 2, 2014): 177–82.

8. Brian Fauteux, "Songs You Need to Hear: Public Radio Partnerships and the Mobility of National Music," *Radio Journal: International Studies in Broadcast and Audio Media* 15, no. 1 (April 1, 2017): 47–63.

9. Monica de la Torre, "*Programas Sin Vergüenza* (Shameless Programs): Mapping Chicanas in Community Radio in the 1970s," *Women's Studies Quarterly WSQ: The 1970s,* Volume 43, Nos. 3–4, (2015).

10. William Hoynes, "Public Broadcasting for the 21st Century: Notes on an Agenda for Reform," *Critical Studies in Media Communication* 24, no. 4 (October 2007): 370–76. https://doi.org/10.1080/07393180701560955.

11. See Andrew Bottomley, *Sound Streams: A Cultural History of Radio-Internet Convergence* (Ann Arbor: University of Michigan Press, 2020); and Jeremy Morris, "Non-Practical Entities: Patents and the Digitization of Culture." *Critical Studies in Media Communication,* 31(3): 212–29.

12. Nikki Usher, "Reshaping the Public Radio Newsroom for the Digital Future," *Radio Journal: International Studies in Broadcast and Audio Media* 10, no. 1 (June 2, 2012): 65–79.

Index

JOSH SHEPPERD is an assistant professor of
media studies at the University of Colorado
Boulder and director of the Sound Submissions
Project at the Library of Congress.

The History of Communication

Heroes and Scoundrels: The Image of the Journalist in Popular Culture
  Matthew C. Ehrlich and Joe Saltzman
The Real Cyber War: The Political Economy of Internet Freedom
  Shawn M. Powers and Michael Jablonski
The Polish Hearst: *Ameryka-Echo* and the Public Role of the Immigrant Press
  Anna D. Jaroszyńska-Kirchmann
Acid Hype: American News Media and the Psychedelic Experience   *Stephen Siff*
Making the News Popular: Mobilizing U.S. News Audiences   *Anthony M. Nadler*
Indians Illustrated: The Image of Native Americans in the Pictorial Press
  John M. Coward
Mister Pulitzer and the Spider: Modern News from Realism to the Digital
  Kevin G. Barnhurst
Media Localism: The Policies of Place   *Christopher Ali*
Newspaper Wars: Civil Rights and White Resistance in South Carolina, 1935–1965
  Sid Bedingfield
Across the Waves: How the United States and France Shaped the International
  Age of Radio   *Derek W. Vaillant*
Race News: Black Reporters and the Fight for Racial Justice in the
  Twentieth Century   *Fred Carroll*
Becoming the Story: War Correspondents since 9/11   *Lindsay Palmer*
Wired into Nature: The Telegraph and the North American Frontier
  James Schwoch
The Enforcers: How Little-Known Trade Reporters Exposed the Keating Five   ·
  and Advanced Business Journalism   *Rob Wells*
Graphic News: How Sensational Images Transformed Nineteenth-Century
  Journalism   *Amanda Frisken*
Front Pages, Front Lines: Media and the Fight for Women's Suffrage
  Edited by Linda Steiner, Carolyn Kitch, and Brooke Kroeger
Journalism and Jim Crow: White Supremacy and the Black Struggle for a
  New America   *Edited by Kathy Roberts Forde and Sid Bedingfield*
The Sunday Paper: A Media History   *Paul Moore and Sandra Gabriele*
A Century of Repression: The Espionage Act and Freedom of the Press
  Ralph Engelman and Carey Shenkman
Eternity in the Ether: A Mormon Media History   *Gavin Feller*
Shadow of the New Deal: The Victory of Public Broadcasting   *Josh Shepperd*

The University of Illinois Press
is a founding member of the
Association of University Presses.

University of Illinois Press
1325 South Oak Street
Champaign, IL 61820-6903
www.press.uillinois.edu